JUSTICE:
ALTERNATIVE POLITICAL PERSPECTIVES

James P. Sterba
University of Notre Dame

Wadsworth Publishing Company
Belmont, California
A Division of Wadsworth, Inc.

Philosophy Editor: Ken King
Production Editor: Jeanne Heise

Printed in the United States of America

1 2 3 4 5 6 7 8 9 10—84 83 82 81 80

Library of Congress Cataloging in Publication Data

Main entry under title:

Justice.

    Bibliography: p.
    1. Justice—Addresses, essays, lectures.
I. Sterba, James P.
JC578.J87   320.5   79-16860
ISBN 0-534-00762-7

To Janet,
A Philosopher's Philosopher

Contents

I
INTRODUCTION

Introduction

James P. Sterba

Virtually all of us become involved at some time or another in disputes about justice. Sometimes our involvement in such disputes is rooted in the fact that we believe ourselves to be victims of some form of injustice; sometimes our involvement is rooted in the fact that others believe us to be the perpetrators or at least the beneficiaries of some form of injustice affecting them. Sometimes the injustice at issue seems to require for its elimination a drastic reform, or even a revolutionary change, in the political system—like the change from free market capitalism to worker-controlled socialism. Sometimes it seems to require for its elimination only some electoral pressure or administrative decision—what might be required, say, in ending a war. But whatever the origin and whatever the practical effect, such disputes about justice are difficult to avoid, especially when dealing with issues (like the distribution of income, the control and use of natural resources, and the distribution of educational and employment opportunities) that have widespread social effects.

But if we can hardly avoid getting involved in disputes about justice, how can we resolve such disputes in a reasonable way? Certainly, if we all share a common conception of justice—if we all agree, for example, to such principles as that justice requires that social goods be distributed "from each according to his choice, to each according to his contribution," (or "from each according to his ability, to each according to his need," or "from each according to his choice, given his assets, to each as he is chosen," or something else instead)—then it would seem that the only problem we shall confront in resolving our disputes about justice is the apparently manageable one of applying our shared conception of justice to the various areas of concern.

But what if we lack such a shared conception of justice? What should we do then? As a first step, we should explore whatever we *do* hold in common; that is, we should explore whatever assumptions and distinctions regarding justice we do hold in common even when our conceptions of justice differ. Such assumptions and distinctions will, in fact, constitute our very "concept of justice," that which makes our alternative conceptions of justice alternative conceptions of *justice*. Thus, one of these assumptions will be the principle that justice requires giving each person his due: while alternative conceptions of justice may differ over just what constitutes a "person's due," (see, for example, the alternative principles mentioned in the last paragraph), all will yet hold this principle in common.

Next, of course, we should critically evaluate the available alternative conceptions of justice. We should, that is, carefully consider and compare whatever reasons have been, or might be, advanced in favor of these conceptions of justice. Hopefully, through this process of critical comparison and evaluation, something approaching a common conception of justice will begin to emerge. But even when this does not occur, those who have carried out this process of critical comparison and evaluation cannot reasonably be held blameworthy for applying whatever conception of justice they have come to regard as the best available.

In sum, reasonably resolving disputes about justice in cases in which we lack a common conception of justice requires us to (1) explore the assumptions and distinctions belonging to the concept of justice and (2) critically evaluate the available alternative conceptions of justice. Indeed, we can hardly be held exempt from this procedure even in those cases in which we *do* share a common conception of justice. For the above procedure ensures a resolution of our disputes about justice that is based on the most reasonable conception of justice available, and this may not, after all, be the conception of justice that just happens to be commonly accepted.

This is not, of course, to suggest that the task of carrying out this twofold procedure is an easy one. Indeed, few of us are confident of having a firm enough grasp on the assumptions and distinctions belonging to the concept of justice, and fewer still are confident of having successfully carried out a full critical evaluation of the available alternative conceptions of justice. An anthology like the present one— containing as it does an initial section of readings on the assumptions and distinctions belonging to the concept of justice drawn from classical and contemporary sources, followed by sections containing classical and contemporary defenses and critiques of competing conceptions of justice—is therefore entirely appropriate. It has, in fact, been designed as an aid in carrying out the twofold procedure required for reasonably resolving disputes about justice.

The Concept of Justice

The first section of readings opens with a selection drawn from Book V of Aristotle's *Nicomachean Ethics*—the classical location for a discussion of the concept of justice. In this selection Aristotle distinguishes between different varieties of justice. He first distinguishes between justice as the whole of virtue and justice as a particular part of virtue. In the former sense justice is understood as what is lawful and the just man is equivalent to the moral man. In the latter sense justice is understood as what is fair or equal and the just man is the man who takes what is his proper share. Aristotle focuses his discussion on justice in this latter sense, which he further divides into distributive justice, corrective justice, and justice in exchange. Each of these varieties of justice, Aristotle claims, can be understood to be concerned with achieving equality. For distributive justice, it is equality between equals; for corrective justice, it is equality between punishment and the crime; and for justice in exchange, it is equality between whatever goods are exchanged. Aristotle also claims that justice has both its natural and its conventional aspects: this twofold character of justice seems to be behind Aristotle's discussion of equity, in which equity is described as a corrective to legal or conventional justice.

Note that few of the distinctions Aristotle makes seem to be tied to the acceptance of any particular conception of justice. One could, for example, accept the view that justice requires equality but then specify the equality that is required in different ways. Even the idea of justice as giving people what they deserve, which has its roots in Aristotle's account of distributive justice, is also subject to various interpretations. For a correct analysis of the concept of desert would show that there is no conceptual difficulty with claiming, for example, that everyone deserves to have his needs satisfied, or that everyone deserves an equal share of the goods distributed in his society.[1] Consequently, Aristotle's account is primarily helpful for getting clear about the distinctions belonging to the concept of justice that can be made without committing oneself to any particular conception of justice.

A number of the distinctions that Aristotle makes are further developed by Stanley I. Benn in selection 2. Aristotle's idea that justice requires treating equals equally and unequals unequally, Benn claims, implies a presumption in favor of equal treatment. According to Benn, this means that people should be treated alike unless relevant differences have been established.

But what differences are relevant? Or put another way, what are the criteria of relevance for resolving disputes about justice? Some philosophers, Benn notes, have offered only purely legal or formal criteria of relevance and so have given up, in effect, the possibility of a nonarbitrary resolution of disputes about justice. At the same time other philosophers have defended the possibility of criteria of relevance that are extralegal and objective, but then have disagreed as to what those criteria are. Thus, some favor social utility as the ultimate criterion, while others favor various nonutilitarian standards. Likewise, as Benn points out, disagreement exists at a more particular level over whether need, merit (desert), and social equality are appropriate criteria for the distribution of social goods.

This disagreement over particular substantive criteria for resolving disputes about justice is the starting point for Nicholas Rescher's discussion in selection 3. In this selection Rescher notes that distributive justice has been held to consist "wholly or primarily" in distribution according to (1) equality, (2) need, (3) ability and/or achievement, (4) effort, (5) productivity, (6) social utility, and (7) supply and demand. Yet Rescher claims that there are serious objections to

---

[1]For further argument, see my article "Justice and the Concept of Desert," *The Personalist* (1976): 188–197.

regarding any one of these "canons" as ultimate for all circumstances. As an alternative, Rescher favors a strategy of weighing the merits of each canon in a case-by-case application. But clearly such a strategy goes beyond a consideration of the assumptions and distinctions belonging to the concept of justice, and amounts to a recommendation for a particular conception of justice. This means that an adequate assessment of Rescher's proposed strategy would ultimately lead us to a critical evaluation of the conceptions of justice defended in the following selections.

Liberal Justice: The Contractual Tradition

A liberal conception of justice can be roughly distinguished from a libertarian conception of justice (which takes liberty to be the ultimate moral ideal) and from a socialist conception of justice (which takes social equality to be the ultimate moral ideal) by its attempt to combine both liberty and social equality—especially in the form of economic liberty and political equality—into one ultimate moral ideal. According to one of its most important defenses, such a liberal conception of justice is derivable from the free agreement of rational agents. Sometimes, as in the writings of John Locke, the free agreement or "contract" is assumed to be an actual agreement to abide by the requirements of liberal justice entered into by rational agents at a particular time and place. But more frequently the "contract" is understood to be a hypothetical agreement; that is, it is simply claimed that rational agents would freely agree to abide by the requirements of liberal justice under certain ideal conditions.

A classical example of the contractual approach to liberal justice is found in the works of Immanuel Kant, from which selection 4 is taken. In this selection Kant claims that a civil state ought to be founded on an original contract satisfying the requirements of freedom (the freedom of each person to seek his happiness in whatever way he sees fit so long as he does not infringe upon the freedom of others to pursue a similar end), equality (the equal right of each person to coerce others to use their freedom in a way that harmonizes with his freedom), and independence (that independence of each citizen that is necessarily presupposed by the free agreement of the original contract).

According to Kant the original contract, which ought to be the foundation of every civil state, does not have to "actually exist as a fact." It suffices that the laws of a civil state are such that people would agree to them under conditions in which the requirements of freedom, equality, and independence obtain. Laws that accord with this original contract would then, Kant claims, give each member of society the right to reach any degree of rank that he could earn through his labor, industry, and good fortune. Thus, the equality demanded by the original contract would not, in Kant's view, exclude a considerable amount of economic liberty.

This Kantian idea of a hypothetical contract as the moral foundation for a liberal conception of justice has been further developed by John Rawls in *A Theory of Justice*. In selection 5, taken from his book, Rawls, like Kant, argues that principles of justice are those principles that free and rational persons who are concerned to advance their own interests would accept in an initial position of equality. Yet Rawls goes beyond Kant by interpreting the conditions of his "original position" to explicitly require a "veil of ignorance." This veil of ignorance, Rawls claims, has the effect of depriving persons in the original position of the knowledge they would need to advance their own interests in ways that are morally arbitrary.

The justification Rawls offers for the conditions he imposes on the original position basically takes two forms. First, Rawls claims that the conditions express weak but widely shared moral presumptions. Second, Rawls assures us that the choice of principles in the original position will always conform to our considered moral judgments. In cases of conflict, this will be accomplished either by revising our considered moral judgments or by revising the particular conditions on the original position that gave rise to the conflict.

Rawls presents the principles of justice he believes would be derived in the original position in two successive formulations. In his first formulation, they are:

I. Special Conception of Justice

   1. Each person is to have an equal right to the most extensive basic liberty compatible with a similar liberty for others.

   2. Social and economic inequalities are to be arranged so that they are both (a) reasonably expected to be to everyone's advantage, and (b) attached to positions and offices open to all.

II. General Conception of Justice

All social values—liberty and opportunity, income and wealth, and the bases of self-respect—are to be distributed equally unless an unequal distribution of any or all of these values is to everyone's advantage.

Later these principles are more accurately formulated as:

I. Special Conception of Justice

   1. Each person is to have an equal right to the most extensive total system of equal basic liberties compatible with a similar system of liberty for all.

   2. Social and economic inequalities are to be arranged so that they are both (a) to the greatest benefit of the least advantaged, consistent with the just savings principle, and (b) attached to offices and positions open to all under conditions of fair equality of opportunity.

II. General Conception of Justice

All social goods—liberty and opportunity, income and wealth, and the bases of self-respect—are to be distributed equally unless an unequal distribution of any or all of these goods is to the advantage of the least favored.

Under both formulations the general conception of justice differs from the special conception of justice by allowing trade-offs between liberty and other social goods. According to Rawls, persons in the original position would want the special conception of justice to be applied in place of the general conception of justice whenever social conditions allowed every representative person effectively to exercise his basic liberties.

Rawls holds that the above principles of justice would be chosen in the original position because persons so situated would find it reasonable to follow the conservative dictates of a "maximin strategy" and thereby secure for themselves the highest minimum payoff. In the final part of the selection, Rawls connects his contractual theory of justice with Kant's conception of autonomy and the categorical imperative.

Rawls' defense of a liberal conception of justice has been challenged in various ways. Some critics have endorsed Rawls' contractual approach while disagreeing with Rawls over what principles of justice would be derived thereby. These critics usually attempt to undermine the use of a maximin strategy in the original position.[2] Other critics, however, have found fault with the contractual approach itself. The criticism that Ronald Dworkin directs at Rawls' theory of justice in selection 6 is of this second sort.

Dworkin argues that hypothetical agreements do not (unlike actual agreements) provide independent arguments for the fairness of those agreements. Thus, Dworkin holds, the fact that a person would freely agree to do something under certain conditions does not provide an independent argument for his doing it or for others forcing him to do it, whereas the fact that a person has agreed to do something (anything?) does provide an independent argument for his doing it or for others forcing him to do it.

According to Dworkin, the true warrant for accepting the principles that Rawls derives from his original position is that these principles give expression to an underlying natural right. This underlying right is not a right to liberty, nor even, presumably, a right to fair treatment, but rather a right to equal concern and respect; and the original position, Dworkin maintains, is simply designed to accord with that right. Dworkin thus concludes that the original position is unnecessary and dispensable, for he assumes that it is always possible to argue directly from each person's equal right to concern and respect.[3]

In selection 7, Richard Miller also directs his criticism of Rawls's theory to the contractual approach itself. However, he does so from the point of view of Marxist social theory. Miller maintains that if certain elements of Marxist social theory are correct then neither Rawls' principles of justice nor any other candidates for "morally acceptable principles" would emerge from the original position.

The elements of Marxist social theory in question are the following: (1) no social arrangement that is acceptable to the best-off class is acceptable to the worst-off class; (2) the best-off class is a ruling class, that is, a class whose interests are served by the major political and ideological institutions; and (3) the need for wealth and power typical of the best-off class is much more acute than what is typical of the rest of society. What Miller is claiming is that if persons in the original position

[2] See, for example, my article "Distributive Justice," *American Journal of Jurisprudence* (1977): 55–79; and John C. Harsanyi, *Essays on Ethics, Social Behavior, and Scientific Explanation* (Boston: D. Reidel Publishing Co., 1976) 37–85.

[3] For a similar line of argument, see Ted Honderich, "The Use of the Basic Proposition of a Theory of Justice," *Mind* (1975): 63–78.

accepted these elements of Marxist social theory (and persons in the original position are presumed to have access to all available general information) then they would not choose Rawls' principles of justice nor any other "morally acceptable principles" you like.

Note that if Miller's critique of Rawls' contractual approach is correct for the context of distributive justice, then a similar critique could be validly directed at the use of Rawls' contractual approach for the context of corrective or retributive justice. This is because at least some criminals or potential criminals would have just as unalterable needs as the members of a capitalist ruling class. Accordingly, a contractual approach to distributive justice and a contractual approach to corrective or retributive justice will succeed or fail together.[4]

Liberal Justice: The Utilitarian Tradition

One way to avoid the challenges that have been directed at a contractual defense of liberal justice is to find some alternative way of defending liberal justice. Historically, utilitarianism has been thought to provide such an alternative defense. What has been claimed is that the requirements of a liberal conception of justice can be derived from considerations of social utility in such a way that following these requirements will result in the maximization of total happiness or satisfaction in society. The best known classical defense of this utilitarian approach is certainly that presented by John Stuart Mill in Chapter 5 of *Utilitarianism*, from which selection 8 is taken.

In this selection Mill surveys various types of actions and situations that are ordinarily described as just or unjust and concludes that justice (by which he understands a liberal conception of justice) simply denotes a certain class of fundamental moral rules, the adherence to which is essential for maximizing social utility. Thus, Mill rejects the idea that (liberal) justice and social utility are ultimately distinct moral ideals, maintaining instead that (liberal) justice is in fact derivable from the moral ideal of social utility.

Nevertheless, various problems remain for the utilitarian defense of liberal justice. Consider, for example, a society in which the members are equally divided between the Privileged Rich and the Alienated Poor, and suppose that the incomes for two alternative social arrangements for this society are the following:

	Social Arrangement A	Social Arrangement B
Privileged Rich	$100,000	$60,000
Alienated Poor	$5,000	$15,000

[4]For further considerations on the possibility of a contractual approach to retributive justice, see my article "Retributive Justice," *Political Theory* (1977): 349–362.

Given these alternatives, considerations of maximizing utility would appear to favor Social Arrangement A over Social Arrangement B. But suppose that liberal justice required a high minimum for each person in society. Then it would seem that liberal justice would favor Social Arrangement B over Social Arrangement A, in apparent conflict with the requirements of social utility. Obviously, the possibility of such a conflict places the utilitarian defense of liberal justice in some doubt. In selection 9 R. M. Hare attempts to remove the grounds for that doubt.

Hare argues that in fashioning a theory of justice we must proceed in accordance with the formal constraints of the concept of justice; that is, our judgments must be universalizable and impartial. But in addition, Hare argues, we must take relevant empirical considerations into account, such as the fact that people experience a declining marginal utility for money and other social goods. For example, considerations of declining marginal utility of money and other social goods, Hare believes, would render a utilitarian approach to a theory of justice moderately egalitarian in its requirements. Applied to our example, considerations of declining marginal utility of money and other social goods would seem to render Social Arrangement B preferable to Social Arrangement A from a utilitarian point of view, thus removing the grounds for thinking that liberal justice and social utility conflict in this case.

Of course, when considerations of declining marginal utility of money and other social goods are taken into account, the utility values for the two alternatives given on page 8 might end up to be something like:

Social Arrangement A		Social Arrangement B
Privileged Rich	55	40
Alienated Poor	10	20

And if they did, then there would still remain a conflict between liberal justice and social utility, with liberal justice favoring Social Arrangement B, and social utility favoring Social Arrangement A . . . unless, of course, additional empirical considerations could be advanced to show that this is not the case.

Still another objection to a utilitarian defense of liberal justice is developed by John Rawls in selection 10. In this selection Rawls criticizes utilitarianism, particularly classical utilitarianism, for applying to society as a whole the principle of rational choice for one person, and thereby treating the desires and satisfactions of separate persons as if they were the desires and satisfactions of just one person. In this way, Rawls claims, utilitarianism fails to preserve the distinction between persons.

What Rawls must be claiming is that even after considerations of declining marginal utility of money and other social goods are taken into account, utilitarianism will still fail to adequately preserve the distinction between persons. But is Rawls right? It may well be that a proper assessment of the relative merits of the contractual and utilitarian approaches to liberal justice will turn on this very issue.

Libertarian Justice

Of course the question of the relative merits of the contractual and the utilitarian defense of a liberal conception of justice appears to be somewhat beside the point to the defender of a libertarian conception of justice. He, after all, believes his conception of justice to be incompatible with a liberal conception of justice. For him, the ultimate moral foundation for a conception of justice is an ideal of liberty. In selection 11, F. A. Hayek contends that such an ideal requires "equality before the law" and "reward according to perceived value" but not "substantial equality" or "reward according to merit." In addition, according to Hayek, the inequalities due to upbringing, inheritance and education that are permitted by an ideal of liberty tend actually to benefit society as a whole.

In basic agreement with Hayek, Milton Friedman argues in selection 12 that the ethical principle governing the distribution of income in a free society is "to each according to what he or the instruments he owns produce." Furthermore, Friedman believes, unless an individual receives all that he produces he will enter into exchanges on the basis of what he can receive rather than what he can produce, and this will work to everyone's disadvantage. Finally, Friedman points out, the inequalities among persons in free societies are not so great when they are compared with those found in noncapitalist societies.

In selection 13, Robert Nozick also endorses the libertarian ideal of a just society, but for him the requirements of that ideal can best be captured by the principle "from each as he chooses, to each as he is chosen." For Nozick, the holdings of persons in society are just if and only if those persons are "entitled" to them by certain principles that specify how those holdings came about. There is a principle of original appropriation, a principle of exchange, and, for situations in which such principles have been violated, a principle of rectification. The principles of appropriation and exchange are said to contain a "Lockean proviso" restricting acquisition and exchange in such a way that no one is thereby made worse off; but since the baseline for comparison is so low, the question of the Lockean proviso being violated arises only in the case of catastrophe.

In Nozick's view, what distinguishes his "entitlement principles" from other principles of justice, such as the classical principle of utility or Rawls' principles of justice, is that the entitlement principles are "historical process principles" rather than "end-state principles"; that is, they specify justice in terms of how holdings came about rather than in terms of how holdings are distributed. By specifying justice in this way, Nozick believes, his entitlement principles avoid the continual interference with people's lives required by end-state conceptions of justice.[5]

Critics of these defenses of a libertarian conception of justice have pursued at least two lines of attack. Some have set out to show that defenders of libertarian justice have incorrectly assessed the implications of their own ideal of liberty— arguing, for example, that the libertarian ideal of liberty lacks the anti-forced

[5]For further discussion of Nozick's critique of alternative conceptions of justice, see my article "In Defense of Rawls Against Arrow and Nozick," *Philosophia* (1977) (Special Issue): 293-303.

welfare and anti-paternalism implications that libertarians have generally believed it to have. Others have set out to show that defenders of libertarian justice have incorrectly assessed the moral status of their ideal—arguing, for example, that other ideals (such as the ideal of social equality) are at least sometimes morally preferable to the ideal of liberty.

In selection 14 James P. Sterba pursues the first line of attack, arguing that defenders of libertarian justice have failed to recognize the welfare implications of their own ideal of liberty. Sterba contends that any act for which others are morally responsible restricts someone's liberty if that act prevents him from doing something he could otherwise do. Utilizing this account of liberty, Sterba then shows that in virtually every case in which persons in need are left alone to care for themselves, their liberty and/or the liberty of others is actually restricted. Finally, in order to determine a morally acceptable distribution of liberty, Sterba employs a Rawlsian contractual procedure and defends the requirement of a high minimum of liberty that results from the libertarian's objection that all that is morally justified is an appeal to charity.

Socialist Justice

Achieving a resolution of the debate between libertarians and their liberal critics will not provide a morally acceptable conception of justice—at least, not if the defenders of a socialist conception of justice are correct. The reason for this, defenders of socialist justice maintain, is that libertarians and their liberal critics both make the same mistake (although in varying degrees) of failing to recognize the ultimate moral significance of an ideal of social equality. To remedy this situation, defenders of a socialist conception of justice have attempted persuasively to present the requirements of their proposed ideal and the various justifications for accepting it.

In the first part of selection 15, which is taken from the *Communist Manifesto*, Karl Marx and Friedrich Engels maintain that the abolition of bourgeois property and bourgeois family structure is a necessary first requirement for building a society according to an ideal of social equality. In the second part of selection 15 Marx provides a much more positive account of what is required to build a society according to such an ideal. Marx claims that the distribution of social goods must conform, at least initially, to the principle "from each according to his ability, to each according to his contribution." But when the highest stage of communist society has been reached, Marx adds, distribution will conform to the principle "from each according to his ability, to each according to his need."

This final principle of socialist justice is discussed and defended by Edward Nell and Onora O'Neill in selection 16. They argue that any incentive problems associated with the principle will be resolved when, quoting Marx, "labor is no longer a means of life but has become life's principal need." They further contend that when it is at last appropriate to apply the final principle of socialist justice there will exist a system for equitably distributing the burdens of nonfulfilling but socially necessary tasks as well as a system for equitably distributing the benefits of goods not required by anyone's needs.

In selection 17 Steven Lukes attempts to ground a demand for the social equality that characterizes the highest stage of socialist society on a principle that defenders of liberal justice simply have to take seriously, namely, "the principle of equality of consideration or respect." According to this principle, all human beings have certain basic attributes that entitle them to be considered or respected as equals. Thus, Lukes's argument parallels the argument that Sterba directed at the libertarian conception of justice. For, Sterba argues that those who accept the ideal of liberty on which libertarian justice is founded should, in all consistency, accept a program of action quite similar to the requirements of liberal justice. Here Lukes argues that those who accept the principle of equality of consideration or respect on which liberal justice is founded should, in all consistency, accept a program of action quite similar to the requirements of socialist justice. Thus, if Lukes and Sterba are both correct, defenders of a libertarian conception of justice as well as defenders of a liberal conception of justice should, in all consistency, accept the requirements of a socialist conception of justice!

In the final selection, John Hospers criticizes socialist justice from the point of view of libertarian justice. Hospers claims that the central planning necessary for maintaining social equality would drastically reduce individual liberty in society. What is important, Hospers concludes, is not that everyone has an equal opportunity in the sense of an equal income but rather that the "lines be left open" from poverty to affluence so that everyone has a chance to rise as far as his ability can carry him.

Obviously, a careful assessment of Hospers' critique of socialist justice would require a careful evaluation of arguments like those presented in the previous selections—arguments designed to establish either (1) the compatibility of the ideals of liberty and social equality, or (2) the moral preferability of one of these ideals over the other.

Carrying out an assessment of this sort is not easy, of course, but since it is required by our twofold procedure for reasonably resolving disputes about justice, it should be given our best efforts.

II
THE CONCEPT OF JUSTICE

1

The Varieties of Justice

Aristotle

With regard to justice[1] and injustice, the points we have to consider are—with what class of actions are they connected, in what sense is justice a middle state, and between what extremes is that which is just intermediate? Our enquiry shall follow the same procedure as our previous investigations.

We observe that by the term justice everybody means that state of character which renders men disposed to act justly, and which causes them to do and to wish what is just; and similarly by injustice they mean the disposition that makes men do and wish what is unjust. Let us then accept these definitions to go upon as broadly correct.

The fact is that it is not the same with a state of character as with the sciences and faculties. It appears that the same science or faculty deals with opposite objects;[2] but a state that produces one result does not also produce the opposite result—for instance, health does not cause us to do actions that are the reverse of healthy, but only those that are healthy: A sound gait in walking means walking like a man in good health, not walking lame.

Hence it is often possible to infer one of two opposite states from the other,

From Chapter V of *Aristotle's Ethics for English Readers*, rendered from the Greek of the *Nicomachean Ethics* by H. Rackham (1943). Reprinted by permission of Basil Blackwell, Publisher.

[1]The Greek term normally thus rendered is stated in what follows to have two senses, the wider sense of righteousness in general, any right conduct in relation to others, and the narrower sense of right conduct in matters involving gain or loss to the agent or to others. It is justice in the latter sense that this chapter deals with; in some places we should rather term it honesty.

[2]For instance, medicine studies both health and disease.

and often states can be identified from the subjects that exhibit them. Thus if we find out what constitutes good bodily condition we learn what bad condition is as well; but we can also learn what good bodily condition is from actual persons that are in good condition, while from knowing what good condition is we can recognize things that produce good condition. If good condition is firmness of flesh, bad condition must necessarily be flabbiness of flesh, and also 'wholesome' must mean productive of firmness of flesh. Also if one of two opposite terms has more than one meaning, it follows as a rule that the other also has more than one meaning—for instance, the terms "just" and "unjust." And "justice" and "injustice" appear to have more than one meaning, but owing to their two meanings not being widely separate, the ambiguity escapes notice and is not rather obvious, as it is in the case of two meanings that are widely separate. Let us then take the different senses in which the word "unjust" is used. A man who breaks the law is unjust, and so also is a man who is grasping and unfair; so that obviously a law-abiding man and a man who is fair in business are both of them just. "Just" therefore denotes both what is lawful and what is fair, and "unjust" denotes both what is unlawful and what is unfair.

As the unjust man is grasping, his injustice will be exercised in regard to things that are good—not all of them but those with which good and bad fortune are concerned, which though always good in the absolute sense are not always good for a particular person. These are the goods that men pray for and seek after, although they ought not to do so; they ought to pray that the things which are good in the absolute sense may also be good for themselves, though choosing the things that are good for themselves. The unjust man does not always choose the larger share—in the case of things that are bad absolutely he chooses the smaller share; but because the smaller quantity of a bad thing seems to be good in a sense, and a grasping nature means one that grasps something good, this makes him appear to be grasping. Let us call him "unfair," as that term includes taking too much of good things and taking too little of bad ones, and covers both.

We saw that the man who breaks the law is unjust and the lawabiding man just. This shows that all that is lawful is just in a sense, since it is the business of legislature to define what is lawful, and the various decisions of the legislature are what we term the principles of justice. Now all the edicts of the laws are aimed either at the common advantage of everybody or at the interest of a ruling class selected by merit or in some other similar way. Consequently in one sense we apply the word "just" to things which produce and preserve happiness, and the things that form part of happiness for the community. And the law prescribes certain conduct: the conduct of a brave man (for instance, not to desert one's post, not to run away in battle, not to throw down one's arms); that of a self-controlled man (for instance, not to commit adultery or violent assault); that of a good-tempered man (for instance, not to strike a person or to use abusive language), and similarly as to all the other forms of virtue—some acts the law enjoins and others it forbids, rightly if the law has been rightly framed and not so well if it has been drafted carelessly.

Justice in this sense then is perfect virtue, though with the qualification that it is virtue in relation to our neighbors. Because of this the view is often held that in the list of virtues justice occupies the top place, and that

Neither the evening nor the morning star[3]
is so sublime; and we have the proverb:
The whole of virtue is comprised in justice.[4]

Justice is perfect because it is our mode of practicing perfect virtue; and it is supremely perfect because its possessor can use it in his relations with others and not only by himself. There are plenty of people who can practice virtue in their personal affairs but who are incapable of displaying it in their relations with others. This shows the truth of the saying of Bias,[5] "Office will show a real man"; when somebody obtains a position of authority he is brought into contact with other people, and is a member of a partnership. For this same reason, justice alone among the virtues is thought to be "another person's good,"[6] because it is exercised in relation to one's neighbors; it does what is in the interest of somebody else, a superior or a partner. The wickedest man therefore is he who exercises his wickedness in his relations with his friends and not merely in his personal affairs; and the best man is the one who practices his virtue not in regard to himself but in relation to someone else, as that is a difficult thing to do.

Justice thus understood therefore is not a part of virtue, but the whole of it; and its opposite, injustice, in not a part of vice, but the whole. The distinction between justice in this sense and virtue is clear from what has been said; they are the same quality of character but differently viewed: what as exercised in relation to others is justice, considered simply as a disposition of a certain sort is virtue.

Justice as a Part of Virtue

But it is justice as a particular part of virtue that we are investigating, that being as we say one sort of justice; and similarly we are considering injustice as a particular vice, not in the sense of wickedness in general.

That there is such a vice is indicated by the following considerations: When a man practices one of the other vices (for instance, when owing to cowardice he throws away his shield,[7] or owing to ill-temper uses abusive language, or owing to meanness refuses to help a friend out of a difficulty with money), he is committing an injustice but he is not taking an unfair share of something. But when he takes an unfair share, he is not displaying one of the vices of the kind specified, and certainly not all of them, but clearly he does display a vice of some sort, as we blame his conduct—in fact he displays injustice. Therefore there is another sort of injustice which is a part of injustice as a whole, and there is a form of unjust action which is a subdivision of unjust and illegal conduct in general. Again, suppose that A commits adultery for gain and gets something by it, whereas B does it out of inclination and

---

[3]A quotation from a play of Euripides that has not come down to us.
[4]From the poet Theognis.
[5]One of the Seven Sages.
[6]Plato, *Republic* 343 c.—the definition given by the sophist Thrasymachus.
[7]I.e., so as to be able to run away quickly.

loses by his indulgence. B would appear to be self-indulgent rather than avaricious, whereas A would seem unjust but not self-indulgent at all. It is clear then that A's motive would be profit. And yet another reason—whereas all other offenses are always attributed to some particular vice; for instance, adultery is ascribed to self-indulgence, desertion of a comrade in battle to cowardice, assault to anger—an offense out of which a man has made a profit is not put down to any other vice but injustice.

Hence it is clear that beside injustice in the wide sense there is another kind of injustice which is a particular form of vice. It bears the same name because it comes under the same general definition—both forms of injustice being exercised in our relations with other people; but injustice in the special sense is concerned with honor or money or security, or perhaps all of these things included under some general term, and its motive is the pleasure derived from gain, whereas injustice in the wide sense is concerned with the whole of the things in relation to which virtue is displayed.

The next step is to ascertain the nature and the attributes of justice in this special sense of the term, as distinct from justice denoting the whole of virtue.

Now we have distinguished two meanings of the term "unjust"—namely, unlawful and unequal or unfair; and we have shown that "just" means both lawful and equal or fair. Injustice of the kind mentioned above corresponds with "unlawful." But the unfair is not the same thing as the unlawful, but is related to it as part to whole—everything unfair is unlawful, but not everything unlawful is unfair. Consequently the unjust and injustice in the special sense are not the same as the unjust and injustice in the wide sense; although they also are related to each other as part to whole—injustice in this sense is a part of injustice in the wide sense, and likewise justice in this sense is a part of justice in the wide sense. We must consequently discuss justice and injustice, and what is just and unjust, in the special sense also. We may therefore leave on one side that form of justice which is co-extensive with virtue as a whole, and the corresponding form of injustice—namely, the exercise of the whole of virtue and of vice in our relations with another person.

It is also clear how we should define what is just and what unjust in the corresponding senses; for almost a majority of the actions ordained by law are those which are prescribed on the basis of virtue taken as a whole, since the law specifies the particular virtues which we are to practice and the particular vices which we are to avoid; and the means for producing virtue as a whole are the regulations laid down by law for education in the duties of a citizen. But in regard to our education as individuals, which renders us simply good *men*, the question whether this is the concern of politics or of another art will have to be decided later;[8] for perhaps to be a good man is not the same thing as to be a good citizen of some particular state.

Special justice, on the other hand, and that which is just in the sense corresponding to it, is of two kinds. One kind is the principle that regulates distributions of honor or money or the other divisible assets of the community, which may be divided among its members in equal or unequal shares. The other kind is that which regulates private transactions. The latter form of justice has two

[8]It is discussed in Aristotle's *Politics*, Book III.

divisions, inasmuch as some transactions are voluntary and others nonvoluntary.[9] Instances of voluntary transactions are selling, buying, lending at interest, lending free of interest, pledging, depositing, letting for hire: these are called voluntary because they are voluntarily entered upon. Of nonvoluntary transactions some are clandestine, such as theft, adultery, poisoning, procuring, enticing slaves to leave their owners, assassination, giving false witness; and some are violent, such as assault, imprisonment, murder, rape, mutilation, abusive language, contumelious treatment.

Distributive and Corrective Justice

Now as an unjust man is unfair and an unjust thing unequal, it is clear that corresponding to the unequal there is a middle point or mean; namely, that which is equal; for any kind of action admitting of more or less also admits what is equal. If then what is unjust is unequal, what is just is equal, as everyone will agree without argument; and since the equal is a mean, the just will be a sort of mean too. Now equality involves at least two terms; it follows therefore not only that the just is a mean and equal, but also that (1) as a mean it implies two extremes, the more and the less, (2) as equal it implies two equal shares, and (3) as just it implies certain persons for whom it is just. Consequently justice involves at least four terms, two persons for whom it is just and two shares which are just. And there will be the same equality between the shares as between the persons, that is, the ratio between the shares will be the same as the ratio between the persons. If the persons are not equal, they will not have equal shares; it is when equals possess or are assigned unequal shares, or persons who are not equal equal shares, that quarrels and complaints arise.

Moreover the same point also clearly follows from the principle of assignment by merit. Everybody agrees that just distribution must be in accordance with merit of some sort, though everybody does not mean the same sort of merit. Democrats take merit to mean free status, adherents of oligarchy take it to mean wealth or noble birth, supporters of aristocracy excellence.

The just then is that which is proportionate and the unjust is that which runs counter to proportion; the man who acts unjustly has too much, and the man who is unjustly treated too little, of the good. In the case of evil, it is the other way about, as the lesser evil is accounted as good in comparison with the greater evil, because the lesser evil is more desirable than the greater, and what is desirable is a good, and what is more desirable a greater good.

This then is one species of justice.

The species of justice that remains is the justice of redress, which operates in the case of voluntary and involuntary transactions. This form of justice has a different specific character from the preceding one. The justice that distributes common property always follows the kind of proportion mentioned above (because in the case of distribution from the common funds of a partnership it will follow the same ratio as that existing between the sums put into the business by the partners);

[9]Viz., lacking the consent of one of the parties.

and the unjust that is opposed to this form of the just is that which violates that proportion. But justice in transactions between individuals, although it is equality of a sort, and injustice inequality, does not go by the kind of proportion mentioned, but by arithmetical proportion.[10] It makes no difference[11] whether a good man has defrauded a bad one or a bad man a good one, nor whether a good man or a bad man has committed adultery; the law only looks at the nature of the injury, and treats the parties as equal if one has done and the other suffered a wrong or if one has inflicted and the other sustained damage. Consequently, in such cases the judge tries to equalize this injustice, which consists in inequality—for even in a case where one person has received and the other has inflicted a blow, or where one has killed and the other been killed, the suffering and the action have been distributed in unequal shares, while the judge's endeavor is to make them equal by means of the penalty he inflicts, taking something away from the gain of the assailant. The term "gain" is applied to such cases in a general sense, even though to some, for instance a person who has inflicted a wound, it is not specially appropriate, and the term "loss" is applied to the sufferer; at all events the terms "gain" and "loss" are employed when the amount of the suffering inflicted has been assessed. Consequently, while equal is intermediate between more and less, gain and loss are at once both more and less in contrary ways—more of what is good and less of what is bad are gain, and more of what is bad and less of what is good are loss, intermediate between them being, as we said, the equal, which we pronounce to be just. Consequently the justice of redress will be what is intermediate between loss and gain. This is why when a dispute arises the parties have recourse to a judge; to go to a judge is to appeal to the just, inasmuch as a judge is virtually justice personified[12]; and they have recourse to a judge as intermediary—indeed, in some countries judges are called "mediators"—on the ground that if the litigants get the medium amount they will get what is just. Thus justice is a sort of medium, as the judge is a medium between the litigants. What he does is to restore equality; it is as if there were a line divided into two unequal parts, and he took away the amount by which the larger segment exceeded half the line and added it to the smaller segment. When the whole has been divided into two equal parts, people say that they "have got their own," having got an equal share. This is the arithmetical mean between the greater amount and the less.

Therefore the just is intermediate between gain and loss due to breach of contract; it consists in having an equal amount both before and after the transaction.

Justice in Exchange

Some people hold the view that mere reciprocity is justice. But reciprocity does not coincide with either distributive justice or with corrective justice; it often conflicts with them—for example, if an officer strikes a man, it is wrong for the man

[10]I.e., two pairs of terms (e.g., 1, 3, 7, 9) the second of which exceeds the first by the same amount as the fourth exceeds the third. We do not call this proportion, but if the third term also exceeds the second by the same amount (e.g., 1, 3, 5, 7), an arithmetical progression.

[11]For corrective justice the merits of the parties are immaterial.

[12]Cf. our expressions "Mr. Justice So-and-so," "Justice of the Peace."

to hit back, but if a man strikes an officer, not only should the officer hit him but he must be punished as well. Further, there is a wide distinction between an act done with the consent of the other party and one done without consent. But in association for exchange this sort of justice, reciprocity, is the bond uniting the parties; but it must be reciprocity on a basis of proportion and not of equality. It is proportionate requital that keeps the state together. Men seek to return either evil for evil, failing which they feel themselves mere slaves, or good for good, in default of which no exchange of goods and services takes place; but it is exchange which holds society together. This is why men build a shrine of the Graces in their cities, as a reminder that favors should be returned, since to return favors received is a characteristic of grace. When somebody has done one a service, it behoves one not only to do him a service in return but also on the next occasion to take the initiative in doing him a service oneself.

Proportional requital is achieved by diagonal conjunction. Let A be a builder, B a shoemaker, C a house, and D a pair of shoes. Then the builder has to take from the shoemaker a part of the produce of his labor and give him in return a part of his own product. If proportionate equality between the products be first established, and then reciprocation takes place, the condition indicated will have been satisfied. But if this is not done, the bargain is not equal, and does not hold, since it may happen that the work of one party is worth more than that of the other, so that they have to be equalized. For two doctors do not combine to exchange their services, but a doctor and a farmer, and in general persons who are different and who may be unequal, but in that case they need to be equated. Consequently exchange of commodities requires that the commodities must be in some way commensurable; and it was to achieve this that money was invented. Money serves as a sort of middle term, as it measures all things, and so indicates their superior or inferior value—just how many shoes are the equivalent of a house or a certain quantity of food. The number of shoes exchanged for a house must correspond to the ratio between a builder and a shoemaker. Failing this, there will be no exchange, and no business will be done. And this cannot be secured unless the goods are equated in some way.

It is therefore necessary to have some one standard of measurement for all commodities, as was said before. And this standard is in reality demand; it is demand which keeps commerce together, since if people were to cease to have wants or if their wants were to alter, exchange will not go on, or it will be on different lines. But it has been agreed to accept money as representing demand. Money is a convention, and we can alter the currency if we choose, rendering the old coinage useless. Thus reciprocity will be achieved when the factors have been equated, bringing it about that as farmer is to shoemaker so the amount of shoemaker's work is to the amount of farmer's work exchanged for it.

That demand serves as a single factor holding commerce together is shown by the fact that when there is no demand for mutual service in the case of both parties or at least of one of the two, exchange of services does not take place. And money serves us as a security for future exchange, if we do not need a thing now; money guarantees that we shall have it if we do need it, as we shall be able to get it by producing the money. Now money fluctuates in value, just like goods; but it tends to be steadier. Consequently all goods must have a price given to them, as then exchange of goods will always be possible, and consequently association between men. Currency therefore is a sort of measure, which equates goods by making them commensurable. In fact there would be no association between man and man if there were no exchange, and no exchange if there were no equalization of values, and no equalization of values if there were no commensurability. No doubt it is not really possible for articles that are so different to be made exactly commensurable in value, but they can be made sufficiently commensurable for the practical purpose of exchange. That is why there has to be a single standard fixed by agreement, making all commodities commensurable; for everything can be measured by money. Let A be a house, B 20 minae and C a bedstead. Then A = B/2 (supposing a house to be worth—that is, equal to—5 minae) and C (the bedstead) = B/10. We can now say how many bedsteads are equal to one house; namely, five. Obviously before money existed this is how the rate of exchange was quoted—five beds for a house; there is no real difference between bartering five bedsteads for a house and buying the house for the price of five bedsteads.

We have now defined "just" and "unjust"; and our definitions show that just action is intermediate between doing injustice and suffering injustice, since the former is to get too much and the latter is to get too little. Justice is a sort of middle state, but not in the same manner as the other virtues are middle states; it is middle because it attaches to a middle amount, injustice being the quality of extremes. Also justice is the virtue which disposes the just man to resolve to act justly, and which leads him, when distributing things between himself and another, not to give himself a larger portion and his neighbor a smaller one of what is desirable, and the other way about in regard to what is detrimental, but to allot shares that are proportionately equal; and similarly when making a distribution between two other persons. Injustice on the contrary stands in the same relation to what is unjust, this being disproportionate excess or deficiency of something useful or harmful. Thus injustice is excess and deficiency in the sense of being productive of excess and deficiency, in one's own case excess of what is simply useful and deficiency of what is harmful, and in the case of others taken as a whole it is the same as in one's own case, but the disproportion may be in either direction.[13] In an unjust distribution to get too little is to suffer injustice and to get too much is to do injustice.

Political Justice and Analogous Kinds of Justice

But it must be borne in mind that what we are investigating is not only justice in the abstract but also political justice. This exists between men living in a community for the purpose of satisfying their needs, men who are free and who enjoy either absolute or proportional equality. Between men who do not fulfill these conditions no political justice exists, but only justice in a special sense and so called by analogy. Justice exists between those whose mutual relations are regulated by law;

[13]When A makes an unjust distribution not between himself and B but between B and C, the result for either B or C may be either too large or too small a share of something beneficial and either too small or too large a share of something detrimental.

and law exists for those between whom there is a possibility of injustice, the administration of the law being the discrimination of what is just and what is unjust. Persons therefore between whom there may be injustice may act unjustly toward each other (although unjust action does not necessarily imply injustice); and unjust action means appropriating too large a share of things essentially good and taking too small a share of things essentially bad. On this account we do not allow a man to govern, but only the law, because a human ruler governs in his own interest and becomes a tyrant; whereas the true function of a ruler is to be the guardian of justice, and therefore of equality. A just ruler, we think, gets no profit out of his office, as he does not assign to himself the larger share of what is essentially good unless such a share is proportionate to his merits. So he labors for the sake of others: this explains the saying "Justice is other men's good." Consequently it is necessary to give him some recompense in the form of honor and privilege. Rulers not content with such rewards become tyrants.

The justice of a master or a father is not the same thing as absolute justice or political justice, but only analogous to them; for there is no such thing as injustice in the absolute sense toward things that belong to one. Slaves, who are a man's chattels, and also children till they reach a certain age and start an independent life, are in a manner part of oneself, and nobody deliberately does harm to himself, so that there is no such thing as being unjust to oneself. Therefore justice and injustice in the political sense are not exercised in these relations, because they are regulated by law, as we saw, and exist between persons naturally governed by law, who, as we saw, are people who have an equal share in governing and being governed. Consequently justice exists in a fuller degree between a man and his wife than between a man and his children and chattels; it is in fact domestic justice. But this also is different from political justice.

Natural and Conventional Justice

Civic justice is partly natural and partly conventional.[14] A natural rule of justice is one which has the same validity everywhere, independently of whether people accept it or not. A conventional rule is a practice that at the outset may equally well be settled one way or the other, but which when once enacted becomes a regulation—for instance, the rule that the ransom for a prisoner of war shall be a mina, or that a certain sacrifice shall consist of one goat or two sheep; as well as enactments dealing with particular cases; for instance, the sacrifice celebrated in honor of Brasidas;[15] and special regulations promulgated by decree. Some people hold that all justice is a matter of fixed regulations, because a law of nature never alters and has the same validity everywhere—for instance, fire burns both here and

[14]The word thus rendered also means "legal."

[15]This Spartan general won the city of Amphipolis from the Athenian Empire, 424 B.C., and fell in defending it two years later. He was consecrated as a local hero, and an annual celebration was held in his honor, with sacrifices and races (for the Greeks races had religious associations).

in Persia—but they see men's conceptions of justice changing. This is not absolutely true, but only with qualifications—among the gods indeed it is perhaps not true at all. But among us, although there is such a thing as natural justice, nevertheless all rules can be altered. For instance, the right hand is naturally stronger than the left, but anybody can train himself to be ambidextrous. And in all other matters the same distinction will apply. But among things which admit of variation, it is not clear what kind is natural and what is not natural but due to convention and based on agreement, as both kinds alike are equally susceptible of change. But nevertheless it is the case that one thing is natural and another not natural. Rules of justice fixed by agreement and for the sake of expediency are like weights and measures. Wine and corn measures are not the same everywhere, but are larger in wholesale and smaller in retail markets. Similarly those rules of justice which are not due to nature but are enacted by man are not the same everywhere, since the constitution of the state is not the same everywhere; yet there is only one form of constitution which is everywhere in accordance with nature, namely the best form. . . .

Justice and Equity

The next subject to discuss is equity and its relation to justice. They appear on examination to be neither absolutely identical nor yet different in kind. Sometimes, it is true, we praise equity and the equitable man, and virtually employ the word as a term of general approval, using "more equitable" to mean merely "better."[16] But sometimes, when we think the matter out, it seems curious that the equitable should be praiseworthy if it is something different from what is just. If they are different, either the just or the equitable is not good, or if both are good, they are the same thing.

These then more or less are the considerations that make the meaning of "equity" a difficult problem. In one way, however, all the different uses of the term are correct, and there is no real inconsistency between them. Although equity is superior to one kind of justice, it is not better than justice as being generically different from it. Justice and equity are the same thing, and both are good, although equity is the better of the two.

The problem arises from the fact that equity, although just, is not justice as enacted by law, but a rectification of legal justice. The reason of this is that all law is universal, but there are some things about which it is not possible to make a universal statement which will be correct. In matters therefore in which a universal statement is necessary but it is not possible for it to be absolutely correct, the law follows the line that is valid as a general rule—though with full recognition of the error involved. Nevertheless this does not make it bad law, for the error does not lie in the law nor in the lawgiver, but in the nature of the case: the material of practical affairs is essentially irregular. When therefore the law lays down a general rule and

[16]In English "reasonable" is similarly used as a term of general approval.

afterwards a case arises that is not covered by the rule, the proper course is to rectify the omission in the law where it is defective and where it errs by oversimplification, and to insert the provision which the author of the law would himself suggest if he were present, and would have inserted if he had been cognizant of the case in question. Therefore while equity is just, and is better than one kind of justice, it is not superior to absolute justice, but only to the error that is caused by the absolute statement of what is just. This is the essential nature of equity—it is a rectification of the law where it is defective owing to its universality. Indeed this is the reason why law does not cover everything: there are some things for which it is impossible to provide by legislation, and consequently they require a special decree. When a thing is indefinite the rule dealing with it is also indefinite, like the mason's rule made of lead that is used by builders in Lesbos. This is not rigid but can be bent to fit the shape of the stone; and similarly a special decree can be adapted to suit the circumstances of the case.

The nature of equity has now been explained, and it has been shown to be just, and to be superior to one kind of justice. And from this it is clear what the equitable man is: he is a man who of set purpose and habitually does what is equitable, and does not stand on his rights unduly but is ready to accept less than his share although he has the law on his side. This quality of character is equity; it is a special kind of justice, not an entirely distinct quality.

Can a Man Treat Himself Unjustly?

The foregoing remarks supply an answer to the question, is it possible for a man to do an injustice to himself? One class of just acts consists of those acts, in conformity with one of the virtues, which are ordained by law. For instance, the law does not sanction suicide, and any form of homicide which it does not expressly permit it must be understood to forbid. Further, when a man in violation of the law voluntarily injures another man (not in retaliation), he acts unjustly ("voluntarily" meaning with a knowledge of the person affected and the instrument employed). Now a man who in a fit of anger stabs himself commits voluntarily an injury that is not a legitimate act of retaliation, and this the law does not permit. He is therefore committing an unjust offense. But against whom? Presumably against the state, not against himself, for he suffers the act voluntarily, and no one is voluntarily treated unjustly. Moreover it is for this that the state inflicts a penalty: suicide is punished by certain marks of dishonor, as an offense against the state.[17]

Secondly, in one sense a man who "acts unjustly" is merely unjust, and not wicked in every way; and in this sense it is not possible to act unjustly toward oneself (this is a different sense of the term from the one above; in one sense injustice is a particular evil quality, and does not imply complete wickedness, so that the unjust act specified does not display general wickedness). For, (1) that would imply that a

[17]At Athens a suicide's hand, as the guilty instrument, was cut off and buried separately from the body.

quality was both present and absent in the same person at the same time, which is impossible. Justice and injustice must always belong to different people. Moreover, (2) to be unjust an act must be voluntary and deliberate, and also unprovoked: a man who retaliates and does to another what that other has done to him is not thought to commit an injustice. But one who does harm to himself is both doing and suffering the same thing at the same time. Again, (3) if it were possible for a man to inflict an injustice on himself, it would be possible voluntarily to suffer injustice. And in addition, (4) acting unjustly means committing a particular act of injustice; for instance, adultery, burglary, theft; but a man cannot commit adultery with his own wife or steal his own property. And broadly speaking, the question "Can a man act unjustly toward himself?" is solved by our answer to the question about suffering injustice voluntarily.

(It is also clear that although both doing and receiving injustice are bad things, the former meaning to have more and the latter to have less than the medium amount, which corresponds to health in the art of medicine and to good bodily condition in the art of athletic training, yet to act unjustly is the worse of the two. For it involves wickedness and deserves reprehension, and its wickedness is complete or nearly complete; but to suffer injustice does not involve wickedness, viz., injustice, in the victim. In itself therefore to suffer injustice is the lesser evil, although it may well be the greater evil incidentally. But with this science is not concerned: it pronounces pleurisy to be a more serious malady than a sprain, in spite of the fact that a sprain might on occasion be a more serious mishap, if owing to it you stumbled in a battle and were taken prisoner and killed by the enemy.)

But in a metaphorical and analogical sense there is such a thing as justice not toward oneself but between the different parts of one's nature, not indeed justice in the full sense of the term but such as exists between master and servant or the head of a household and the members of his family. For in the discourses on these questions[18] distinction is made between the rational and irrational parts of the soul; and this has suggested the view that there is such a thing as injustice toward oneself, because these parts of the self may thwart each other in their respective desires, and consequently there is a sort of mutual justice between them as there is between ruler and subject.

[18]Plato's *Republic* and the writings of Plato's pupils in the Academy.

2

The Nature of Justice

Stanley I. Benn

Although "justice" is sometimes used as a synonym for "law" or "lawfulness," it has a broader sense, closer to "fairness." Questions of justice, according to Hume, Mill, and others, presuppose conflicts of interest; there would be no point in talking about justice, according to Hume, but for the limitations of human benevolence and the competition for scarce goods. Justice presupposes people pressing claims and justifying them by rules or standards. This distinguishes it from charity, benevolence, or generosity. No one can claim alms or gifts as a right. However, although this account is appropriate to questions of distributive justice, where the problem is to allocate benefits, it is not so obviously true of corrective (or retributive) justice. It is farfetched to describe a criminal trial as a conflict between an accused man's interest in being let alone and the community's interest (if it has one) in punishing him. Nevertheless, sentencing criminals and giving judgment in favor of one party to a dispute rather than another have this in common with distribution—that they all may involve overriding a claim and treating one person more harshly than another. All presuppose general principles by which such distinctions are regulated and justified.

Just Actions and Decisions

Aristotle's analysis of justice is the key to its meaning at the level of the particular act or decision. Justice, he said, consists in treating equals equally and unequals unequally but in proportion to their relevant differences. This involves,

From "Justice," *The Encyclopedia of Philosophy* (1967), pp. 298-301. Reprinted by permission of Macmillan Publishing Co., Inc.

first, the idea of impartiality; the honest judge considers only the features of the case that are relevant in law. Justice is no respecter of persons; wealth or status will influence judgment only if it makes a difference in law (for example, in taxation cases or the privilege of a member of Parliament in libel actions). Impartiality implies a kind of equality—not that all cases should be treated alike but that the onus rests on whoever would treat them differently to distinguish them in relevant ways. It is not for a judge to decide the respects in which men are equal but to decide whether the respects in which they are unequal are relevant to the issues in the case. That is what is really meant by the right to equal consideration—to be treated alike unless relevant differences have been proved.

These principles are not limited, of course, to the law. Many philosophers would regard it as characteristic of all moral judgments that the agent places his own interest on the same footing as the interests of others affected by his action, and this distinguishes moral judgments from prudential judgments, in which the agent assumes a position of privilege. The principle of impartiality is closely related, in this regard, to Kant's categorical imperative.

Is there a general duty to act justly? For a judge this is necessarily entailed by his function. Deciding issues according to law means taking account only of those features of a case to which the law attaches significance. But considering the question more generally, the very idea of moral justification implies impartiality and reference to rules. To ask a man why he allots more to A than to B is usually to ask for precisely the kind of justification implied in Aristotle's definition. One might explain a decision by reference to personal preferences; one could not justify it in this way. John Rawls has argued that we are rationally committed to acting justly by our very position as persons engaged with others in joint practices designed to promote common or complementary interests. We cannot reasonably expect other people to respect our interests unless we are prepared to respect theirs, and, as Leibniz put it, a man has grounds for complaint if, should you refuse to do something he asks you to do, he can judge that you would have made the same request in his place. The duty of justice, or fair dealing, according to Rawls, would emerge from the reciprocal recognition by a community of rational egoists that they had similar (and competing) interests and that no one could count on getting his way against all the rest. . . .

A somewhat similar argument, but couched in a transcendental form, is offered by del Vecchio. Consciousness of oneself as a subject of experience implies, according to del Vecchio, the awareness (and therefore the existence) of objects of experience ("not-self"), but it implies, too, the possibility that one is oneself the object of experience of other experiencing subjects. The very fact of consciousness implies at least the possibility of someone besides oneself who could be a subject of claims. To recognize the existence of another person would therefore be to acknowledge the initial equality or parity of two subjects standing toward each other in this reciprocal experience relationship. It is doubtful, however, whether del Vecchio is entitled to infer from consciousness of another person's existence a duty to respect his interests.

Moral reciprocity—doing to others as one would have them do to oneself and giving an equal return for benefits received—is closely linked to impartiality, for to be impartial between oneself and someone else would mean doing nothing to profit at his expense. From this follow ideas such as a fair wage, a just price, and a fair exchange (what Aristotle called "commutative justice"), as opposed to exploitation and profiteering. It may be difficult, of course, to evaluate benefits exchanged, and the only measure available may be a market price or some conventional standard. For instance, how can one evaluate domestic service without taking for granted a wage structure in which types of work are roughly graded according to accepted standards like skill and responsibility? And for any individual worker the just wage is necessarily related to the idea of "the wage for the job."

Justice considered as reciprocity is often held to require returning evil for evil as much as good for good (*lex talionis*). In this case punishment would be paying back what is due. Mill sought to reconcile retaliative justice with utilitarianism, arguing that the natural impulse to retaliate is moralized as a sentiment of justice by confining it to those cases where the injury is to society at large and where retaliative justice has a useful deterrent function. However, although the duty of reciprocity may spring from our recognition of other men, just as much as ourselves, as persons with interests and claims deserving of respect, we cannot infer from that a duty to *attack* their interests whenever they attack either our own or even those of society at large.

Criteria of a Just Rule or Practice

Although Aristotle respected the law-bound decision as the work of "passionless reason," he held, nevertheless, that because legislators could never foresee all the cases that would fall under a rule, it must be too rigid to do justice on every occasion. The equity jurisdiction of the English Court of Chancery grew up as a way of providing discretionary remedies where none was to be had in law. Again, in some branches of law judges rely on standards rather than strict rules and precedents, enjoying, in effect, wide discretion, or the law authorizes administrators to decide cases on their merits in the light of very general canons of policy, subject only to procedural safeguards of impartiality.

But if the law can be too rigid to do justice, does this not imply some extralegal canons of justice, by which perhaps the rules of law themselves might be assessed? Or again, what help is it to say, as we did earlier, that doing justice consists in making only *relevant* distinctions if the criteria of relevance are themselves in dispute? A judge may enforce a racial segregation law with strict impartiality and yet commit injustice if the distinctions embodied in the law are not themselves relevant.

Legal positivists are skeptical of nonlegal criteria of justice. Alf Ross, for instance, has declared that to use the word "just" as a description of a rule or general order, rather than of a particular decision in accordance with the rule, is merely to express emotion, like "banging on the table." Thrasymachus, caricatured in Book I of Plato's *Republic*, held that justice is simply what is advantageous to the stronger. The modern Marxist is more sophisticated; what is considered just, he holds, depends on the conflicting economic interests in a society, and law reflects those of the dominant class. Hobbes is often said to have been a positivist because he maintained that "just" and "unjust" presuppose a coercive power capable of enforcing obligations and that no complaint of injustice could be made against the sovereign legislator. But since he admitted that the sovereign may act inequitably, that is, contrary to natural law, canons of legal criticism beyond positive law do exist; it is only that the subject is not entitled to use them.

The idea of a law behind the law, the standard of justice to which positive law must conform, is exemplified in the "immutable and unwritten laws of Heaven" to which Sophocles' Antigone appeals against the decrees of Creon. In Stoic philosophy and in Roman jurisprudence this becomes a universal law of nature, equally accessible to all men through reason. Aquinas Christianized this theory by treating human law as the local application of natural law, which was itself an expression of God's rational will guiding the universe. By the early seventeenth century Grotius could argue that even if one could suppose that God did not exist, one would still be bound by the law of nature, since it derived from the two human qualities of sociability and rationality. Our need of society dictates the minimum conditions for social harmony. Natural law thus came to be regarded (for example, by Locke) as a universal test of the justice of positive law.

Classical natural law theory took too little account, no doubt, of the variety of legal institutions and moral standards and of their dependence on social and economic conditions. Modern natural-law theorists admit this. What are constant, they would say, are the formal criteria of justice rather than the substantive rules. They insist, however, that a just law formalizes a pre-existing, objective, juridical relationship, that it does not create justice but recognizes and attaches sanctions to what already exists, and that it can be rationally established independently of positive law. A highly abstract generalized theory of this kind was put forward, in Kantian terms, by Stammler. It is based on the principle that a person subjected to legal norms "must be respected as an end in himself, and treated as a participant in the community." But this is really to abandon the notion of a law behind the law and to offer, instead, formal or procedural criteria for rational criticism of positive law. Justice, in this sense, would be objective in that it would not be a matter of fiat but would be the subject of reasoned argument and justification. But it is doubtful whether there would now be any point in talking about justice as if it were something pre-existent—there to be discovered, like a new galaxy.

Almost as ancient as this kind of theory is the argument of Glaucon in the *Republic* (358–359) and Callicles in the *Gorgias* (483) that justice is conventional. Epicurus, denying that there ever was an absolute justice, declared: "Justice and injustice do not exist in relation to beings who have not been able to make a compact with the object of avoiding mutual harm" (*Doctrines and Maxims*). A compact, however, seems to imply that the duty to act justly stems from the duty to keep a promise, and that, as Hume pointed out, is no easier to establish. The strength of the conventionalist position is illustrated by Rawls's view of a just order as that body of principles that *anyone* might recognize as in his interest to maintain, given that others, on whose acquiescence he depends, have interests that conflict with his own. Although the rules might appear to discriminate against him on some given occasion, he would be able to see the point, nevertheless, of having those rules. This was, broadly, Hume's opinion. Justice, he held, was conventional in the sense of being necessary to society. Though there were discrepancies in detail, men's ideas on justice corresponded in essentials because they arose from needs common to all social situations. These rules were binding by custom and convention but were justified by their public utility.

Hume's view is close, therefore, to that of the utilitarians, which Samuel Butler attacked on the grounds that many acts promoting public utility might yet be acts of evident injustice. To rob Peter to pay Paul would be unjust in Butler's view, even though Paul gained more in happiness than Peter lost. Hume's position, however, is that the rules of justice serve the public interest only if decisions are regularly made in accordance with them, even though in some particular cases the public interest might be better served by departing from them. For the rules give security of expectation, which is their virtue, only if they are practices. Moreover, although one might have one's own views of what the rules ought to be, the just man would not act on them since the public interest is best served by supporting the social order, whatever its faults. Like Bentham, Hume stressed that "public utility requires that property should be regulated by general inflexible rules." This is the approach that Sidgwick called "conservative justice." He said that one could always argue against a change in the rules that people would be treated differently from the way others similarly placed had been treated theretofore. (Perelman has suggested this as a reason why all juridical systems are traditionalist, as in their attachment to precedent.) However, Sidgwick argued that conservative justice cannot be absolute. If the rule is contrary to the public interest, it is not, from a utilitarian standpoint, in accordance with "ideal justice." Nevertheless, it is commonly allowed that if normal expectations *are* disappointed, there ought to be compensation.

Rawls has challenged the view that a practice is just if it answers most fully to wants and interests. Justice is not the outcome but is presupposed by such a calculation. Any interest not compatible with justice ought not to be counted. Classical utilitarianism is at fault, according to Rawls, because it permits one to give as a reason why slavery is unjust that the advantages to the slaveholder do not outweigh the disadvantages to the slave and to society at large. Justice, understood as fairness, would not admit to the calculation the advantages of the slaveholder as such because his role could not be mutually acknowledged as part of an acceptable practice by all parties involved. It would not be thought relevant for one person, engaged with another in a common practice and accused by him of injustice, to answer that nevertheless it allowed of the greatest satisfaction of desire.

Classical utilitarianism is least satisfactory in its treatment of justice. The argument that adhering to rules gives greater general satisfaction than deciding every case on its happiness-producing merits does not meet the objection that a rule would still be unjust which deprived a tiny minority of the basic conditions for a decent life, even though it gave great satisfaction to everyone else. The Benthamite saving clause—"each to count for one and for no more than one"—attempts to write the principle of impartiality into the foundations of the system but does not meet the objection. One has to make the further assumptions that the more desires one has satisfied, the less one values the satisfaction and that there is an interpersonal equivalence of satisfactions all the way up the scale. One might then argue that the cost in satisfaction to a sacrificed minority would be so great that whatever the additional satisfaction to the majority, it must be less. But this is a quite arbitrary postulate, to avoid the conflict between the theory and our moral sentiments.

Criteria of Distributive Justice

It would be generally agreed that doing justice means treating equals equally and unequals according to their relevant inequalities. Disagreements arise over the criteria of relevance—that is, over the rule to be applied. Distribution (for example, of income, taxation, social service benefits, rations) may be organized on any of at least three principles of justice: arithmetical equality, merit (or desert), or need. Where no good ground can be shown for treating people differently, they clearly ought to be treated alike. This is the procedural presupposition of justice. The principle "one man, one vote" asserts that there are no differences between persons that would justify a differential franchise. This is not the case with progressive taxation, where capacity to pay is taken as a ground for discrimination.

Rewards or earnings are regulated by criteria of merit or desert, varying with the kind of treatment. Athletic prowess, said Aristotle, is rightly rewarded by prizes, nobility of birth and character by political honors and office. Wages are regulated according to skill, responsibility, industriousness, and similar factors. The only kind of reasons one could give for using such criteria, however, would be in the utilitarian terms of public interest, such as stimulating production.

Some social reformers have believed that distribution according to works should be replaced entirely by distribution according to need. Need criteria presuppose some standard condition that a person would fall short of were the need not satisfied and that falling short of it would be a bad thing—a hardship. Special disabilities involve special needs, calling for special treatment if the standard is to be reached. Needs are therefore claims, grounded on a standard to which a person is entitled simply as a person, irrespective of merit or desert. (There are also functional needs, like the plumber's need for tools, which would have to be justified in utilitarian terms.) The working of need criteria in general bears out the criticisms made earlier of utilitarian theories based on the satisfaction of desires. If it is prima facie unjust to give well-fed men television sets while others starve, it is not because that is not the way to maximize satisfaction. It is, rather, that the degree of urgency of a need depends on how far leaving it unsatisfied deprives an individual of the normal standard to which he is entitled as a person.

Justice and Integrity

Justice has been treated here as a particular virtue. Some philosophers, however, have meant by it an all-embracing virtue, closer to righteousness than to fairness. Contact with the narrower sense is to some extent preserved, however, in that justice is thought of as apportioning to each particular virtue or excellence its proper sphere. Plato's just state is that in which every man does the job to which he is best fitted, under the direction of the wisest; the just man is the one in whom the parts of the soul are harmoniously governed by reason. This conception may not be so far from our notion of a just man as one who possesses integrity, who lives according to consistent principles and is not to be diverted from them by consideration of gain, desire, or passion. However, justice in this sense has been the preoccupation of moralists rather than moral philosophers.

3

The Canons of Distributive Justice

Nicholas Rescher

In the course of the long history of discussions on the subject, distributive justice has been held to consist, wholly or primarily, in the treatment of all people:

1. as equals (except possibly in the case of certain "negative" distributions such as punishments)
2. according to their needs
3. according to their ability or merit or achievements
4. according to their efforts and sacrifices
5. according to their actual productive contribution
6. according to the requirements of the common good, or the public interest, or the welfare of mankind, or the greater good of a greater number
7. according to a valuation of their socially useful services in terms of their scarcity in the essentially economic terms of supply and demand

Correspondingly, seven "canons" of distributive justice result, depending upon which of these factors is taken as the ultimate or primary determinant of individual claims; namely, the canons of equality, need, ability, effort, productivity, public utility, and supply and demand. Brief consideration must be given to each of these proposed conceptions of justice.[1]

From *Distributive Justice* (1966), pp. 73–83. Reprinted by permission of the author.

[1]All of these canons except number 3 (the Canon of Ability) are competently and instructively discussed from an essentially economic point of view—from the special angle of the idea of a just wage or income—in ch. 14 of John A. Ryan, *Distributive Justice* (3rd ed.), New York: Macmillan, 1942.

The Canon of Equality

This canon holds that justice consists in the treatment of people as equals. Here we have the *egalitarian* criterion of (idealistic) democratic theorists. The shortcomings of this canon have already been canvassed in considerable detail . . . to the effect that the principle is oblivious to the reality of differential claims and desert. It is vulnerable to all the same lines of objection which hold against the type of just-wage principle advocated by G. B. Shaw—to let all who contribute to the production of the social-economic product share in it equally.[2] Moreover, the specification of the exact way in which equality is to be understood is by no means so simple and straightforward as it seems on first view. Is one, for example, to think of the type of fixed constant equality that is at issue in a sales tax, or the "equal burden" type of differential equality at issue in a graduated income tax; and more generally, is the "equality" at issue strict equality, equality of sacrifice, equality of opportunity-and-risk, equality of rights, or equality of "consideration," etc.?[3]

A rule of strict equality violates the most elemental requisites of the concept of justice itself: justice not only requires the equal treatment of equals, as the canon at issue would certainly assure, but also under various circumstances requires the converse, the (appropriately measured) unequal treatment of unequals, a requisite which the canon violates blatantly. In any distribution among individuals whose legitimate claims with respect to this distribution are diverse, the treatment of people as equals without reference to their differential claims outrages rather than implements our sense of justice.

The Canon of Need

This canon holds that justice consists in the treatment of people according

[2]Ryan, *Distributive Justice* (3rd ed.), pp. 180–181: "According to the rule of arithmetical equality, all persons who contribute to the product should receive the same amount of remuneration. With the exception of Bernard Shaw, no important writer defends this rule to-day. It is unjust because it would treat unequals equally. Although men are equal as moral entities, as human persons, they are unequal in desires, capacities, and powers. An income that would fully satisfy the needs of one man would meet only 75 per cent., or 50 per cent., of the capacities of another. To allot them equal amounts of income would be to treat them unequally with regard to the requisites of life and self development. To treat them unequally in these matters would be to treat them unequally as regards the real and only purpose of property rights. That purpose is welfare. Hence the equal moral claims of men which admittedly arise out of their moral equality must be construed as claims to equal degrees of welfare, not to equal amounts of external goods. . . . Moreover, the rule of equal incomes is socially impracticable. It would deter the great majority of the more efficient from putting forth their best efforts and turning out their maximum product. As a consequence, the total volume of product would be so diminished as to render the share of the great majority of persons smaller than it would have been under a rational plan of unequal distribution."

[3]Regarding these problems, see S. I. Benn and R. S. Peters, *Social Principles and the Democratic State* (London: Allen & Unwin, 1959), ch. 5, "Justice and Equality."

to their needs. Here we have the *socialistic* principle of the idealistic socialistic and communist theoreticians: "to each according to his needs."[4] Basically this principle is closely allied with the preceding one, and is, like it, one of *rectification*: recognizing that as things stand, men come into the world with different possessions and opportunities as well as differences in natural endowments, the principle professes to treat them, not equally, but so as to *make* them as equal as possible.

Regarding this principle, it has been said:

> If the task of distribution were entirely independent of the process of production, this rule would be ideal [from the standpoint of justice]; for it would treat men as equal in those respects in which they are equal; namely, as beings endowed with the dignity and the potencies of personality; and it would treat them as unequal in those respects in which they are unequal; that is, in their desires and capacities.[5]

This limitation of the rule is of itself too narrow. The principle does recognize inequalities, but it recognizes only one sort; it rides roughshod not only over the matter of productive contributions but over all other ways of grounding legitimate claims (e.g., those based on kinship, on [nonproductive] services rendered, on contracts and compacts, etc.) that make for relevant differences, i.e., inequalities, among the potential recipients of a distribution. Nor, for that matter, is the principle as clear-cut as it seems on first view: by the time anything like an adequate analysis of "need" has been provided, the principle covers a wide-ranging area.[6] For example, are we to interpret the "needs" at issue as *real* needs or as *felt* needs?

The Canon of Ability and/or Achievement

This canon holds that justice consists in the treatment of people according to their abilities. Here we have the *meritarian* criterion going back to Aristotle and echoed by the (Jeffersonian) theorists of a "natural aristocracy of ability." Natural ability, however, is a latent quality which subsists in the mode of potentiality. It represents natural endowments that can be cultivated to varying degrees and may or may not become operative and actually put to work. To allocate rewards with reference solely to innate ability, unqualified by considerations of how the abilities in question are used or abused, would be to act in a way that is patently unjust. Moreover, a question can validly be raised as to the propriety of having natural

[4]The formula "From each according to his abilities; to each according to his needs" was first advanced by the early French socialists of the Utopian school, and was officially adopted by German socialists in the Gotha Program of 1875.

[5]Ryan, *Distributive Justice* (3rd ed.), p. 181.

[6]See Benn and Peters, *Social Principles and the Democratic State*, pp. 141–148.

ability—which is, after all, wholly a "gift of the gods" and in no way a matter of desert—count as the sole or even the primary basis of claims.[7]

This objection might be countered by granting that it may hold for *natural* (or innate) ability, but that it fails to be applicable when the "ability" at issue is an *acquired* ability, or perhaps even more aptly, a *demonstrated* ability of the persons at issue, as determined by their achievements. This is the criterion naturally used in giving grades to students and prizes to tennis players (where need, for instance, and effort are deliberately discounted). But in this case the canon becomes transformed, in its essentials, into the Canon of Productivity, which will be dealt with below.

The Canon of Effort

This canon holds that justice consists in the treatment of people according to their efforts and sacrifices on their own behalves, or perhaps on behalf of their group (family, society, fellowmen). Here we have the *puritanical* principle espoused by theorists of a "Puritan ethic," who hold that God helps (and men should help) those who help themselves. Burke lauded the "natural society" in which "it is an invariable law that a man's acquisitions are in proportion to his labors."[8] Think also of the historic discussions of a just wage and the traditional justification of differential wage scales. On the question of wages, classical socialists such as Fourier and St. Simon argued that the wage should be inversely proportioned to the intrinsic pleasantness (interest, appeal, prestige) of the task. (Presumably, thus, the policeman walking the beat shall receive more than the captain sitting at headquarters.) But the difficulties of this standpoint lie on the surface, e.g., the difficulty of maintaining morale and discipline in a setting in which the claims of ability and responsibility go unrecognized.

Moreover, the principle ignores the fact that effort is of its very nature a many-sided thing: it can be either fruitful or vain, well-directed or misguided, properly applied or misapplied, availing or unavailing, etc. To allocate rewards by effort as such without reference to its nature and direction is to ignore a key facet of just procedure—to fail to make a distinction that makes a difference. Also, to reward by effort rather than achievement is socially undesirable: it weakens incentive and encourages the inefficient, the untalented, the incompetent.

The Canon of Productivity

This canon holds that justice consists in the treatment of people according

[7]"That part of a man's income which he owes to the possession of extraordinary natural abilities is a free boon to him; and from an abstract point of view bears some resemblance to the rent of other free gifts of nature. . . ." A. Marshall, *Principles of Economics* (8th ed., London: Macmillan, 1920), p. 664. The receipt of such "rents" is surely a matter of capitalizing on public necessity rather than one of obtaining the just reward due to individual desert.

[8]Edmund Burke, *Vindication of a Natural Society*, cited by E. Halévy in *The Growth of Philosophic Radicalism*, tr. Mary Morris, p. 216.

to their actual productive contribution to their group.[9] Here we have the essentially economic principle of the social-welfare-minded *capitalistic* theoreticians. The claim-bases at issue here are primarily those traditionally considered in economics: services rendered, capital advanced, risks run, and the like. Much is to be said on behalf of this principle as a *restricted* rule, governing the division of proceeds and profits resulting from a common productive enterprise; but it is clearly defective as a general principle of distributive justice, simply because it is an overly limited single-factor criterion. The principle is prepared to put aside all considerations not only of unmerited claims in general, but also of merited claims when merited through extra-productive factors such as need and effort.

Yet one cannot fail to be impressed by the appeal to justice of such an argument as the following:

> When men of equal productive power are performing the same kind of labour, superior amounts of product do represent superior amounts of effort. . . . If men are unequal in productive power their products are obviously not in proportion to their efforts. Consider two men whose natural physical abilities are so unequal that they can handle with equal effort shovels differing in capacity by fifty per cent. Instances of this kind are innumerable in industry. If these two men are rewarded according to productivi-ty, one will get fifty per cent more compensation than the other. Yet the surplus received by the more fortunate man does not represent any action or quality for which he is personally responsible. It corresponds to no larger output of personal effort, no superior exercise of will, no greater personal desert.[10]

Note here the criticism of a (restricted) purely economic application of the principle by an appeal to one's sense of justice. If such an appeal is to be given but the slightest (even if not ultimately decisive) weight, as I think it must, then the canon in question must *a fortiori* be at once abandoned as an exclusive and exhaustive general principle of distributive justice.

The Canon of Social Utility

This canon holds that justice consists in the treatment of people according to the best prospects for advancing the common good, or the public interest, or the welfare of mankind, or the greater good of a greater number. The theory has two basic variants, according as one resorts to a distinction between the common good of men considered *collectively*, as constituting a social group with some sort of life of its own, or merely *distributively*, as an aggregation of separate individuals. In the former

---

[9]Two alternative constructions of the principle arise, according as the "productive contribution" at issue is construed as the *total* contribution, or as solely the *net* contribution, i.e., the part that is available for consumption by others after deletion of the producers' own share.
[10]Ryan, *Distributive Justice* (3rd ed.), pp. 183–184.

case we have the "public interest," expedientialist variant of the canon with roots going back to Hebraic theology, Stoic philosophy, and Roman jurisprudence (*pro bono publico*). In the second case we have the *utilitarian* and more modern, individualistic version of the canon.

The same fundamental criticism (already dwelt upon at considerable length in our preceding discussion) can be deployed against both versions of the theory: an individual's *proper share viewed from the angle of the general good* cannot be equated with his *just share* pure and simple, because there is no "pre-established harmony" to guarantee that all of the individual's legitimate claims (the authoritative determinants of his just share) be recognized and acceded to when "the *general* good" becomes the decisive criterion. And insofar as these legitimate claims are disallowed—or *could* be disallowed—in a patently unjust (though socially advantageous) way, the principle of the primacy of the general good exhibits a feature which precludes its acceptance as a principle of justice.

The Canon of Supply and Demand

This canon holds that justice consists in the treatment of people according to a valuation of their socially useful—or perhaps merely desired—contributions, these being evaluated not on the basis of the value of the product (as with the Canon of Productivity, above), but on the basis of relative scarcity of the service. Here we have the essentially economic principle of the more hard-boiled "play of the market" school of laissez-faire theoreticians. The train dispatcher would thus deserve a larger part of the proceeds of the joint operation than the conductor, the general manager more than the section foreman, the buyer more than the salesgirl, because—while in each case both kinds of contribution are alike essential to the enterprise—the former type of labor calls for skills that are relatively scarcer, being less plentifully diffused throughout the working population. Such valuation then rests not upon the relative extent or intrinsic merit of the contribution made, but upon the fact that that contribution is viewed by the community as necessary or desirable, and can either be made successfully by fewer people, or else involves such expenditures, risks, hardships, or hazards that fewer people are willing to undertake the task. (Throughout recent years successful entertainers have been remunerated more highly than successful physicians—and on this principle, justly so.)

As a criterion of justice, this canon suffers from the same general defects as does the Canon of Productivity which it seeks to qualify. Not only does it put aside any accommodation of unmerited claims, but also any claims based upon factors (such as individual need and expenditure of effort) which have no basis in the making of a productive contribution to felt social needs.

Our Own Position: The Canon of Claims

One and the same shortcoming runs through all of the above canons of distributive justice: they are all *monistic*. They all recognize but one solitary, homogeneous mode of claim production (be it need, effort, productivity, or whatever), to the exclusion of all others. A single specific ground of claim establishment is canonized as uniquely authoritative, and all the others dismissed. As a result, these canons all suffer the aristocratic fault of hyperexclusiveness. As we see it, they err not so much in commission as in omission.

To correct this failing requires that we go from a concept of claim establishment that is monistic and homogeneous to one that is pluralistic and heterogeneous. To do so we put forward, as representing (in essentials) our own position on the issue of distributive justice, the Canon of Claims: Distributive justice consists in the treatment of people *according to their legitimate claims*, positive and negative. This canon shifts the burden to—and thus its implementation hinges crucially upon—the question of the nature of legitimate claims, and of the machinery for their mutual accommodation in cases of plurality, and their reconciliation in cases of conflict. To say this is not a criticism of the principle, but simply the recognition of an inevitable difficulty which must be encountered by any theory of distributive justice at the penalty of showing itself grossly inadequate.

The Canon of Claims plainly avoids the fault of overrestrictiveness: indeed, it reaches out to embrace all the other canons. From its perspective each canon represents one particular sort of ground (need, effort, productivity, etc.) on whose basis certain legitimate claims—upon whose accommodation it insists—can be advanced. The evaluation of these claims in context, and their due recognition under the circumstances, is in our view the key element of distributive justice.

We must be prepared to take such a multifaceted approach to claims because of the propriety of recognizing different kinds of claim-grounds as appropriate types of distribution. Our society inclines to the view that in the case of wages, desert is to be measured according to productivity of contribution qualified by supply-and-demand considerations; in the case of property income, by productivity considerations; in public-welfare distributions, by need qualifed to avoid the demoralization inherent in certain types of means-tests; and in the negative distributions of taxation, by ability-to-pay qualified by social-utility considerations. The list could be extended and refined at great length but is already extensive enough to lend support to our pluralistic view of claims.

One important consequence of our canon must be noted. With it, the concept of justice is no solitarily self-sufficient ultimate, but becomes dependent upon the articulation of certain coordinate ideas, namely, those relating to claims and their establishment. The unraveling of the short thesis that distributive justice requires (in general) the accommodation of legitimate claims is but the preface of a long story about claims, a story for which there is neither need nor space here. Moreover, since claims themselves are not (at any rate, not in general) established by considerations of abstract justice, but are in large part grounded in positive law, the heavy dependence of justice upon a body of positive law may be seen. Where abstract justice might countenance various alternative divisions, the law specifies one particular procedure that underwrites a certain specific set of claims. That law shall embody considerations of justice is a trite thesis, but that there is a converse requirement resulting in mutual dependence is less frequently observed.

In espousing the Canon of Claims we may note that the search for a canon of distributive justice is carried back to the Roman jurists' view that the definitive principle of justice is inherent in the dictum *suum cuique tribuens*—"giving each his own." To the question *What is his own?* we have given the answer *What he deserves!*; that is, a share ideally equal—or at any rate generally proportional—to his legitimate claims.

III
LIBERAL JUSTICE

Section A
The Contractual Tradition: Defenses and Critiques

4

The Contractual Basis for a Just Society

Immanuel Kant

Among all the contracts by which a large group of men unites to form a society, . . . the contract establishing a *civil constitution* . . . is of an exceptional nature. For while, so far as its execution is concerned, it has much in common with all others that are likewise directed toward a chosen end to be pursued by joint effort, it is essentially different from all others in the principle of its constitution. . . . In all social contracts, we find a union of many individuals for some common end which they all *share*. But a union as an end in itself which they all *ought to share* and which is thus an absolute and primary duty in all external relationships whatsoever among human beings (who cannot avoid mutually influencing one another), is only found in a society insofar as it constitutes a civil state, i.e. a commonwealth. . . .

The civil state, regarded purely as a lawful state, is based on the following *a priori* principles:

1. the *freedom* of every member of society as a *human being*
2. the *equality* of each with all the others as a *subject*
3. the *independence* of each member of a commonwealth as a *citizen*

These principles are not so much laws given by an already established state, as laws by which a state can alone be established in accordance with pure rational principles of external human right. Thus:

1. Man's *freedom* as a human being, as a principle for the constitution of a commonwealth, can be expressed in the following formula. No one can compel me to

From *Kant's Political Writings*, edited by Hans Reiss and translated by H. B. Nisbet (1970), pp. 73–81. Reprinted by permission of Cambridge University Press.

be happy in accordance with his conception of the welfare of others, for each may seek his happiness in whatever way he sees fit, so long as he does not infringe upon the freedom of others to pursue a similar end which can be reconciled with the freedom of everyone else within a workable general law—i.e., he must accord to others the same right as he enjoys himself. A government might be established on the principle of benevolence toward the people, like that of a father toward his children. Under such a *paternal government* . . . the subjects, as immature children who cannot distinguish what is truly useful or harmful to themselves, would be obliged to behave purely passively and to rely upon the judgement of the head of state as to how they *ought* to be happy, and upon his kindness in willing their happiness at all. Such a government is the greatest conceivable *despotism*, i.e., a constitution which suspends the entire freedom of its subjects, who thenceforth have no rights whatsoever. The only conceivable government for men who are capable of possessing rights, even if the ruler is benevolent, is not a *paternal* but a *patriotic* government. . . . A *patriotic* attitude is one where everyone in the state, not excepting its head, regards the commonwealth as a maternal womb, or the land as the paternal ground from which he himself sprang and which he must leave to his descendants as a treasured pledge. Each regards himself as authorized to protect the rights of the commonwealth by laws of the general will, but not to submit it to his personal use at his own absolute pleasure. This right of freedom belongs to each member of the commonwealth as a human being, insofar as each is a being capable of possessing rights.

2. Man's equality as a subject might be formulated as follows. Each member of the commonwealth has rights of coercion in relation to all the others, except in relation to the head of state. For he alone is not a member of the commonwealth, but its creator or preserver, and he alone is authorized to coerce others without being subject to any coercive law himself. But all who are subject to laws are the subjects of a state, and are thus subject to the right of coercion along with all other members of the commonwealth; the only exception is a single person (in either the physical or the moral sense of the word), the head of state, through whom alone the rightful coercion of all others can be exercised. For if he too could be coerced, he would not be the head of state, and the hierarchy of subordination would ascend infinitely. But if there were two persons exempt from coercion, neither would be subject to coercive laws, and neither could do to the other anything contrary to right, which is impossible.

This uniform equality of human beings as subjects of a state is, however, perfectly consistent with the utmost inequality of the mass in the degree of its possessions, whether these take the form of physical or mental superiority over others, or of fortuitous external property and of particular rights (of which there may be many) with respect to others. Thus the welfare of the one depends very much on the will of the other (the poor depending on the rich), the one must obey the other (as the child its parents or the wife her husband), the one serves (the laborer) while the other pays, etc. Nevertheless, they are all equal as subjects *before the law*, which, as the pronouncement of the general will, can only be single in form, and which concerns the form of right and not the material or object in relation to which I possess rights. For no one can coerce anyone else other than through the public law and its executor, the head of state, while everyone else can resist the others in the same way and to the same degree. No one, however, can lose this authority to coerce others and to have rights toward them except through committing a crime. And no one can voluntarily renounce his rights by a contract or legal transaction to the effect that he has no rights but only duties, for such a contract would deprive him of the right to make a contract, and would thus invalidate the one he had already made.

From this idea of the equality of men as subjects in a commonwealth, there emerges this further formula: every member of the commonwealth must be entitled to reach any degree of rank which a subject can earn through his talent, his industry and his good fortune. And his fellow-subjects may not stand in his way by *hereditary* prerogatives or privileges of rank and thereby hold him and his descendants back indefinitely.

All right consists solely in the restriction of the freedom of others, with the qualification that their freedom can co-exist with my freedom within the terms of a general law; and public right in a commonwealth is simply a state of affairs regulated by a real legislation which conforms to this principle and is backed up by power, and under which a whole people live as subjects in a lawful state. . . . This is what we call a civil state, and it is characterized by equality in the effects and countereffects of freely willed actions which limit one another in accordance with the general law of freedom. Thus the *birthright* of each individual in such a state (i.e., before he has performed any acts which can be judged in relation to right) is absolutely *equal* as regards his authority to coerce others to use their freedom in a way which harmonizes with his freedom. Since birth is not an act on the part of the one who is born, it cannot create any inequality in his legal position and cannot make him submit to any coercive laws except insofar as he is a subject, along with all the others, of the one supreme legislative power. Thus no member of the commonwealth can have a hereditary privilege as against his fellow-subjects; and no one can hand down to his descendants the privileges attached to the rank he occupies in the commonwealth, nor act as if he were qualified as a ruler by birth and forcibly prevent others from reaching the higher levels of the hierarchy (which are *superior* and *inferior*, but never *imperans* and *subiectus*) through their own merit. He may hand down everything else, so long as it is material and not pertaining to his person, for it may be acquired and disposed of as property and may over a series of generations create considerable inequalities in wealth among the members of the commonwealth (the employee and the employer, the landowner and the agricultural servants, etc.). But he may not prevent his subordinates from raising themselves to his own level if they are able and entitled to do so by their talent, industry and good fortune. If this were not so, he would be allowed to practise coercion without himself being subject to coercive countermeasures from others, and would thus be more than their fellow-subject. No one who lives within the lawful state of a commonwealth can forfeit this equality other than through some crime of his own, but never by contract or through military force. . . . For no legal transaction on his part or on that of anyone else can make him cease to be his own master. He cannot become like a domestic animal to be employed in any chosen capacity and retained therein without consent for any desired period, even with the reservation (which is at times sanctioned by religion, as among the Indians) that he may not be maimed or killed. He can be considered happy in any condition so long as he is aware that, if he does not reach the same level as others, the fault lies either with himself (i.e., lack of ability or serious endeavour) or with circumstances for which he cannot blame others, and not with the irresistible will of any outside party. For as far as right is concerned, his fellow-subjects have no advantage over him.

    3. The *independence* . . . of a member of the commonwealth as a *citizen*, i.e., as a co-legislator, may be defined as follows. In the question of actual legislation, all who are free and equal under existing public laws may be considered equal, but not as regards the right to make these laws. Those who are not entitled to this right are nonetheless obliged, as members of the commonwealth, to comply with these laws, and they thus likewise enjoy their protection (not as *citizens* but as co-beneficiaries of this protection). For all right depends on laws. But a public law which defines for everyone that which is permitted and prohibited by right, is the act of a public will, from which all right proceeds and which must not therefore itself be able to do an injustice to any one. And this requires no less than the will of the entire people (since all men decide for all men and each decides for himself). For only toward oneself can one never act unjustly. But on the other hand, the will of another person cannot decide anything for someone without injustice, so that the law made by this other person would require a further law to limit his legislation. Thus an individual will cannot legislate for a commonwealth. For this requires freedom, equality and *unity* of the will of *all* the members. And the prerequisite for unity, since it necessitates a general vote (if freedom and equality are both present), is independence. The basic law, which can come only from the general, united will of the people, is called the *original contract*.

    Anyone who has the right to vote on this legislation is a *citizen* . . . (i.e., citizen of a state). . . . The only qualification required by a citizen (apart, of course, from being an adult male) is that he must be his *own master* . . . , and must have some *property* (which can include any skill, trade, fine art or science) to support himself. In cases where he must earn his living from others, he must earn it only by *selling* that which is his,[1] and not by allowing others to make use of him; for he must in the true sense of the word *serve* no one but the commonwealth. In this respect, artisans and large or small landowners are all equal, and each is entitled to one vote only. As for landowners, we leave aside the question of how anyone can have rightfully acquired

---

[1]He who does a piece of work (*opus*) can sell it to someone else, just as if it were his own property. But guaranteeing one's labor (*praestatio operae*) is not the same as selling a commodity. The domestic servant, the shop assistant, the laborer, or even the barber, are merely laborers (*operarii*), not *artists* (*artifices*, in the wider sense) or members of the state, and are thus unqualified to be citizens. And although the man to whom I give my firewood to chop and the tailor to whom I give material to make into clothes both appear to have a similar relationship toward me, the former differs from the latter in the same way as the barber from the wigmaker (to whom I may in fact have given the requisite hair) or the laborer from the artist or tradesman, who does a piece of work which belongs to him until he is paid for it. For the latter, in pursuing his trade, exchanges his property with someone else (*opus*), while the former allows someone else to make use of him. But I do admit that it is somewhat difficult to define the qualifications which entitle anyone to claim the status of being his own master.

more land than he can cultivate with his own hands (for acquisition by military seizure is not primary acquisition), and how it came about that numerous people who might otherwise have acquired permanent property were thereby reduced to serving someone else in order to live at all. It would certainly conflict with the above principle of equality if a law were to grant them a privileged status so that their descendants would always remain feudal landowners, without their land being sold or divided by inheritance and thus made useful to more people; it would also be unjust if only those belonging to an arbitrarily selected class were allowed to acquire land, should the estates in fact be divided. The owner of a large estate keeps out as many smaller property owners (and their votes) as could otherwise occupy his territories. He does not vote on their behalf, and himself has only *one* vote. It should be left exclusively to the ability, industry and good fortune of each member of the commonwealth to enable each to acquire a part and all to acquire the whole, although this distinction cannot be observed within the general legislation itself. The number of those entitled to vote on matters of legislation must be calculated purely from the number of property owners, not from the size of their properties.

Those who possess this right to vote must agree *unanimously* to the law of public justice, or else a legal contention would arise between those who agree and those who disagree, and it would require yet another higher legal principle to resolve it. An entire people cannot, however, be expected to reach unanimity, but only to show a majority of votes (and not even of direct votes, but simply of the votes of those delegated in a large nation to represent the people). Thus the actual principle of being content with majority decisions must be accepted unanimously and embodied in a contract; and this itself must be the ultimate basis on which a civil constitution is established.

Conclusion

This, then, is an *original contract* by means of which a civil and thus completely lawful constitution and commonwealth can alone be established. But we need by no means assume that this contract . . . , based on a coalition of the wills of all private individuals in a nation to form a common, public will for the purposes of rightful legislation, actually exists as a *fact*, for it cannot possibly be so. Such an assumption would mean that we would first have to prove from history that some nation, whose rights and obligations have been passed down to us, did in fact perform such an act, and handed down some authentic record or legal instrument, orally or in writing, before we could regard ourselves as bound by a preexisting civil constitution. It is in fact merely an *idea* of reason, which nonetheless has undoubted practical reality; for it can oblige every legislator to frame his laws in such a way that they could have been produced by the united will of a whole nation, and to regard each subject, insofar as he can claim citizenship, as if he had consented within the general will. This is the test of the rightfulness of every public law. For if the law is such that a whole people could not *possibly* agree to it (for example, if it stated that a certain class of *subjects* must be privileged as a hereditary *ruling class*), it is unjust; but if it is at least *possible* that a people could agree to it, it is our duty to consider the law as just, even if the people is at present in such a position or attitude of mind that it would probably refuse its consent if it were consulted.[2] But this restriction obviously applies only to the judgment of the legislator, not to that of the subject. Thus if a people, under some existing legislation, were asked to make a judgment which in all probability would prejudice its happiness, what should it do? Should the people not oppose the measure? The only possible answer is that they can do nothing but obey. For we are not concerned here with any happiness which the subject might expect to derive from the institutions or administration of the commonwealth, but primarily with the rights which would thereby be secured for everyone. And this is the highest principle from which all maxims relating to the commonwealth must begin, and which cannot be qualified by any other principles. No generally valid principle of legislation can be based on happiness. For both the current circumstances and the highly conflicting and variable illusions as to what happiness is (and no one can prescribe to others how they should attain it) make all fixed principles impossible, so that happiness alone can never be a suitable principle of legislation. The doctrine that *salus publica suprema civitatis lex est*[3] retains its value and authority undiminished; but the public welfare which demands *first* consideration lies precisely in that legal constitution which guarantees everyone his freedom within the law, so that each remains free to seek his happiness in whatever way he thinks best, so long as he does not violate the lawful freedom and rights of his fellow subjects at large. If the supreme power makes laws which are primarily directed toward happiness (the affluence of the citizens, increased population, etc.), this cannot be regarded as the end for which a civil constitution was established, but only as a means of *securing the rightful state*, especially against external enemies of the people. The head of state must be authorized to judge for himself whether such measures are necessary for the commonwealth's prosperity, which is required to maintain its strength and stability both internally and against external enemies. The aim is not, as it were, to make the people happy against its will, but only to ensure its continued existence as a commonwealth.[4] The legislator may indeed err in judging whether or not the measures he adopts are *prudent*, but not in deciding whether or not the law harmonizes with the principle of right. For he has ready to hand as an infallible *a*

---

[2]If, for example, a war tax were proportionately imposed on all subjects, they could not claim, simply because it is oppressive, that it is unjust because the war is in their opinion unnecessary. For they are not entitled to judge this issue, since it is at least *possible* that the war is inevitable and the tax indispensable, so that the tax must be deemed rightful in the judgment of the subjects. But if certain estate owners were oppressed with levies for such a war, while others of the same class were exempted, it is easily seen that a whole people could never agree to a law of this kind, and it is entitled at least to make representations against it, since an unequal distribution of burdens can never be considered just.

[3]"The public welfare is the supreme law of the state."

[4]Measures of this kind might include certain restrictions on imports, so that the means of livelihood may be developed for the benefit of the subjects themselves and not as an advantage to foreigners or an encouragement for their industry. For without the prosperity of the people, the state would not have enough strength to resist external enemies or to preserve itself as a commonwealth.

priori standard, the idea of an original contract, and he need not wait for experience to show whether the means are suitable, as would be necessary if they were based on the principle of happiness. For so long as it is not self-contradictory to say that an entire people could agree to such a law, however painful it might seem, then the law is in harmony with right. But if a public law is beyond reproach (i.e., *irreprehensible*) with respect to right, it carries with it the authority to coerce those to whom it applies, and conversely, it forbids them to resist the will of the legislator by violent means. In other words, the power of the state to put the law into effect is also *irresistible*, and no rightfully established commonwealth can exist without a force of this kind to suppress all internal resistance. For such resistance would be dictated by a maxim which, if it became general, would destroy the whole civil constitution and put an end to the only state in which men can possess rights.

5

Justice as Rational Choice
Behind a Veil of Ignorance

John Rawls

My aim is to present a conception of justice which generalizes and carries to a higher level of abstraction the familiar theory of the social contract as found, say, in Locke, Rousseau, and Kant.[1] In order to do this we are not to think of the original contract as one to enter a particular society or to set up a particular form of government. Rather, the guiding idea is that the principles of justice for the basic structure of society are the object of the original agreement. They are the principles that free and rational persons concerned to further their own interests would accept in an initial position of equality as defining the fundamental terms of their association. These principles are to regulate all further agreements; they specify the kinds of social cooperation that can be entered into and the forms of government that can be established. This way of regarding the principles of justice I shall call justice as fairness.

Thus we are to imagine that those who engage in social cooperation choose together, in one joint act, the principles which are to assign basic rights and duties

From *A Theory of Justice* (1971), pp. 11-22, 60-65, 150-156, 302-303, 252-257. Reprinted by permission of the publishers from *A Theory of Justice* by John Rawls, Cambridge, Mass.: The Belknap Press of Harvard University Press, Copyright © 1971 by the President and Fellows of Harvard College.

[1]As the text suggests, I shall regard Locke's *Second Treatise of Government*, Rousseau's *The Social Contract*, and Kant's ethical works beginning with *The Foundations of the Metaphysics of Morals* as definitive of the contract tradition. For all of its greatness, Hobbes's *Leviathan* raises special problems. A general historical survey is provided by J. W. Gough, *The Social Contract*, 2nd ed. (Oxford, The Clarendon Press, 1957), and Otto Gierke, *Natural Law and the Theory of Society*, trans. with an introduction by Ernest Barker (Cambridge, The University Press, 1934). A presentation of the contract view as primarily an ethical theory is to be found in G. R. Grice, *The Grounds of Moral Judgment* (Cambridge, The University Press, 1967). . . .

and to determine the division of social benefits. Men are to decide in advance how they are to regulate their claims against one another and what is to be the foundation charter of their society. Just as each person must decide by rational reflection what constitutes his good—that is, the system of ends which it is rational for him to pursue—so a group of persons must decide once and for all what is to count among them as just and unjust. The choice which rational men would make in this hypothetical situation of equal liberty, assuming for the present that this choice problem has a solution, determines the principles of justice.

In justice as fairness the original position of equality corresponds to the state of nature in the traditional theory of the social contract. This original position is not, of course, thought of as an actual historical state of affairs, much less as a primitive condition of culture. It is understood as a purely hypothetical situation characterized so as to lead to a certain conception of justice.[2] Among the essential features of this situation is that no one knows his place in society, his class position or social status, nor does any one know his fortune in the distribution of natural assets and abilities, his intelligence, strength, and the like. I shall even assume that the parties do not know their conceptions of the good or their special psychological propensities. The principles of justice are chosen behind a veil of ignorance. This ensures that no one is advantaged or disadvantaged in the choice of principles by the outcome of natural chance or the contingency of social circumstances. Since all are similarly situated and no one is able to design principles to favor his particular condition, the principles of justice are the result of a fair agreement or bargain. For given the circumstances of the original position, the symmetry of everyone's relations to each other, this initial situation is fair between individuals as moral persons; that is, as rational beings with their own ends and capable, I shall assume, of a sense of justice. The original position is, one might say, the appropriate initial status quo, and thus the fundamental agreements reached in it are fair. This explains the propriety of the name "justice as fairness": it conveys the idea that the principles of justice are agreed to in an initial situation that is fair. The name does not mean that the concepts of justice and fairness are the same, any more than the phrase "poetry as metaphor" means that the concepts of poetry and metaphor are the same.

Justice as fairness begins, as I have said, with one of the most general of all choices which persons might make together, namely, with the choice of the first principles of a conception of justice which is to regulate all subsequent criticism and reform of institutions. Then, having chosen a conception of justice, we can suppose that they are to choose a constitution and a legislature to enact laws, and so on, all in accordance with the principles of justice initially agreed upon. Our social situation is

[2]Kant is clear that the original agreement is hypothetical. See *The Metaphysics of Morals*, pt. I (*Rechtslehre*), especially §§ 47, 52; and pt. II of the essay "Concerning the Common Saying: This May Be True in Theory but It Does Not Apply in Practice," in *Kant's Political Writings*, ed. Hans Reiss and trans. by H. B. Nisbet (Cambridge, The University Press, 1970), pp. 73–87. See Georges Vlachos, *La Pensée politique de Kant* (Paris, Presses Universitaires de France, 1962), pp. 326–335; and J. G. Murphy, *Kant: The Philosophy of Right* (London, Macmillan, 1970), pp. 109–112, 133–136, for a further discussion.

just if it is such that by this sequence of hypothetical agreements we would have contracted into the general system of rules which defines it. Moreover, assuming that the original position does determine a set of principles (that is, that a particular conception of justice would be chosen), it will then be true that whenever social institutions satisfy these principles those engaged in them can say to one another that they are cooperating on terms to which they would agree if they were free and equal persons whose relations with respect to one another were fair. They could all view their arrangements as meeting the stipulations which they would acknowledge in an initial situation that embodies widely accepted and reasonable constraints on the choice of principles. The general recognition of this fact would provide the basis for a public acceptance of the corresponding principles of justice. No society can, of course, be a scheme of cooperation which men enter voluntarily in a literal sense; each person finds himself placed at birth in some particular position in some particular society, and the nature of this position materially affects his life prospects. Yet a society satisfying the principles of justice as fairness comes as close as a society can to being a voluntary scheme, for it meets the principles which free and equal persons would assent to under circumstances that are fair. In this sense its members are autonomous and the obligations they recognize self-imposed.

One feature of justice as fairness is to think of the parties in the initial situation as rational and mutually disinterested. This does not mean that the parties are egoists; that is, individuals with only certain kinds of interests, say in wealth, prestige, and domination. But they are conceived as not taking an interest in one another's interests. They are to presume that even their spiritual aims may be opposed, in the way that the aims of those of different religions may be opposed. Moreover, the concept of rationality must be interpreted as far as possible in the narrow sense, standard in economic theory, of taking the most effective means to given ends. I shall modify this concept to some extent . . . , but one must try to avoid introducing into it any controversial ethical elements. The initial situation must be characterized by stipulations that are widely accepted.

In working out the conception of justice as fairness one main task clearly is to determine which principles of justice would be chosen in the original position. To do this we must describe this situation in some detail and formulate with care the problem of choice which it presents. It may be observed, however, that once the principles of justice are thought of as arising from an original agreement in a situation of equality, it is an open question whether the principle of utility would be acknowledged. Offhand it hardly seems likely that persons who view themselves as equals, entitled to press their claims upon one another, would agree to a principle which may require lesser life prospects for some simply for the sake of a greater sum of advantages enjoyed by others. Since each desires to protect his interests, his capacity to advance his conception of the good, no one has a reason to acquiesce in an enduring loss for himself in order to bring about a greater net balance of satisfaction. In the absence of strong and lasting benevolent impulses, a rational man would not accept a basic structure merely because it maximized the algebraic sum of advantages irrespective of its permanent effects on his own basic rights and interests. Thus it seems that the principle of utility is incompatible with the conception of social cooperation among equals for mutual advantage. It appears to be inconsistent with the idea of reciprocity implicit in the notion of a well-ordered society. Or, at any rate, so I shall argue.

I shall maintain instead that the persons in the initial situation would choose two rather different principles: the first requires equality in the assignment of basic rights and duties, while the second holds that social and economic inequalities; for example, inequalities of wealth and authority; are just only if they result in compensating benefits for everyone, and in particular for the least advantaged members of society. These principles rule out justifying institutions on the grounds that the hardships of some are offset by a greater good in the aggregate. It may be expedient but it is not just that some should have less in order that others may prosper. But there is no injustice in the greater benefits earned by a few provided that the situation of persons not so fortunate is thereby improved. The intuitive idea is that since everyone's well-being depends upon a scheme of cooperation without which no one could have a satisfactory life, the division of advantages should be such as to draw forth the willing cooperation of everyone taking part in it, including those less well situated. Yet this can be expected only if reasonable terms are proposed. The two principles mentioned seem to be a fair agreement on the basis of which those better endowed, or more fortunate in their social position, neither of which we can be said to deserve, could expect the willing cooperation of others when some workable scheme is a necessary condition of the welfare of all.[3] Once we decide to look for a conception of justice that nullifies the accidents of natural endowment and the contingencies of social circumstance as counters in quest for political and economic advantage, we are led to these principles. They express the result of leaving aside those aspects of the social world that seem arbitrary from a moral point of view.

The problem of the choice of principles, however, is extremely difficult. I do not expect the answer I shall suggest to be convincing to everyone. It is, therefore, worth noting from the outset that justice as fairness, like other contract views, consists of two parts: (1) an interpretation of the initial situation and of the problem of choice posed there, and (2) a set of principles which, it is argued, would be agreed to. One may accept the first part of the theory (or some variant thereof), but not the other, and conversely. The concept of the initial contractual situation may seem reasonable although the particular principles proposed are rejected. To be sure, I want to maintain that the most appropriate conception of this situation does lead to principles of justice contrary to utilitarianism and pefectionism, and therefore that the contract doctrine provides an alternative to these views. Still, one may dispute this contention even though one grants that the contractarian method is a useful way of studying ethical theories and of setting forth their underlying assumptions.

Justice as fairness is an example of what I have called a contract theory. Now there may be an objection to the term "contract" and related expressions, but I think it will serve reasonably well. Many words have misleading connotations which at first are likely to confuse. The terms "utility" and "utilitarianism" are surely no exception. They too have unfortunate suggestions which hostile critics have been willing to exploit; yet they are clear enough for those prepared to study utilitarian

[3]For the formulation of this intuitive idea I am indebted to Allan Gibbard.

doctrine. The same should be true of the term "contract" applied to moral theories. As I have mentioned, to understand it one has to keep in mind that it implies a certain level of abstraction. In particular, the content of the relevant agreement is not to enter a given society or to adopt a given form of government, but to accept certain moral principles. Moreover, the undertakings referred to are purely hypothetical: a contract view holds that certain principles would be accepted in a well-defined initial situation.

The merit of the contract terminology is that it conveys the idea that principles of justice may be conceived as principles that would be chosen by rational persons, and that in this way conceptions of justice may be explained and justified. The theory of justice is a part, perhaps the most significant part, of the theory of rational choice. Furthermore, principles of justice deal with conflicting claims upon the advantages won by social cooperation; they apply to the relations among several persons or groups. The word "contract" suggests this plurality as well as the condition that the appropriate division of advantages must be in accordance with principles acceptable to all parties. The condition of publicity for principles of justice is also connoted by the contract phraseology. Thus, if these principles are the outcome of an agreement, citizens have a knowledge of the principles that others follow. It is characteristic of contract theories to stress the public nature of political principles. Finally there is the long tradition of the contract doctrine. Expressing the tie with this line of thought helps to define ideas and accords with natural piety. There are then several advantages in the use of the term "contract." With due precautions taken, it should not be misleading.

A final remark. Justice as fairness is not a complete contract theory. For it is clear that the contractarian idea can be extended to the choice of more or less an entire ethical system; that is, to a system including principles for all the virtues and not only for justice. Now for the most part I shall consider only principles of justice and others closely related to them; I make no attempt to discuss the virtues in a systematic way. Obviously if justice as fairness succeeds reasonably well, a next step would be to study the more general view suggested by the name "rightness as fairness." But even this wider theory fails to embrace all moral relationships, since it would seem to include only our relations with other persons and to leave out of account how we are to conduct ourselves toward animals and the rest of nature. I do not contend that the contract notion offers a way to approach these questions, which are certainly of the first importance; and I shall have to put them aside. We must recognize the limited scope of justice as fairness and of the general type of view that it exemplifies. How far its conclusions must be revised once these other matters are understood cannot be decided in advance.

The Original Position and Justification

I have said that the original position is the appropriate initial status quo which insures that the fundamental agreements reached in it are fair. This fact yields the name "justice as fairness." It is clear, then, that I want to say that one conception of justice is more reasonable than another, or justifiable with respect to it, if rational persons in the initial situation would choose its principles over those of the other for the role of justice. Conceptions of justice are to be ranked by their acceptability to persons so circumstanced. Understood in this way the question of justification is settled by working out a problem of deliberation: we have to ascertain which principles it would be rational to adopt given the contractual situation. This connects the theory of justice with the theory of rational choice.

If this view of the problem of justification is to succeed, we must, of course, describe in some detail the nature of this choice problem. A problem of rational decision has a definite answer only if we know the beliefs and interests of the parties, their relations with respect to one another, the alternatives between which they are to choose, the procedure whereby they make up their minds, and so on. As the circumstances are presented in different ways, correspondingly different principles are accepted. The concept of the original position, as I shall refer to it, is that of the most philosophically favored interpretation of this initial choice situation for the purposes of a theory of justice.

But how are we to decide what is the most favored interpretation? I assume, for one thing, that there is a broad measure of agreement that principles of justice should be chosen under certain conditions. To justify a particular description of the intial situation one shows that it incorporates these commonly shared presumptions. One argues from widely accepted but weak premises to more specific conclusions. Each of the presumptions should by itself be natural and plausible; some of them may seem innocuous or even trivial. The aim of the contract approach is to establish that taken together they impose significant bounds on acceptable principles of justice. The ideal outcome would be that these conditions determine a unique set of principles; but I shall be satisfied if they suffice to rank the main traditional conceptions of social justice.

One should not be misled, then, by the somewhat unusual conditions which characterize the original position. The idea here is simply to make vivid to ourselves the restrictions that it seems reasonable to impose on arguments for principles of justice, and therefore on these principles themselves. Thus it seems reasonable and generally acceptable that no one should be advantaged or disadvantaged by natural fortune or social circumstances in the choice of principles. It also seems widely agreed that it should be impossible to tailor principles to the circumstances of one's own case. We should ensure further that particular inclinations and aspirations, and persons' conceptions of their good, do not affect the principles adopted. The aim is to rule out those principles that it would be rational to propose for acceptance, however little the chance of success, only if one knew certain things that are irrelevant from the standpoint of justice. For example, if a man knew that he was wealthy, he might find it rational to advance the principle that various taxes for welfare measures be counted unjust; if he knew that he was poor, he would most likely propose the contrary principle. To represent the desired restrictions one imagines a situation in which everyone is deprived of this sort of information. One excludes the knowledge of those contingencies which sets men at odds and allows them to be guided by their prejudices. In this manner the veil of ignorance is arrived at in a natural way. This concept should cause no difficulty if we keep in mind the constraints on arguments that it is meant to express. At any time we can enter the original position, so to speak, simply by following a certain procedure; namely, by arguing for principles of justice in accordance with these restrictions.

It seems reasonable to suppose that the parties in the original position are equal. That is, all have the same rights in the procedure for choosing principles; each can make proposals, submit reasons for their acceptance, and so on. Obviously the purpose of these conditions is to represent equality between human beings as moral persons, as creatures having a conception of their good and capable of a sense of justice. The basis of equality is taken to be similarity in these two respects. Systems of ends are not ranked in value; and each man is presumed to have the requisite ability to understand and to act upon whatever principles are adopted. Together with the veil of ignorance, these conditions define the principles of justice as those which rational persons concerned to advance their interests would consent to as equals when none are known to be advantaged or disadvantaged by social and natural contingencies.

There is, however, another side to justifying a particular description of the original position. This is to see if the principles which would be chosen match our considered convictions of justice or extend them in an acceptable way. We can note whether applying these principles would lead us to make the same judgments about the basic structure of society which we now make intuitively and in which we have the greatest confidence; or whether, in cases where our present judgments are in doubt and given with hesitation, these principles offer a resolution which we can affirm on reflection. There are questions which we feel sure must be answered in a certain way. For example, we are confident that religious intolerance and racial discrimination are unjust. We think that we have examined these things with care and have reached what we believe is an impartial judgment not likely to be distorted by an excessive attention to our own interests. These convictions are provisional fixed points which we presume any conception of justice must fit. But we have much less assurance as to what is the correct distribution of wealth and authority. Here we may be looking for a way to remove our doubts. We can check an interpretation of the initial situation, then, by the capacity of its principles to accommodate our firmest convictions and to provide guidance where guidance is needed.

In searching for the most favored description of this situation we work from both ends. We begin by describing it so that it represents generally shared and preferably weak conditions. We then see if these conditions are strong enough to yield a significant set of principles. If not, we look for further premises equally reasonable. But if so, and these principles match our considered convictions of justice, then so far well and good. But presumably there will be discrepancies. In this case we have a choice. We can either modify the account of the initial situation or we can revise our existing judgments, for even the judgments we take provisionally as fixed points are liable to revision. By going back and forth, sometimes altering the conditions of the contractual circumstances, at others withdrawing our judgments and conforming them to principle, I assume that eventually we shall find a description of the initial situation that both expresses reasonable conditions and yields principles which match our considered judgments duly pruned and adjusted. This state of affairs I refer to as reflective equilibrium.[4] It is an equilibrium because at last our principles and judgments coincide; and it is reflective since we know to what principles our judgments conform and the premises of their derivation. At the moment everything is in order. But this equilibrium is not necessarily stable. It is liable to be upset by further examination of the conditions which should be imposed on the contractual situation and by particular cases which may lead us to revise our judgments. Yet for the time being we have done what we can to render coherent and to justify our convictions of social justice. We have reached a conception of the original position.

I shall not, of course, actually work through this process. Still, we may think of the interpretation of the original position that I shall present as the result of such a hypothetical course of reflection. It represents the attempt to accommodate within one scheme both reasonable philosophical conditions on principles as well as our considered judgments of justice. In arriving at the favored interpretation of the initial situation there is no point at which an appeal is made to self-evidence in the traditional sense either of general conceptions or particular convictions. I do not claim for the principles of justice proposed that they are necessary truths or derivable from such truths. A conception of justice cannot be deduced from self-evident premises or conditions on principles; instead, its justification is a matter of the mutual support of many considerations, of everything fitting together into one coherent view.

A final comment. We shall want to say that certain principles of justice are justified because they would be agreed to in an initial situation of equality. I have emphasized that this original position is purely hypothetical. It is natural to ask why, if this agreement is never actually entered into, we should take any interest in these principles, moral or otherwise. The answer is that the conditions embodied in the description of the original position are ones that we do in fact accept. Or if we do not, then perhaps we can be persuaded to do so by philosophical reflection. Each aspect of the contractual situation can be given supporting grounds. Thus what we shall do is to collect together into one conception a number of conditions on principles that we are ready upon due consideration to recognize as reasonable. These constraints express what we are prepared to regard as limits on fair terms of social cooperation. One way to look at the idea of the original position, therefore, is to see it as an expository device which sums up the meaning of these conditions and helps us to extract their consequences. On the other hand, this conception is also an intuitive notion that suggests its own elaboration, so that led on by it we are drawn to define more clearly the standpoint from which we can best interpret moral relationships. We need a conception that enables us to envision our objective from afar: the intuitive notion of the original position is to do this for us. . . .

[4]The process of mutual adjustment of principles and considered judgments is not peculiar to moral philosophy. See Nelson Goodman, *Fact, Fiction, and Forecast* (Cambridge, Mass., Harvard University Press, 1955), pp. 65–68, for parallel remarks concerning the justification of the principles of deductive and inductive inference.

Two Principles of Justice

I shall now state in a provisional form the two principles of justice that I believe would be chosen in the original position. In this section I wish to make only the most general comments, and therefore the first formulation of these principles is tentative. As we go on I shall run through several formulations and approximate step by step the final statement to be given much later. I believe that doing this allows the exposition to proceed in a natural way.

The first statement of the two principles reads as follows:

First: each person is to have an equal right to the most extensive basic liberty compatible with a similar liberty for others.

Second: social and economic inequalities are to be arranged so that they are both (a) reasonably expected to be to everyone's advantage, and (b) attached to positions and offices open to all.

There are two ambiguous phrases in the second principle, namely "everyone's advantage" and "open to all." Determining their sense more exactly will lead to a second formulation of the principle. . . .

By way of general comment, these principles primarily apply, as I have said, to the basic structure of society. They are to govern the assignment of rights and duties and to regulate the distribution of social and economic advantages. As their formulation suggests, these principles presuppose that the social structure can be divided into two more or less distinct parts, the first principle applying to the one, the second to the other. They distinguish between those aspects of the social system that define and secure the equal liberties of citizenship and those that specify and establish social and economic inequalities. The basic liberties of citizens are, roughly speaking, political liberty (the right to vote and to be eligible for public office) together with freedom of speech and assembly; liberty of conscience and freedom of thought; freedom of the person along with the right to hold (personal) property; and freedom from arbitrary arrest and seizure as defined by the concept of the rule of law. These liberties are all required to be equal by the first principle, since citizens of a just society are to have the same basic rights.

The second principle applies, in the first approximation, to the distribution of income and wealth and to the design of organizations that make use of differences in authority and responsibility, or chains of command. While the distribution of wealth and income need not be equal, it must be to everyone's advantage, and at the same time, positions of authority and offices of command must be accessible to all. One applies the second principle by holding positions open, and then, subject to this constraint, arranges social and economic inequalities so that everyone benefits.

These principles are to be arranged in a serial order with the first principle prior to the second. This ordering means that a departure from the institutions of equal liberty required by the first principle cannot be justified by, or compensated for, by greater social and economic advantages. The distribution of wealth and income, and the hierarchies of authority, must be consistent with both the liberties of equal citizenship and equality of opportunity.

It is clear that these principles are rather specific in their content, and their acceptance rests on certain assumptions that I must eventually try to explain and justify. A theory of justice depends upon a theory of society in ways that will become evident as we proceed. For the present, it should be observed that the two principles (and this holds for all formulations) are a special case of a more general conception of justice that can be expressed as follows:

> All social values—liberty and opportunity, income and wealth, and the bases of self-respect—are to be distributed equally unless an unequal distribution of any, or all, of these values is to everyone's advantage.

Injustice, then, is simply inequalities that are not to the benefit of all. Of course, this conception is extremely vague and requires interpretation.

As a first step, suppose that the basic structure of society distributes certain primary goods, that is, things that every rational man is presumed to want. These goods normally have a use whatever a person's rational plan of life. For simplicity, assume that the chief primary goods at the disposition of society are rights and liberties, powers and opportunities, income and wealth. (Later on . . . the primary good of self-respect has a central place.) These are the social primary goods. Other primary goods such as health and vigor, intelligence and imagination, are natural goods; although their possession is influenced by the basic structure, they are not so directly under its control. Imagine, then, a hypothetical initial arrangement in which all the social primary goods are equally distributed: everyone has similar rights and duties, and income and wealth are evenly shared. This state of affairs provides a benchmark for judging improvements. If certain inequalities of wealth and organizational powers would make everyone better off than in this hypothetical starting situation, then they accord with the general conception.

Now it is possible, at least theoretically, that by giving up some of their fundamental liberties men are sufficiently compensated by the resulting social and economic gains. The general conception of justice imposes no restrictions on what sort of inequalities are permissible; it only requires that everyone's position be improved. We need not suppose anything so drastic as consenting to a condition of slavery. Imagine instead that men forgo certain political rights when the economic returns are significant and their capacity to influence the course of policy by the exercise of these rights would be marginal in any case. It is this kind of exchange which the two principles as stated rule out; being arranged in serial order they do not permit exchanges between basic liberties and economic and social gains. The serial ordering of principles expresses an underlying preference among primary social goods. When this preference is rational so likewise is the choice of these principles in this order.

In developing justice as fairness I shall, for the most part, leave aside the general conception of justice and examine instead the special case of the two principles in serial order. The advantage of this procedure is that from the first the matter of priorities is recognized and an effort made to find principles to deal with it. One is led to attend throughout to the conditions under which the acknowledgment of the absolute weight of liberty with respect to social and economic advantages, as defined by the lexical order of the two principles, would be reasonable. Offhand, this ranking appears extreme and too special a case to be of much interest; but there is more justification for it than would appear at first sight. Or at any rate, so I shall maintain. . . . Furthermore, the distinction between fundamental rights and liberties and economic and social benefits marks a difference among primary social goods that one should try to exploit. It suggests an important division in the social system. Of course, the distinctions drawn and the ordering proposed are bound to be at best only approximations. There are surely circumstances in which they fail. But it is essential to depict clearly the main lines of a reasonable conception of justice; and under many conditions, anyway, the two principles in serial order may serve well enough. When necessary we can fall back on the more general conception.

The fact that the two principles apply to institutions has certain consequences. Several points illustrate this. First of all, the rights and liberties referred to by these principles are those that are defined by the public rules of the basic structure. Whether men are free is determined by the rights and duties established by the major institutions of society. Liberty is a certain pattern of social forms. The first principle simply requires that certain sorts of rules, those defining basic liberties, apply to everyone equally and that they allow the most extensive liberty compatible with a like liberty for all. The only reason for circumscribing the rights defining liberty and making men's freedom less extensive than it might otherwise be is that these equal rights as institutionally defined would interfere with one another.

Another thing to bear in mind is that when principles mention persons, or require that everyone gain from an inequality, the reference is to representative persons holding the various social positions, or offices, or whatever, established by the basic structure. Thus in applying the second principle I assume that it is possible to assign an expectation of well-being to representative individuals holding these positions. This expectation indicates their life prospects as viewed from their social station. In general, the expectations of representative persons depend upon the distribution of rights and duties throughout the basic structure. When this changes, expectations change. I assume, then, that expectations are connected: by raising the prospects of the representative man in one position we presumably increase or decrease the prospects of representative men in other positions. Since it applies to institutional forms, the second principle (or rather the first part of it) refers to the expectations of representative individuals. As I shall discuss below, neither principle applies to distributions of particular goods to particular individuals who may be identified by their proper names. The situation where someone is considering how to allocate certain commodities to needy persons who are known to him is not within the scope of the principles. They are meant to regulate basic institutional arrangements. We must not assume that there is much similarity from the standpoint of justice between an administrative allotment of goods to specific persons and the appropriate design of society. Our common sense intuitions for the former may be a poor guide to the latter.

Now the second principle insists that each person benefit from permissible inequalities in the basic structure. This means that it must be reasonable for each relevant representative man defined by this structure, when he views it as a going concern, to prefer his prospects with the inequality, to his prospects without it. One is not allowed to justify differences in income or organizational powers on the ground that the disadvantages of those in one position are outweighed by the greater advantages of those in another. Much less can infringements of liberty be counterbalanced in this way. Applied to the basic structure, the principle of utility would have us maximize the sum of expectations of representative men (weighted by the number of persons they represent, on the classical view); and this would permit us to compensate for the losses of some by the gains of others. Instead, the two principles require that everyone benefit from economic and social inequalities.

The Reasoning Leading to the Two Principles of Justice

It will be recalled that the general conception of justice as fairness requires that all primary social goods be distributed equally unless an unequal distribution would be to everyone's advantage. No restrictions are placed on exchanges of these goods and therefore a lesser liberty can be compensated for by greater social and economic benefits. Now looking at the situation from the standpoint of one person selected arbitrarily, there is no way for him to win special advantages for himself. Nor, on the other hand, are there grounds for his acquiescing in special disadvantages. Since it is not reasonable for him to expect more than an equal share in the division of social goods, and since it is not rational for him to agree to less, the sensible thing for him to do is to acknowledge as the first principle of justice one requiring an equal distribution. Indeed, this principle is so obvious that we would expect it to occur to anyone immediately.

Thus, the parties start with a principle establishing equal liberty for all, including equality of opportunity, as well as an equal distribution of income and wealth. But there is no reason why this acknowledgment should be final. If there are inequalities in the basic structure that work to make everyone better off in comparison with the benchmark of initial equality, why not permit them? The immediate gain which a greater equality might allow can be regarded as intelligently invested in view of its future return. If, for example, these inequalities set up various incentives which succeed in eliciting more productive efforts, a person in the original position may look upon them as necessary to cover the costs of training and to encourage effective performance. One might think that ideally individuals should want to serve one another. But since the parties are assumed not to take an interest in one another's interests, their acceptance of these inequalities is only the acceptance of the relations in which men stand in the circumstances of justice. They have no grounds for complaining of one another's motives. A person in the original position would, therefore, concede the justice of these inequalities. Indeed, it would be shortsighted of him not to do so. He would hesitate to agree to these regularities only if he would be dejected by the bare knowledge or perception that others were better situated; and I have assumed that the parties decide as if they are not moved by envy. In order to make the principle regulating inequalities determinate, one looks at the system from the standpoint of the least advantaged representative man. Inequalities are permissible when they maximize, or at least all contribute to, the long-term expectations of the least fortunate group in society.

Now this general conception imposes no constraints on what sorts of inequalities are allowed, whereas the special conception, by putting the two principles in serial order (with the necessary adjustments in meaning), forbids exchanges between basic liberties and economic and social benefits. I shall not try to justify this ordering here. . . . But roughly, the idea underlying this ordering is that if the parties assume that their basic liberties can be effectively exercised, they will not exchange a lesser liberty for an improvement in economic well-being. It is only when social conditions do not allow the effective establishment of these rights that one can concede their limitation; and these restrictions can be granted only to the extent that they are necessary to prepare the way for a free society. The denial of equal liberty can be defended only if it is necessary to raise the level of civilization so that in due course these freedoms can be enjoyed. Thus in adopting a serial order we are in effect making a special assumption in the original position, namely, that the parties know that the conditions of their society, whatever they are, admit the effective realization of the equal liberties. The serial ordering of the two principles of justice eventually comes to be reasonable if the general conception is consistently followed. This lexical ranking is the long-run tendency of the general view. For the most part I shall assume that the requisite circumstances for the serial order obtain.

It seems clear from these remarks that the two principles are at least a plausible conception of justice. The question, though, is how one is to argue for them more systematically. Now there are several things to do. One can work out their consequences for institutions and note their implications for fundamental social policy. In this way they are tested by a comparison with our considered judgments of justice. . . . But one can also try to find arguments in their favor that are decisive from the standpoint of the original position. In order to see how this might be done, it is useful as a heuristic device to think of the two principles as the maximin solution to the problem of social justice. There is an analogy between the two principles and the maximin rule for choice under uncertainty.[5] This is evident from the fact that the two principles are those a person would choose for the design of a society in which his enemy is to assign him his place. The maximin rule tells us to rank alternatives by their worst possible outcomes: we are to adopt the alternative the worst outcome of which is superior to the worst outcomes of the others. The persons in the original position do not, of course, assume that their initial place in society is decided by a malevolent opponent. As I note below, they should not reason from false premises. The veil of ignorance does not violate this idea, since an absence of information is not misinformation. But that the two principles of justice would be

[5]An accessible discussion of this and other rules of choice under uncertainty can be found in W. J. Baumol, *Economic Theory and Operations Analysis*, 2nd ed. (Englewood Cliffs, N. J., Prentice-Hall, 1965), ch. 24. Baumol gives a geometric interpretation of these rules, including the diagram used . . . to illustrate the difference principle. See pp. 558–562. See also R. D. Luce and Howard Raiffa, *Games and Decisions* (New York, John Wiley and Sons, Inc., 1957), ch. XIII, for a fuller account.

chosen if the parties were forced to protect themselves against such a contingency explains the sense in which this conception is the maximin solution. And this analogy suggests that if the original position has been described so that it is rational for the parties to adopt the conservative attitude expressed by this rule, a conclusive argument can indeed be constructed for these principles. Clearly the maximin rule is not, in general, a suitable guide for choices under uncertainty. But it is attractive in situations marked by certain special features. My aim, then, is to show that a good case can be made for the two principles based on the fact that the original position manifests these features to the fullest possible degree, carrying them to the limit, so to speak.

Consider the gain-and-loss table below. It represents the gains and losses for a situation which is not a game of strategy. There is no one playing against the person making the decision; instead he is faced with several possible circumstances which may or may not obtain. Which circumstances happen to exist does not depend upon what the person choosing decides or whether he announces his moves in advance. The numbers in the table are monetary values (in hundreds of dollars) in comparison with some initial situation. The gain (g) depends upon the individual's decision (d) and the circumstances (c). Thus $g = f(d,c)$. Assuming that there are three possible decisions and three possible circumstances, we might have this gain-and-loss table.

Decisions	Circumstances		
	c_1	c_2	c_3
d_1	-7	8	12
d_2	-8	7	14
d_3	5	6	8

The maximin rule requires that we make the third decision. For in this case the worst that can happen is that one gains five hundred dollars, which is better than the worst for the other actions. If we adopt one of these we may lose either eight or seven hundred dollars. Thus, the choice of d_3 maximizes $f(d,c)$ for that value of c which for a given d, minimizes f. The term "maximin" means the *maximum minimorum*; and the rule directs our attention to the worst that can happen under any proposed course of action, and to decide in the light of that.

Now there appear to be three chief features of situations that give plausibility to this unusual rule.[6] First, since the rule takes no account of the likelihoods of the possible circumstances, there must be some reason for sharply discounting estimates of these probabilities. Offhand, the most natural rule of choice would seem to be to compute the expectation of monetary gain for each decision and then to adopt the course of action with the highest prospect. (This expectation is defined as follows: let us suppose that g_{ij} represent the numbers in the gain-and-loss table, where i is the row index and j is the column index; and let p_i, $j = 1$,

---

[6]Here I borrow from William Fellner, *Probability and Profit* (Homewood, Ill., Richard D. Irwin, 1965), pp. 140–142, where these features are noted.

2, 3, be the likelihoods of the circumstances, with $\Sigma p_j = 1$. Then the expectation for the ith decision is equal to $\Sigma p_j g_{ij}$.) Thus it must be, for example, that the situation is one in which a knowledge of likelihoods is impossible, or at best extremely insecure. In this case it is unreasonable not to be skeptical of probabilistic calculations unless there is no other way out, particularly if the decision is a fundamental one that needs to be justified to others.

The second feature that suggests the maximin rule is the following: the person choosing has a conception of the good such that he cares very little, if anything, for what he might gain above the minimum stipend that he can, in fact, be sure of by following the maximin rule. It is not worthwhile for him to take a chance for the sake of a further advantage, especially when it may turn out that he loses much that is important to him. This last provision brings in the third feature; namely, that the rejected alternatives have outcomes that one can hardly accept. The situation involves grave risks. Of course these features work most effectively in combination. The paradigm situation for following the maximin rule is when all three features are realized to the highest degree. This rule does not, then, generally apply, nor of course is it self-evident. Rather, it is a maxim, a rule of thumb, that comes into its own in special circumstances. Its application depends upon the qualitative structure of the possible gains and losses in relation to one's conception of the good, all this against a background in which it is reasonable to discount conjectural estimates of likelihoods.

It should be noted, as the comments on the gain-and-loss table say, that the entries in the table represent monetary values and not utilities. This difference is significant since for one thing computing expectations on the basis of such objective values is not the same thing as computing expected utility and may lead to different results. The essential point, though, is that in justice as fairness the parties do not know their conception of the good and cannot estimate their utility in the ordinary sense. In any case, we want to go behind de facto preferences generated by given conditions. Therefore expectations are based upon an index of primary goods and the parties make their choice accordingly. The entries in the example are in terms of money and not utility to indicate this aspect of the contract doctrine.

Now, as I have suggested, the original position has been defined so that it is a situation in which the maximin rule applies. In order to see this, let us review briefly the nature of this situation with these three special features in mind. To begin with, the veil of ignorance excludes all but the vaguest knowledge of likelihoods. The parties have no basis for determining the probable nature of their society, or their place in it. Thus they have strong reasons for being wary of probability calculations if any other course is open to them. They must also take into account the fact that their choice of principles should seem reasonable to others, in particular their descendants, whose rights will be deeply affected by it. There are further grounds for discounting that I shall mention as we go along. For the present it suffices to note that these considerations are strengthened by the fact that the parties know very little about the gain-and-loss table. Not only are they unable to conjecture the likelihoods of the various possible circumstances, they cannot say much about what the possible circumstances are, much less enumerate them and foresee the outcome of each alternative available. Those deciding are much more in the dark than the illustration by a numerical table suggests. It is for this reason that I have spoken of an analogy with the maximin rule.

Several kinds of arguments for the two principles of justice illustrate the second feature. Thus, if we can maintain that these principles provide a workable theory of social justice, and that they are compatible with reasonable demands of efficiency, then this conception guarantees a satisfactory minimum. There may be, on reflection, little reason for trying to do better. Thus much of the argument. . . is to show, by their application to the main questions of social justice, that the two principles are a satisfactory conception. These details have a philosophical purpose. Moreover, this line of thought is practically decisive if we can establish the priority of liberty, the lexical ordering of the two principles. For this priority implies that the persons in the original position have no desire to try for greater gains at the expense of the equal liberties. The minimum assured by the two principles in lexical order is not one that the parties wish to jeopardize for the sake of greater economic and social advantages. . . .

Finally, the third feature holds if we can assume that other conceptions of justice may lead to institutions that the parties would find intolerable. For example, it has sometimes been held that under some conditions the utility principle (in either form) justifies, if not slavery or serfdom, at any rate serious infractions of liberty for the sake of greater social benefits. We need not consider here the truth of this claim, or the likelihood that the requisite conditions obtain. For the moment, this contention is only to illustrate the way in which conceptions of justice may allow for outcomes which the parties may not be able to accept. And having the ready alternative of the two principles of justice which secure a satisfactory minimum, it seems unwise, if not irrational, for them to take a chance that these outcomes are not realized.

So much, then, for a brief sketch of the features of situations in which the maximin rule comes into its own and of the way in which the arguments for the two principles of justice can be subsumed under them. . . .

The Final Formulation of the
Principles of Justice

. . . I now wish to give the final statement of the two principles of justice for institutions. For the sake of completeness, I shall give a full statement including earlier formulations.

First Principle

Each person is to have an equal right to the most extensive total system of equal basic liberties compatible with a similar system of liberty for all.

Second Principle

Social and economic inequalities are to be arranged so that they are both:

(a) to the greatest benefit of the least advantaged, consistent with the just savings principle, and

(b) attached to offices and positions open to all under conditions of fair equality of opportunity.

First Priority Rule (The Priority of Liberty)

The principles of justice are to be ranked in lexical order and therefore liberty can be restricted only for the sake of liberty. There are two cases:

(a) a less extensive liberty must strengthen the total system of liberty shared by all;

(b) a less than equal liberty must be acceptable to those with the lesser liberty.

Second Priority Rule (The Priority of Justice over Efficiency and Welfare)

The second principle of justice is lexically prior to the principle of efficiency and to that of maximizing the sum of advantages; and fair opportunity is prior to the difference principle. There are two cases:

(a) an inequality of opportunity must enhance the opportunities of those with the lesser opportunity;

(b) an excessive rate of saving must on balance mitigate the burden of those bearing this hardship.

General Conception

All social primary goods—liberty and opportunity, income and wealth, and the bases of self-respect—are to be distributed equally unless an unequal distribution of any or all of these goods is to the advantage of the least favored.

By way of comment, these principles and priority rules are no doubt incomplete. Other modifications will surely have to be made, but I shall not further complicate the statement of the principles. It suffices to observe that when we come to nonideal theory, we do not fall back straightway upon the general conception of justice. The lexical ordering of the two principles, and the valuations that this ordering implies, suggest priority rules which seem to be reasonable enough in many cases. By various examples I have tried to illustrate how these rules can be used and to indicate their plausibility. Thus the ranking of the principles of justice in ideal theory reflects back and guides the application of these principles to nonideal situations. It identifies which limitations need to be dealt with first. The drawback of the general conception of justice is that it lacks the definite structure of the two principles in serial order. In more extreme and tangled instances of nonideal theory there may be no alternative to it. At some point the priority of rules for nonideal cases will fail; and indeed, we may be able to find no satisfactory answer at all. But we must try to postpone the day of reckoning as long as possible, and try to arrange society so that it never comes. . . .

The Kantian Interpretation

Kant held, I believe, that a person is acting autonomously when the principles of his action are chosen by him as the most adequate possible expression of his nature as a free and equal rational being. The principles he acts upon are not adopted because of his social position or natural endowments, or in view of the particular kind of society in which he lives or the specific things that he happens to want. To act on such principles is to act heteronomously. Now the veil of ignorance deprives the persons in the original position of the knowledge that would enable them to choose heteronomous principles. The parties arrive at their choice together as free and equal rational persons knowing only that those circumstances obtain which give rise to the need for principles of justice.

To be sure, the argument for these principles does add in various ways to Kant's conception. For example, it adds the feature that the principles chosen are to apply to the basic structure of society; and premises characterizing this structure are used in deriving the principles of justice. But I believe that this and other additions are natural enough and remain fairly close to Kant's doctrine, at least when all of his ethical writings are viewed together. Assuming, then, that the reasoning in favor of the principles of justice is correct, we can say that when persons act on these principles they are acting in accordance with principles that they would choose as rational and independent persons in an original position of equality. The principles of their actions do not depend upon social or natural contingencies, nor do they reflect the bias of the particulars of their plan of life or the aspirations that motivate them. By acting from these principles persons express their nature as free and equal rational beings subject to the general conditions of human life. For to express one's nature as a being of a particular kind is to act on the principles that would be chosen if this nature were the decisive determining element. Of course, the choice of the parties in the original position is subject to the restrictions of that situation. But when we knowingly act on the principles of justice in the ordinary course of events, we deliberately assume the limitations of the original position. One reason for doing this, for persons who can do so and want to, is to give expression to one's nature.

The principles of justice are also categorical imperatives in Kant's sense. For by a categorical imperative Kant understands a principle of conduct that applies to a person in virtue of his nature as a free and equal rational being. The validity of the principle does not presuppose that one has a particular desire or aim. Whereas a hypothetical imperative by contrast does assume this: it directs us to take certain steps as effective means to achieve a specific end. Whether the desire is for a particular thing, or whether it is for something more general, such as certain kinds of agreeable feelings or pleasures, the corresponding imperative is hypothetical. Its applicability depends upon one's having an aim which one need not have as a condition of being a rational human individual. The argument for the two principles of justice does not assume that the parties have particular ends, but only that they desire certain primary goods. These are things that it is rational to want whatever else one wants. Thus given human nature, wanting them is part of being rational; and while each is presumed to have some conception of the good, nothing is known about his final ends. The preference for primary goods is derived, then, from only the most general assumptions about rationality and the conditions of human life. To act from the principles of justice is to act from categorical imperatives in the sense that they apply to us whatever in particular our aims are. This simply reflects the fact that no such contingencies appear as premises in their derivation.

We may note also that the motivational assumption of mutual disinterest accords with Kant's notion of autonomy, and gives another reason for this condition. So far this assumption has been used to characterize the circumstances of justice and to provide a clear conception to guide the reasoning of the parties. We have also seen that the concept of benevolence, being a second-order notion, would not work out well. Now we can add that the assumption of mutual disinterest is to allow for freedom in the choice of a system of final ends.[7] Liberty in adopting a conception of the good is limited only by principles that are deduced from a doctrine which imposes no prior constraints on these conceptions. Presuming mutual disinterest in the original position carries out this idea. We postulate that the parties have opposing claims in a suitably general sense. If their ends were restricted in some specific way, this would appear at the outset as an arbitrary restriction on freedom. Moreover, if the parties were conceived as altruists, or as pursuing certain kinds of pleasures, then the principles chosen would apply, as far as the argument would have shown, only to persons whose freedom was restricted to choices compatible with altruism or hedonism. As the argument now runs, the principles of justice cover all persons with rational plans of life, whatever their content, and these principles represent the appropriate restrictions on freedom. Thus it is possible to say that the constraints on conceptions of the good are the result of an interpretation of the contractual situation that puts no prior limitations on what men may desire. There are a variety of reasons, then, for the motivational premise of mutual disinterest. This premise is not only a matter of realism about the circumstances of justice or a way to make the theory manageable. It also connects up with the Kantian idea of autonomy. . . .

The original position may be viewed, then, as a procedural interpretation of Kant's conception of autonomy and the categorical imperative. The principles regulative of the kingdom of ends are those that would be chosen in this position, and the description of this situation enables us to explain the sense in which acting from these principles expresses our nature as free and equal rational persons. No longer are these notions purely transcendent and lacking explicable connections with human conduct, for the procedural conception of the original position allows us to make these ties. . . .

[7]For this point I am indebted to Charles Fried.

6

Hypothetical Contracts and Rights

Ronald Dworkin

I trust that it is not necessary to describe John Rawls's famous idea of the original position in any great detail.[1] It imagines a group of men and women who come together to form a social contract. Thus far it resembles the imaginary congresses of the classical social contract theories. The original position differs, however, from these theories in its description of the parties. They are men and women with ordinary tastes, talents, ambitions, and convictions, but each is temporarily ignorant of these features of his own personality, and must agree upon a contract before his self-awareness returns.

Rawls tries to show that if these men and women are rational, and act only in their own self-interest, they will choose his two principles of justice. These provide, roughly, that every person must have the largest political liberty compatible with a like liberty for all, and that inequalities in power, wealth, income, and other resources must not exist except insofar as they work to the absolute benefit of the worst-off members of society. Many of Rawls's critics disagree that men and women in the original position would inevitably choose these two principles. The principles are conservative, and the critics believe they would be chosen only by men who were conservative by temperament, and not by men who were natural gamblers. I do not think this criticism is well-taken, but in this essay, at least, I mean to ignore the point. I am interested in a different issue.

Suppose that the critics are wrong, and that men and women in the original position would in fact choose Rawls's two principles as being in their own best

From *Taking Rights Seriously* (1977), pp. 150–159, 177–183. Reprinted by permission of the author.

[1]John Rawls, *A Theory of Justice* (Cambridge, Mass.: Harvard University Press, 1971).

interest. Rawls seems to think that that fact would provide an argument in favor of these two principles as a standard of justice against which to test actual political institutions. But it is not immediately plain why this should be so.

If a group contracted in advance that disputes amongst them would be settled in a particular way, the fact of that contract would be a powerful argument that such disputes should be settled in that way when they do arise. The contract would be an argument in itself, independent of the force of the reasons that might have led different people to enter the contract. Ordinarily, for example, each of the parties supposes that a contract he signs is in his own interest; but if someone has made a mistake in calculating his self-interest, the fact that he did contract is a strong reason for the fairness of holding him nevertheless to the bargain.

Rawls does not suppose that any group ever entered into a social contract of the sort he describes. He argues only that if a group of rational men did find themselves in the predicament of the original position, they would contract for the two principles. His contract is hypothetical, and hypothetical contracts do not supply an independent argument for the fairness of enforcing their terms. A hypothetical contract is not simply a pale form of an actual contract; it is no contract at all.

If, for example, I am playing a game, it may be that I would have agreed to any number of ground rules if I had been asked in advance of play. It does not follow that these rules may be enforced against me if I have not, in fact, agreed to them. There must be reasons, of course, why I would have agreed if asked in advance, and these may also be reasons why it is fair to enforce these rules against me even if I have not agreed. But my hypothetical agreement does not count as a reason, independent of these other reasons, for enforcing the rules against me, as my actual agreement would have.

Suppose that you and I are playing poker and we find, in the middle of a hand, that the deck is one card short. You suggest that we throw the hand in, but I refuse because I know I am going to win and I want the money in the pot. You might say that I would certainly have agreed to that procedure had the possibility of the deck being short been raised in advance. But your point is not that I am somehow committed to throwing the hand in by an agreement I never made. Rather you use the device of a hypothetical agreement to make a point that might have been made without that device, which is that the solution recommended is so obviously fair and sensible that only someone with an immediate contrary interest could disagree. Your main argument is that your solution is fair and sensible, and the fact that I would have chosen it myself adds nothing of substance to that argument. If I am able to meet the main argument nothing remains, rising out of your claim that I would have agreed, to be answered or excused.

In some circumstances, moreover, the fact that I would have agreed does not even suggest an independent argument of this character. Everything depends on your reasons for supposing that I would have agreed. Suppose you say that I would have agreed, if you had brought up the point and insisted on your solution, because I very much wanted to play and would have given in rather than miss my chance. I might concede that I would have agreed for that reason, and then add that I am lucky that you did not raise the point. The fact that I would have agreed if you had insisted neither adds nor suggests any argument why I should agree now. The point is not that it would have been unfair of you to insist on your proposal as a condition of playing; indeed, it would not have been. If you had held out for your proposal, and I had agreed, I could not say that my agreement was in any way nullified or called into question because of duress. But if I had not in fact agreed, the fact that I would have in itself means nothing.

I do not mean that it is never relevant, in deciding whether an act affecting someone is fair, that he would have consented if asked. If a doctor finds a man unconscious and bleeding, for example, it might be important for him to ask whether the man would consent to a transfusion if he were conscious. If there is every reason to think that he would, that fact is important in justifying the transfusion if the patient later, perhaps because he has undergone a religious conversion, condemns the doctor for having proceeded. But this sort of case is beside the present point, because the patient's hypothetical agreement shows that his will was inclined toward the decision at the time and in the circumstances that the decision was taken. He has lost nothing by not being consulted at the appropriate time, because he would have consented if he had been. The original position argument is very different. If we take it to argue for the fairness of applying the two principles we must take it to argue that because a man would have consented to certain principles if asked in advance, it is fair to apply those principles to him later, under different circumstances, when he does not consent.

But that is a bad argument. Suppose I did not know the value of my painting on Monday; if you had offered me $100 for it then I would have accepted. On Tuesday I discovered it was valuable. You cannot argue that it would be fair for the courts to make me sell it to you for $100 on Wednesday. It may be my good fortune that you did not ask me on Monday, but that does not justify coercion against me later.

We must therefore treat the argument from the original position as we treat your argument in the poker game; it must be a device for calling attention to some independent argument for the fairness of the two principles—an argument that does not rest on the false premise that a hypothetical contract has some pale binding force. What other argument is available? One might say that the original position shows that the two principles are in the best interests of every member of any political community, and that it is fair to govern in accordance with them for that reason. It is true that if the two principles could be shown to be in everyone's interest, that would be a sound argument for their fairness, but it is hard to see how the original position can be used to show that they are.

We must be careful to distinguish two senses in which something might be said to be in my interest. It is in my *antecedent* interest to make a bet on a horse that, all things considered, offers the best odds, even if, in the event, the horse loses. It is in my *actual* interest to bet on the horse that wins, even if the bet was, at the time I made it, a silly one. If the original position furnishes an argument that it is in everyone's interest to accept the two principles over other possible bases for a constitution, it must be an argument that uses the idea of antecedent and not actual interest. It is not in the actual best interests of everyone to choose the two principles, because when the veil of ignorance is lifted some will discover that they would have been better off if some other principle, like the principle of average utility, had been chosen.

A judgment of antecedent interest depends upon the circumstances under which the judgment is made, and, in particular, upon the knowledge available to the man making the judgment. It might be in my antecedent interest to bet on a certain horse at given odds before the starting gun, but not, at least at the same odds, after he has stumbled on the first turn. The fact, therefore, that a particular choice is in my interest at a particular time, under conditions of great uncertainty, is not a good argument for the fairness of enforcing that choice against me later under conditions of much greater knowledge. But that is what, on this interpretation, the original position argument suggests, because it seeks to justify the contemporary use of the two principles on the supposition that, under conditions very different from present conditions, it would be in the antecedent interest of everyone to agree to them. If I have bought a ticket on a longshot it might be in my antecedent interest, before the race, to sell the ticket to you for twice what I paid; it does not follow that it is fair for you to take it from me for that sum when the longshot is about to win.

Someone might now say that I have misunderstood the point of the special conditions of uncertainty in the original position. The parties are made ignorant of their special resources and talents to prevent them from bargaining for principles that are inherently unfair because they favor some collection of resources and talents over others. If the man in the original position does not know his special interests, he cannot negotiate to favor them. In that case, it might be said, the uncertainty of the original position does not vitiate the argument from antecedent interest as I have suggested, but only limits the range within which self-interest might operate. The argument shows that the two principles are in everyone's interest once obviously unfair principles are removed from consideration by the device of uncertainty. Since the only additional knowledge contemporary men and women have over men and women in the original position is knowledge that they ought not to rely upon in choosing principles of justice, their antecedent interest is, so far as it is relevant, the same, and if that is so the original position argument does offer a good argument for applying the two principles to contemporary politics.

But surely this confuses the argument that Rawls makes with a different argument that he might have made. Suppose his men and women had full knowledge of their own talents and tastes, but had to reach agreement under conditions that ruled out, simply by stipulation, obviously unfair principles like those providing special advantage for named individuals. If Rawls could show that, once such obviously unfair principles had been set aside, it would be in the interest of everyone to settle for his two principles, that would indeed count as an argument for the two principles. My point—that the antecedent self-interest of men in the original position is different from that of contemporary men—would no longer hold because both groups of men would then have the same knowledge about themselves, and be subject to the same moral restrictions against choosing obviously unfair principles.

Rawls's actual argument is quite different, however. The ignorance in which his men must choose affects their calculations of self-interest, and cannot be described merely as setting boundaries within which these calculations must be applied. Rawls supposes, for example, that his men would inevitably choose conservative principles because this would be the only rational choice, in their ignorance, for self-interested men to make. But some actual men, aware of their own talents, might well prefer less conservative principles that would allow them to take advantage of the resources they know they have. Someone who considers the original position an argument for the conservative principles, therefore, is faced with this choice. If less conservative principles, like principles that favor named individuals, are to be ruled out as obviously unfair, then the argument for the conservative principles is complete at the outset, on grounds of obvious fairness alone. In that case neither the original position nor any considerations of self-interest it is meant to demonstrate play any role in the argument. But if less conservative principles cannot be ruled out in advance as obviously unfair, then imposing ignorance on Rawls's men, so that they prefer the more conservative principles, cannot be explained simply as ruling out obviously unfair choices. And since this affects the antecedent self-interest of these men, the argument that the original position demonstrates the antecedent self-interest of actual men must therefore fail. This same dilemma can, of course, be constructed for each feature of the two principles.

I recognize that the argument thus far seems to ignore a distinctive feature of Rawls's methodology, which he describes as the technique of seeking a "reflective equilibrium" between our ordinary, unreflective moral beliefs and some theoretical structure that might unify and justify these ordinary beliefs.[2] It might now be said that the idea of an original position plays a part in this reflective equilibrium, which we will miss if we insist, as I have, on trying to find a more direct, one-way argument from the original position to the two principles of justice.

The technique of equilibrium does play an important role in Rawls's argument, and it is worth describing that technique briefly here. The technique assumes that Rawls's readers have a sense, which we draw upon in our daily life, that certain particular political arrangements or decisions, like conventional trials, are just and others, like slavery, are unjust. It assumes, moreover, that we are each able to arrange these immediate intuitions or convictions in an order that designates some of them as more certain than others. Most people, for example, think that it is more plainly unjust for the state to execute innocent citizens of its own than to kill innocent foreign civilians in war. They might be prepared to abandon their position on foreign civilians in war, on the basis of some argument, but would be much more reluctant to abandon their view on executing innocent countrymen.

It is the task of moral philosophy, according to the technique of equilibrium, to provide a structure of principles that supports these immediate convictions about which we are more or less secure, with two goals in mind. First, this structure of principles must explain the convictions by showing the underlying

---

[2]pp. 48 ff.

assumptions they reflect; second, it must provide guidance in those cases about which we have either no convictions or weak or contradictory convictions. If we are unsure, for example, whether economic institutions that allow great disparity of wealth are unjust, we may turn to the principles that explain our confident convictions, and then apply these principles to that difficult issue.

But the process is not simply one of finding principles that accommodate our more or less settled judgments. These principles must support, and not merely account for, our judgments, and this means that the principles must have independent appeal to our moral sense. It might be, for example, that a cluster of familiar moral convictions could be shown to serve an undeserving policy— perhaps, that the standard judgments we make without reflection serve the purpose of maintaining one particular class in political power. But this discovery would not vouch for the principle of class egoism; on the contrary, it would discredit our ordinary judgments, unless some other principle of a more respectable sort could be found that also fits our intuitions, in which case it would be this principle and not the class-interest principle that our intuitions would recommend.

It might be that no coherent set of principles could be found that has independent appeal and that supports the full set of our immediate convictions; indeed it would be surprising if this were not often the case. If that does happen, we must compromise, giving way on both sides. We might relax, though we could not abandon, our initial sense of what might be an acceptable principle. We might come to accept, for example, after further reflection, some principle that seemed to us initially unattractive, perhaps the principle that men should sometimes be made to be free. We might accept this principle if we were satisfied that no less harsh principle could support the set of political convictions we were especially reluctant to abandon. On the other hand, we must also be ready to modify or adjust, or even to give up entirely, immediate convictions that cannot be accommodated by any principle that meets our relaxed standards; in adjusting these immediate convictions we will use our initial sense of which seem to us more and which less certain, though in principle no immediate conviction can be taken as immune from reinspection or abandonment if that should prove necessary. We can expect to proceed back and forth between our immediate judgments and the structure of explanatory principles in this way, tinkering first with one side and then the other, until we arrive at what Rawls calls the state of reflective equilibrium in which we are satisfied, or as much satisfied as we can reasonably expect.

It may well be that, at least for most of us, our ordinary political judgments stand in this relation of reflective equilibrium with Rawls's two principles of justice, or, at least, that they could be made to do so through the process of adjustment just described. It is nevertheless unclear how the idea of the original position fits into this structure or, indeed, why it has any role to play at all. The original position is not among the ordinary political convictions that we find we have, and that we turn to reflective equilibrium to justify. If it has any role, it must be in the process of justification, because it takes its place in the body of theory we construct to bring our convictions into balance. But if the two principles of justice are themselves in reflective equilibrium with our convictions, it is unclear why we need the original position to supplement the two principles on the theoretical side of the balance. What can the idea contribute to a harmony already established?

We should consider the following answer. It is one of the conditions we impose on a theoretical principle, before we allow it to figure as a justification of our convictions, that the people the principle would govern would have accepted that principle, at least under certain conditions, if they had been asked, or at least that the principle can be shown to be in the antecedent interest of every such person. If this is so, then the original position plays an essential part in the process of justification through equilibrium. It is used to show that the two principles conform to this established standard of acceptability for political principles. At the same time, the fact that the two principles, which do conform to that standard, justify our ordinary convictions in reflective equilibrium reinforces our faith in the standard and encourages us to apply it to other issues of political or moral philosophy.

This answer does not advance the case that the original position furnishes an argument for the two principles, however; it merely restates the ideas we have already considered and rejected. It is certainly not part of our established political traditions or ordinary moral understanding that principles are acceptable only if they would be chosen by men in the particular predicament of the original position. It is, of course, part of these traditions that principles are fair if they have in fact been chosen by those whom they govern, or if they can at least be shown to be in their antecedent common interest. But we have already seen that the original position device cannot be used to support either of these arguments in favor of applying the two principles to contemporary politics. If the original position is to play any role in a structure of principles and convictions in reflective equilibrium, it must be by virtue of assumptions we have not yet identified.

It is time to reconsider an earlier assumption. So far I have been treating the original position construction as if it were either the foundation of Rawls's argument or an ingredient in a reflective equilibrium established between our political intuitions and his two principles of justice. But, in fact, Rawls does not treat the original position that way. He describes the construction in these words:

> I have emphasized that this original position is purely hypotheti-
> cal. It is natural to ask why, if this agreement is never actually
> entered into, we should take any interest in these principles, moral
> or otherwise. The answer is that the conditions embodied in the
> description of the original position are ones that we do in fact
> accept. Or if we do not, then perhaps we can be persuaded to do so
> by philosophical reflection. Each aspect of the contractual
> situation can be given supporting grounds. . . . On the other
> hand, this conception is also an intuitive notion that suggests its
> own elaboration, so that led on by it we are drawn to define more
> clearly the standpoint from which we can best interpret moral
> relationships. We need a conception that enables us to envision

our objective from afar: the intuitive notion of the original position is to do this for us.[3]

This description is taken from Rawls's first statement of the original position. It is recalled and repeated in the very last paragraph of [his] book.[4] It is plainly of capital importance, and it suggests that the original position, far from being the foundation of his argument, or an expository device for the technique of equilibrium, is one of the major substantive products of the theory as a whole. Its importance is reflected in another crucial passage. Rawls describes his moral theory as a type of psychology. He wants to characterize the structure of our (or, at least, one person's) capacity to make moral judgments of a certain sort; that is, judgments about justice. He thinks that the conditions embodied in the original position are the fundamental "principles governing our moral powers, or more specifically, our sense of justice."[5] The original position is therefore a schematic representation of a particular mental process of at least some, and perhaps most, human beings, just as depth grammar, he suggests, is a schematic presentation of a different mental capacity.

All this suggests that the original position is an intermediate conclusion, a halfway point in a deeper theory that provides philosophical arguments for its conditions. In the next part of this essay I shall try to describe at least the main outlines of this deeper theory. I shall distinguish three features of the surface argument of the book—the technique of equilibrium, the social contract, and the original position itself—and try to discern which of various familiar philosophical principles or positions these represent.

First, however, I must say a further word about Rawls's exciting, if imprecise, idea that the principles of this deeper theory are constitutive of our moral capacity. That idea can be understood on different levels of profundity. It may mean, at its least profound, that the principles that support the original position as a device for reasoning about justice are so widely shared and so little questioned within a particular community, for whom the book is meant, that the community could not abandon these principles without fundamentally changing its patterns of reasoning and arguing about political morality. It may mean, at its most profound, that these principles are innate categories of morality common to all men, imprinted in their neural structure, so that man could not deny these principles short of abandoning the power to reason about morality at all.

I shall be guided, in what follows, by the less profound interpretation, though what I shall say, I think, is consistent with the more profound. I shall assume, then, that there is a group of men and women who find, on reading Rawls, that the original position does strike them as a proper "intuitive notion" from which to think about problems of justice, and who would find it persuasive, if it could be

[3]pp. 21-2.
[4]p. 587.
[5]p. 51.

demonstrated that the parties to the original position would in fact contract for the two principles he describes. I suppose, on the basis of experience and the literature, that this group contains a very large number of those who think about justice at all, and I find that I am a member myself. I want to discover the hidden assumptions that bend the inclinations of this group that way, and I shall do so by repeating the question with which I began. Why does Rawls's argument support his claim that his two principles are principles of justice? My answer is complex and it will take us, at times, far from his text, but not, I think, from its spirit. . . .

The Original Position

I said that the use of a social contract, in the way that Rawls uses it, presupposes a deep theory that assumes natural rights. I want now to describe, in somewhat more detail, how the device of a contract applies that assumption. It capitalizes on the idea, mentioned earlier, that some political arrangements might be said to be in the antecedent interest of every individual even though they are not, in the event, in his actual interest.

Everyone whose consent is necessary to a contract has a veto over the terms of that contract, but the worth of that veto, to him, is limited by the fact that his judgment must be one of antecedent rather than actual self-interest. He must commit himself, and so abandon his veto, at a time when his knowledge is sufficient only to allow him to estimate the best odds, not to be certain of his bet. So the contract situation is in one way structurally like the situation in which an individual with specific political rights confronts political decisions that may disadvantage him. He had a limited, political right to veto these, a veto limited by the scope of the rights he has. The contract can be used as a model for the political situation by shaping the degree or character of a party's ignorance in the contractual situation so that this ignorance has the same force on his decision as the limited nature of his rights would have in the political situation.

This shaping of ignorance to suit the limited character of political rights is most efficiently done simply by narrowing the individual goals that the parties to the contract know they wish to pursue. If we take Hobbes's deep theory, for example, to propose that men have a fundamental natural right to life, so that it is wrong to take their lives, even for social goals otherwise proper, we should expect a contract situation of the sort he describes. Hobbes's men and women, in Rawls's phrase, have lexically ordered security of life over all other individual goals; the same situation would result if they were simply ignorant of any other goals they might have and unable to speculate about the chances that they have any particular one or set of these.

The ignorance of the parties in the original position might thus be seen as a kind of limiting case of the ignorance that can be found, in the form of a distorted or eccentric ranking of interests, in classical contract theories and that is natural to the contract device. The original position is a limiting case because Rawls's men are not simply ignorant of interests beyond a chosen few; they are ignorant of all the interests they have. It would be wrong to suppose that this makes them incapable of any judgments of self-interest. But the judgments they make must nevertheless be very abstract; they must allow for any combination of interests, without the benefit of any supposition that some of these are more likely than others.

The basic right of Rawls's deep theory, therefore, cannot be a right to any particular individual goal, like a right to security of life, or a right to lead a life according to a particular conception of the good. Such rights to individual goals may be produced by the deep theory, as rights that men in the original position would stipulate as being in their best interest. But the original position cannot itself be justified on the assumption of such a right, because the parties to the contract do not know that they have any such interest or rank it lexically ahead of others.

So the basic right of Rawls's deep theory must be an abstract right, that is, not a right to any particular individual goal. There are two candidates, within the familiar concepts of political theory, for this role. The first is the right to liberty, and it may strike many readers as both plausible and comforting to assume that Rawls's entire structure is based on the assumption of a fundamental natural right to liberty — plausible because the two principles that compose his theory of justice give liberty an important and dominant place, and comforting because the argument attempting to justify that place seems uncharacteristically incomplete.[6]

Nevertheless, the right to liberty cannot be taken as the fundamental right in Rawls's deep theory. Suppose we define general liberty as the overall minimum possible constraints, imposed by government or by other men, on what a man might want to do.[7] We must then distinguish this general liberty from particular liberties, that is, freedom from such constraints on particular acts thought specially important, like participation in politics. The parties to the original position certainly have, and know that they have, an interest in general liberty, because general liberty will, *pro tanto*, improve their power to achieve any particular goals they later discover themselves to have. But the qualification is important, because they have no way of knowing that general liberty will in fact improve this power overall, and every reason to suspect that it will not. They know that they might have other interests, beyond general liberty, that can be protected only by political constraints on acts of others.

So if Rawlsian men must be supposed to have a right to liberty of some sort, which the contract situation is shaped to embody, it must be a right to particular liberties. Rawls does name a list of basic liberties, and it is these that his men do choose to protect through their lexically ordered first principle of justice.[8] But Rawls plainly casts this principle as the product of the contract rather than as a condition of it. He argues that the parties to the original position would select these basic liberties to protect the basic goods they decide to value, like self-respect, rather than taking these liberties as goals in themselves. Of course they might, in fact, value the activities protected as basic liberties for their own sake, rather than as means to some other goal or interest. But they certainly do not know that they do.

The second familiar concept of political theory is even more abstract than

[6]See Hart, 'Rawls on Liberty and Its Priority,' 40 *U. Chi. L. Rev.* 534 (1973).
[7]Cf. Rawls's definition of liberty at p. 202.
[8]p. 61.

liberty. This is equality, and in one way Rawlsian men and women cannot choose other than to protect it. The state of ignorance in the original position is so shaped that the antecedent interest of everyone must lie, as I said, in the same solution. The right of each man to be treated equally without regard to his person or character or tastes is enforced by the fact that no one else can secure a better position by virtue of being different in any such respect. In other contract situations, when ignorance is less complete, individuals who share the same goal may nevertheless have different antecedent interests. Even if two men value life above everything else, for example, the antecedent interest of the weaker might call for a state monopoly of force rather than some provision for private vengeance, but the antecedent interest of the stronger might not. Even if two men value political participation above all else, the knowledge that one's views are likely to be more unorthodox or unpopular than those of the other will suggest that his antecedent interest calls for different arrangements. In the original position no such discrimination of antecedent interests can be made.

It is true that, in two respects, the principles of justice that Rawls thinks men and women would choose in the original position may be said to fall short of an egalitarian ideal. First, they subordinate equality in material resources, when this is necessary, to liberty of political activity, by making the demands of the first principle prior to those of the second. Second, they do not take account of relative deprivation, because they justify any inequality when those worse off are better off than they would be, in absolute terms, without that inequality.

Rawls makes plain that these inequalities are required, not by some competing notion of liberty or some overriding goal, but by a more basic sense of equality itself. He accepts a distinction between what he calls two conceptions of equality:

> Some writers have distinguished between equality as it is invoked in connection with the distribution of certain goods, some of which will almost certainly give higher status or prestige to those who are more favored, and equality as it applies to the respect which is owed to persons irrespective of their social position. Equality of the first kind is defined by the second principle of justice. . . . But equality of the second kind is fundamental.[9]

We may describe a right to equality of the second kind, which Rawls says is fundamental, in this way. We might say that individuals have a right to equal concern and respect in the design and administration of the political institutions that govern them. This is a highly abstract right. Someone might argue, for example, that it is satisfied by political arrangements that provide equal opportunity for office and position on the basis of merit. Someone else might argue, to the contrary, that it is satisfied only by a system that guarantees absolute equality of income and status, without regard to merit. A third man might argue that equal concern and respect is provided by that system, whatever it is, that improves the average welfare of all

[9]p. 511.

citizens counting the welfare of each on the same scale. A fourth might argue, in the name of this fundamental equality, for the priority of liberty, and for the other apparent inequalities of Rawls's two principles.

The right to equal concern and respect, then, is more abstract than the standard conceptions of equality that distinguish different political theories. It permits arguments that this more basic right requires one or another of these conceptions as a derivative right or goal.

The original position may now be seen as a device for testing these competing arguments. It supposes, reasonably, that political arrangements that do not display equal concern and respect are those that are established and administered by powerful men and women who, whether they recognize it or not, have more concern and respect for members of a particular class, or people with particular talents or ideals, than they have for others. It relies on this supposition in shaping the ignorance of the parties to the contract. Men who do not know to which class they belong cannot design institutions, consciously or unconsciously, to favor their own class. Men who have no idea of their own conception of the good cannot act to favor those who hold one ideal over those who hold another. The original position is well designed to enforce the abstract right to equal concern and respect, which must be understood to be the fundamental concept of Rawls's deep theory.

If this is right, then Rawls must not use the original position to argue for this right in the same way that he uses it, for example, to argue for the rights to basic liberties embodied in the first principle. The text confirms that he does not. It is true that he once says that equality of respect is "defined" by the first principle of justice.[10] But he does not mean, and in any case he does not argue, that the parties choose to be respected equally in order to advance some more basic right or goal. On the contrary, the right to equal respect is not, on his account, a product of the contract, but a condition of admission to the original position. This right, he says, is "owed to human beings as moral persons," and follows from the moral personality that distinguishes humans from animals. It is possessed by all men who can give justice, and only such men can contract.[11] This is one right, therefore, that does not emerge from the contract, but is assumed, as the fundamental right must be, in its design.

Rawls is well aware that his argument for equality stands on a different footing from his argument for the other rights within his theory:

> Now of course none of this is literally argument. I have not set out the premises from which this conclusion follows, as I have tried to do, albeit not very rigorously, with the choice of conceptions of justice in the original position. Nor have I tried to prove that the characterization of the parties must be used as the basis of equality. Rather this interpretation seems to be the natural completion of justice as fairness.[12]

[10]*Id.*

[11]Chapter 77.

[12]p. 509.

It is the "natural completion," that is to say, of the theory as a whole. It completes the theory by providing the fundamental assumption that charges the original position, and makes it an "intuitive notion" for developing and testing theories of justice.

We may therefore say that justice as fairness rests on the assumption of a natural right of all men and women to equality of concern and respect, a right they possess not by virtue of birth or characteristic or merit or excellence but simply as human beings with the capacity to make plans and give justice. Many readers will not be surprised by this conclusion, and it is, as I have said, reasonably clear from the text. It is an important conclusion, nevertheless, because some forms of criticism of the theory, already standard, ignore it. I shall close this long essay with one example.

One form of criticism has been expressed to me by many colleagues and students, particularly lawyers. They point out that the particular political institutions and arrangements that Rawls says men in the original position would choose are merely idealized forms of those now in force in the United States. They are the institutions, that is, of liberal constitutional democracy. The critics conclude that the fundamental assumptions of Rawls's theory must, therefore, be the assumptions of classical liberalism, however they define these, and that the original position, which appears to animate the theory, must somehow be an embodiment of these assumptions. Justice as fairness therefore seems to them, in its entirety, a particularly subtle rationalization of the political status quo, which may safely be disregarded by those who want to offer a more radical critique of the liberal tradition.

If I am right, this point of view is foolish, and those who take it lose an opportunity, rare for them, to submit their own political views to some form of philosophical examination. Rawls's most basic assumption is not that men have a right to certain liberties that Locke or Mill thought important, but that they have a right to equal respect and concern in the design of political institutions. This assumption may be contested in many ways. It will be denied by those who believe that some goal, like utility or the triumph of a class or the flowering of some conception of how men should live, is more fundamental than any individual right, including the right to equality. But it cannot be denied in the name of any more radical concept of equality, because none exists.

Rawls does argue that this fundamental right to equality requires a liberal constitution, and supports an idealized form of present economic and social structures. He argues, for example, that men in the original position would protect the basic liberties in the interest of their right to equality, once a certain level of material comfort has been reached, because they would understand that a threat to self-respect, which the basic liberties protect, is then the most serious threat to equal respect. He also argues that these men would accept the second principle in preference to material equality because they would understand that sacrifice out of envy for another is a form of subordination to him. These arguments may, of course, be wrong. I have certainly said nothing in their defense here. But the critics of liberalism now have the responsibility to show that they are wrong. They cannot say that Rawls's basic assumptions and attitudes are too far from their own to allow a confrontation.

7

Rawls and Marxism

Richard Miller

In *A Theory of Justice*, John Rawls claims that all of the most fundamental questions about justice, including questions about an individual's duty to help achieve justice, can be settled from the standpoint of the original position.[1] He proposes, as a criterion of social justice, the so-called "difference principle," the principle that basic institutions ought to maximize the life prospects of the worst-off.[2] And he presents this standard as a morally realistic one, in that people in societies that do not yet fulfill it ought to accept advances toward it (at least if these advances do not conflict with the maximization of equal basic liberties or with fair equality of opportunity), and ought, to some extent, to help achieve such advances.[3]

I shall try to show that these claims, taken together, presuppose a relatively low estimate of the extent and consequences of social conflict. In particular, if a Marxist analysis of social conflict is right in certain respects, a commitment to accept advances toward the difference principle in societies that do not embody it would not emerge from the original position. Thus, if these Marxist ideas are correct, either the difference principle is unrealistic, in that people do not have a duty to accept and to further its realization, or there are fundamental issues concerning justice (for example, this issue of moral realism), that cannot be resolved from the standpoint of the original position.

From "Rawls and Marxism," *Philosophy and Public Affairs* (1974), pp. 167–180. Reprinted by permission of the author and Princeton University Press.

[1] John Rawls, *A Theory of Justice* (Cambridge, Mass., 1971), pp. 11, 17, 115, 333f. Otherwise unidentified page references in the notes that follow are to this volume.

[2] Pp. 60f., 75ff.

[3] Pp. 115, 246, 288f., 334. On the priority of the principles of equal liberties and equal opportunity, see note 7, below.

In Rawls's "ideal contractualism," principles concerning justice are seen as agreements that would be made by rational deliberants seeking to pursue their interests behind a veil of ignorance which excludes knowledge of what one's place in society and one's special interests are. This is, of course, a very rough statement, but most refinements on it go beyond the needs of this essay. There are, however, a few details of Rawls's theory that need further elaboration, for the sake of my subsequent arguments.

In the original position, one does not know what one's social position or one's special needs and interests are. And in deciding the most general questions about justice, one does not know what particular form of society (e.g., slave-holding, feudal, capitalist) one lives in.[4] But one does know "the general facts about human society."[5] Thus, if Marxist social theory is correct, the general facts contained in this theory would be known in the original position, and could affect its outcome.

In defining the agreements Rawls believes would emerge from the original position, it will be helpful to distinguish the outcomes Rawls thinks he *has* established in his book, from the outcomes he thinks *can* be established by ideal contractualism. In particular, Rawls claims to have actually derived a commitment to support the difference principle in circumstances of "strict compliance," i.e., in any society the basic institutions of which conform to the difference principle and the members of which regard the latter as a principle of justice and willingly do what it requires.[6] But he surely regards it as *possible* to derive a commitment to accept and, to some extent, to further advances toward the difference principle in any society within the "circumstances of justice," i.e., in any society with respect to which questions of justice can appropriately be raised. For he says the difference principle applies throughout the circumstances of justice.[7] As noted before, he regards it as a duty to help realize principles of justice. And he sees all fundamental questions concerning justice as being decidable by determining what commitments would emerge from the original position. Thus some commitment to uphold the difference principle, even when strict compliance has not been achieved, ought to emerge from the original position.

Of course, that the text of Rawls's book implies a commitment to there

---

[4]P. 137.

[5]*Ibid.* Rawls goes on to say, "They understand political affairs and the principles of economic theory. . . . Indeed the parties are presumed to know whatever general facts affect the choice of the principles of justice."

[6]The derivation is contained in sections 26, 29, and 51. For the restriction to circumstances of strict compliance, see pp. 8, 288f., 334. This restriction was also imposed in unpublished comments of Rawls in response to David Lyons's paper at the 1972 A.P.A. symposium on *A Theory of Justice.* I should add that a reader who favors a less restrictive interpretation of Rawls's claims will find the conflict I sketch between Rawls and Marx all the more acute.

[7]Pp. 125, 126. Strictly speaking, the difference principle is always to be fulfilled insofar as this does not conflict with the principle of greatest equal liberty or the principle of fair equality of opportunity (pp. 61, 302f.). Also, an expanded version of the difference principle, in which liberty, opportunity, and self-respect are counted among the relevant goods, holds universally (pp. 62f.). In this essay, all discussions of the difference principle are to be understood as bearing on these two restricted claims. There is little danger of resulting oversimplification, for we shall not be concerned with conflicts between the (narrower) difference principle and principles that override it.

being an ideal contractualist account of the duty to uphold Rawlsian justice does not show that this commitment is central to Rawls's theory. But in fact this claim of Rawls cannot be rejected without casting doubt on the whole ideal contractualist approach. To begin with, the view that people in less than just societies have no duty to help achieve justice, or even to accept advances in this direction, is monstrous, and more than a bit absurd. After all, a slave owner who refuses to let his slaves go free, when this would require only moderate financial losses, would not be a just man because he believed slavery to be an unjust institution. Indeed, we would regard this belief as playing a trivial role in his sense of justice. But if the assertion of principles of justice for institutions must be accompanied by the requirement that these principles be upheld, a moral outlook appealed to in support of the former claim should provide support for the latter. Certainly, if ideal contractualism is supposed to tell us how basic institutions should operate, but must be abandoned when we ask how people should behave in less than ideal circumstances, it cannot be the satisfactory end result of moral reflection that Rawls wants it to be. Thus, the importance of the idea of an ideal contractualist account of the duty to help achieve justice is much greater than might be thought from the few paragraphs Rawls devotes directly to this claim.

I shall be arguing that certain aspects of Marxism (and not very hard-line ones) would preclude the requisite agreement to uphold the difference principle throughout the circumstances of justice. In particular, I shall argue that this commitment would not be made if *some* societies in the circumstances of justice display the following three features: no social arrangement that is acceptable to the best-off class is acceptable to the worst-off class; the best-off class is a ruling class, i.e., one whose interests are served by the major political and ideological institutions; the need for wealth and power typical of the best-off class is much more acute than that typical of the rest of society. This piece of Marxism is, of course, less controversial than Marx's whole theory, in which these features are said to hold true of all nonprimitive societies. But certain of the claims I have sketched can be so understood that it is implausible that they should hold true of any society. And, of course, the question of whether there is an obligation to uphold the difference principle in a society like our own will be an implicit concern in my arguments, even though I do not explicitly address myself to it. For these reasons, I would like to spell out in more detail the ways in which the above three properties might obtain in various societies.

To begin with, Marx claims that in any society, from the dissolution of primitive communism to the overthrow of capitalism, there is no social contract that the best-off class and the worst-off one will acquiesce in, except as a result of defeat in class struggle or a tactical retreat to preserve long-term advantages. For example, Marx would say that no aristocracy has reduced feudal obligations, no bourgeoisie has reduced the length or pace of the working day, except in response to the actual or potential militancy of peasants or of workers, usually in alliance with other classes. And no peasantry or proletariat has accepted an economic arrangement for long without fighting against it, whether in peasant uprisings, militant strikes, or revolutions. For Marx, this determination of social affairs by what Rawls would call "threat advantage" reflects people's rational pursuit of their self-interests. Moreover, improvements in the relative position of the worst-off class cannot, in

Marx's view, be brought about by appeals to any universal sense of justice. Even when such a sense exists, no appropriate consensus can be achieved as to whether the demands of justice have in fact been fulfilled. For instance, capitalists, as a class, have always insisted that a proposed reduction of the working day, e.g., from twelve or more hours to ten, would do immeasurable harm to workers by destroying the capitalist economy on whose existence workers' welfare depends.[8]

The second Marxist idea I shall emphasize is the notion that the best-off class is a ruling class, one whose interests are served by all major institutions. Marx and Engels emphasize two aspects of this rule, the repressive and the ideological. In their view, the official instruments of coercion are employed, in almost all crucial instances of class conflict, in favor of the best-off class. Thus, to take some dramatic examples, the police, the army, and the courts were used in the United States and Great Britain to break up meetings in support of the ten-hour day, not meetings against it. In the fight for industrial unionism in this country in the twenties and thirties, they were used to protect strikebreakers and threaten sit-down strikers, not the other way around. In addition to institutions of repression, ideological institutions, in the Marxist view, help to maintain the special status of the best-off class. For example, in the Middle Ages, the Church tended to teach that submission to the dominant social order was an expression of piety. In nineteenth-century England, according to Marx, as class struggle became more intense, academic economists mostly became "hired prizefighters" of the bourgeoisie,[9] arguing, e.g., that abolishing tariffs on grain would immensely enrich workers and that a ten-hour workday would reduce profits to zero.[10] To take a present-day American example, many Marxists would now argue that the media and the schools foster anti-Black racism because it serves to divide those having common interests against American big business.

The third Marxist idea to which I shall refer is, strictly speaking, an extrapolation from Marx's writings, and not taken directly from them. Marx seems to regard a typical member of the best-off class in an exploitive society as having an especially acute need for wealth and power. He would, I think, have accepted the following estimate of how acute these needs usually are: the need for wealth and power of a typical member of the best-off class is sufficiently great that such a person would be miserable if his society were transformed to accord with the egalitarian demands of the difference principle. Indeed, this misery would be so great that the possibility of such unhappiness would dissuade someone in the original position from committing himself to help realize the difference principle, when the veil of ignorance is lifted. (I shall spell out this claim in more detail later on.)

While this specific estimate of ruling-class needs cannot, of course, be found in Marx, it is, I think, a reasonable extrapolation from Marx's writings. Some such radical estimate of how much greater a lord's needs are than a serf's, or how much greater a capitalist's are than a worker's, is suggested by Marx's comments on the immense differences between what workers in different societies regard as

[8]See Karl Marx, *Capital* (Moscow, n.d.), 1, chap. 9. sec. 3, "Senior's 'Last Hour.'"
[9]*Ibid.*, 1, "Preface to the Second German Edition," p. 25.
[10]*Ibid.*, 1, p. 25 and chap. 9, sec. 3.

"necessities of life."[11] It also seems implicit in his historical writings. For example, in Marx's account, the factions of the French bourgeoisie who overthrew Louis Philippe risked large-scale social disorder to escape a subordination to other factions that allowed the worst-off factions wealth and power beyond the dreams of most of the French working class, or, indeed, most workers in the Paris Commune, twenty years later. The general idea that classes differ in their needs, and not just in the degree to which their needs are satisfied, is almost explicitly stated in one of Marx's last writings, his notes on Wagner's *Lehrbuch der politischen Oekonomie*, when he criticizes some remarks of Wagner's on the "natural" needs of Man: "[If 'Man'] means Man, as a category, he has . . . no . . . needs at all. If it means man confronting nature by himself, one has in mind a non-social animal. If it means a man who is already to be found in some form of society . . . one must begin by presenting the particular character of this social man, i.e., the particular character of the community in which he lives, since here production, and thus *the means by which he maintains his existence* already have a social character."[12] This idea is, in turn, a special case of Marx's general thesis that "the social being [of men] determines their consciousness."[13]

If some societies in the circumstances of justice have the three features I have sketched, then, I shall try to show, no commitment to uphold the difference principle throughout the circumstances of justice would emerge from the original position.[14] To organize my argument, I shall take advantage of a certain feature of Rawls's exposition. His arguments for the difference principle often look like arguments for a commitment to participate in the immediate realization of the difference principle, once the veil of ignorance is lifted.[15] As I have mentioned, I do not think Rawls actually means to put forward such an argument within the confines of his book. He means only to argue for a commitment to uphold the

[11]See, for example, *ibid.*, 1, chap. 6, "The Buying and Selling of Labor-Power," p. 168: "On the other hand, the number and extent of his [the wage-laborer's] so-called necessary wants, as also the modes of satisfying them, are themselves the product of historical development, and depend therefore to a great extent on the degree of civilization of a country, more particularly on the conditions under which, and consequently on the habits and degree of comfort in which, the class of free laborers has been formed."

There is a discussion to the same effect in *Wages, Price and Profit*, in which Marx speaks of "a *traditional standard of life*" as "the satisfaction of certain wants springing from the social conditions in which people are placed and reared up," and contrasts "the English standard of life" with "the Irish standard"; "the standard of life of a German peasant" with that "of a Livonian peasant" (*Selected Works in One Volume* [New York, 1970], p. 225). See also *Wage-Labor and Capital, ibid.*, pp. 84f.

[12]Marx's emphasis. See Marx and Engels, *Werke* (Berlin, 1958), 19, p. 362. The idea that needs differ significantly among different classes or socio-economic groups is not, of course, by any means confined to Marxist or left-wing writers. See, for example, Emile Durkheim, "Anomic Suicide," in *Suicide* (New York, 1951), pp. 249ff.

[13]Preface to the *Critique of Political Economy*, in Marx and Engels, *Selected Works*, p. 182.

[14]One clear and immediate corollary will be that if present-day society has these features, no commitment to uphold the difference principle in the present day would emerge.

[15]These arguments, in sections 26 and 29, are actually presented as arguments for Rawls's two principles of justice, in serial order. But they are fairly characterized as "Rawls's arguments for the difference principle," since no other derivation of that principle is given in Rawls's book.

difference principle in a society in which the principle has already been stably realized and everyone has a psychology supporting compliance with it. Nevertheless, the considerations Rawls brings forward in these arguments, considerations concerning the strains of commitment, rationality, self-respect, and stability, seem the ones that would be appealed to in support of a commitment to uphold the difference principle in less than ideal circumstances. In fact, it will be helpful to examine Rawls's arguments in turn, first taking each as if it *were* an argument for a commitment to realize the difference principle as soon as possible, then seeing if such an argument could be modified so as to generate a commitment to gradual realization. It might seem that working in this way I will tie my arguments too closely to special features of Rawls's text. But I think the reader will find that if the putative arguments I construct conflict with Marxist social theory, it seems quite unlikely that any argument for a commitment to uphold the difference principle throughout the circumstances of justice could accord with relevant aspects of Marxism.

One final comment may be necessary, before setting out my main arguments, in order for their import not to be misunderstood. I shall be maintaining that Rawls is tacitly committed to a social hypothesis than can reasonably be argued either way, i.e., that the Marxist analysis I have just sketched is wrong throughout the circumstances of justice. I should note that I do not at all intend to criticize Rawls for developing a moral theory based on controversial factual assumptions. Indeed, it seems unlikely he could have written a book of such merit and importance if he had not been willing to commit himself to empirical claims. My intention in this essay is, rather, to show what some of Rawls's implicit assumptions are. By that token, I shall be arguing that some of his claims must be rejected if these assumptions are held to be false.

On the Derivation of the
Difference Principle

I shall now consider Rawls's main attempts to derive the difference principle from the original position. In the chapter entitled "Some Main Grounds for the Two Principles of Justice" Rawls begins with the argument that his standard of social justice uniquely satisfies the following constraint: ". . . they [the bargainers in the original position] consider the strains of commitment. They cannot enter into agreements that may have consequences they cannot accept. They will avoid those that they can adhere to only with great difficulty."[16] Rawls argues along these lines against the principle of utility, noting that it will probably be a standard one cannot adhere to if it turns out to demand that one make great sacrifices simply to create more happiness for mankind as a whole.

Taken as an argument for a commitment to realize the difference principle as soon as possible, such reasoning from the strains of commitment seems subject to the charge Rawls makes against utilitarianism. It might be said that the best-off

[16]P. 176.

people will generally find it intolerable to give up great advantages in order to maximize the situation of the worst-off. This is, of course, a claim that Marxists would make. They would claim that the best-off people in any exploitive society cannot be made to give up their privileges except by force. In support of this claim, they would argue, for example, that no dominant exploitive class has voluntarily given up its rule, no matter how unjust. If Marxist social theory is right, at least when applied to some societies, someone in the original position would foresee that the difference principle may be intolerable for him, if he turns out to be a typical member of a dominant exploitive class. Thus, he could not accept, as grounds for a commitment to help realize the difference principle, an argument that this commitment, unlike its rivals, will be one he can live up to, no matter what social position he turns out to occupy.

In his book Rawls advances certain considerations that might be taken to show that in the original position one can foresee oneself as fulfilling a commitment to the difference principle, even if one turns out to be among the best-off. Most notably, in the chapter "On the Tendency to Equality," Rawls argues, in the following terms, that the difference principle is a "principle of mutual benefit":

> to begin with, it is clear that the well-being of each [i.e., both the best-off and the worst-off] depends on a scheme of social cooperation without which no one could have a satisfactory life. Secondly, we can ask for the willing cooperation of everyone only if the terms of the scheme are reasonable. The difference principle, then, seems to be a fair basis on which those better endowed, or more fortunate in their social circumstances, could expect others to collaborate with them when some workable arrangement is a necessary condition of the good of all.[17]

Such a line of reasoning is inadequate to establish the tolerability of commitment to the difference principle, if the best-off are a *ruling class* in an exploitive society. In a system which is in fact thoroughly exploitive, a ruling class can, for centuries, maintain as much willing cooperation as it needs, because ideological institutions serve its interests, while restraining most who do not cooperate and dissuading most who are tempted not to, by employing the coercive apparatus of the state. In such a situation, the rewards of exploitation for the ruling class far outweigh the costs to it of maintaining cooperation in an exploitive society. (Note that most of these costs are not supplied by the ruling class at all, but by workers who supply taxes and, in times of war, their lives.) Thus, if the best-off are sometimes a ruling class, of the sort just described, someone in the original position would foresee that if he turns out to be one of the best-off, his interests may not lie in the realization of Rawls's standard of social justice.

Of course, there is nothing in Marxist social theory to indicate one is *likely* to find it impossible to live up to a commitment to help realize the difference principle. To the contrary, the sort of exploitive ruling class I have described is supposed to be a small minority in any society. But an argument that one is quite

[17]P. 103.

unlikely to find commitment to the difference principle intolerable could not be successfully advanced behind the veil of ignorance. For, as Rawls indicates on several occasions, if reasoning from the respective likelihoods of one's occupying various social positions were admitted in the original position, the social ideal chosen would be some version of the principle of average utility.[18] Thus, if probabilistic reasoning were admitted (and Rawls thinks it should not be), the resultant commitment would be to help maximize the welfare of the average person, or something of the sort.

Let us suppose that if the sort of exploitive ruling class Marx describes has, at times, existed, the reasoning about the strains of commitment that Rawls uses against utilitarianism would also count against a commitment to help realize the difference principle immediately, or, in any case, as soon as possible after the veil of ignorance is lifted. It might still seem possible that the argument from the strains of commitment might persuade one to help maintain some *gradual* course of development toward full realization. Ideal contractualism might thus lead to a view according to which one sometimes has a duty to accept (and, perhaps, to promote) a certain incremental advance toward the realization of the difference principle, without having a duty to accept any advance beyond this increment. An example of such a gradualist moral claim, though admittedly an extreme one, is the view that slaveholders are obliged to accept emancipation with compensation, but not to accept uncompensated emancipation involving considerable financial sacrifice.

One thing to be said about the gradualist position is that it is repugnant to many people's considered moral judgments. Many would say that if the difference principle defines the requirements of perfect social justice, everyone should willingly accept its immediate realization. Indeed, many would say that everyone who can be helpful in realizing perfect social justice should take an active part in this process, if no great effort is involved.

In any case, an argument from the strains of commitment would not in fact support a gradualist commitment to the difference principle, if exploitive classes such as Marx describes have existed. For on the latter assumption every course of development leading to the difference principle will be more than some social class can willingly accept. Roughly speaking, there will be at least some circumstances in which any rate of change is either too fast for the best-off or too slow for the worst-off. The gradual realization of Rawls's principle will require a narrowing of the gap between best-off and worst-off, until Rawls's standard is satisfied. In the process, wealth, power, and status of the best-off will be progressively reduced. There are, presumably, definite limits to the size of the reduction an upper class can be expected to accept willingly in a given generation. They may accept a greater advance toward equality as a concession to force or the prospect of it. (Thus, the prospect of further social turmoil is sometimes said to be the cause of ultimate corporate acceptance of New Deal legislation.) But in a society for which a Marxist analysis holds true, the best-off will not accept an advance toward equality beyond a certain limit as a voluntary expression of their sense of justice. On the other hand, there are definite lower limits to the rate of advance typical members of the worst-off class find

[18]Pp. 154, 164f., 168f.

acceptable. They may settle for less out of fear, or a misguided perception of social reality, but not out of a feeling that in the actual social setting justice requires no quicker rate of progress. According to the view of class conflict characteristic of, though by no means special to, Marxist social theory, these two ranges of tolerability do not, as a rule, intersect. An advance that is not too much for the best-off class is, characteristically, too little for the worst-off class. Thus, Marx (e.g., in the beginning of Part I of the *Manifesto*) characterizes the whole course of social development as a more or less veiled civil war. And a great many people who do not discern such conflict in the most advanced societies would still claim that in some less advanced societies (where the circumstances of justice obtain) there is no course of action that is relevantly tolerable to all classes. Given such assumptions as these, the reasoning from the strains of commitment that Rawls directs against utilitarianism could also be directed against a commitment to accept any course of development leading to the difference principle.

It should be noted that there is a second sort of objection that might be raised against a gradualist version of Rawls's tolerability argument. Assuming that upper class needs do not change as the gap between best-off and worst-off narrows, the question of tolerability is simply postponed, since the cumulative results of change will eventually become intolerable from the standpoint of the best-off. Marxists and many others would reject the possibility of an appropriate gradual reduction of upper-class needs. They would, for example, point to many upper classes of the past that have responded more and more vigorously as their status has been eroded, even entering when necessary into civil wars. They would also claim that no substantial long-run decline in upper-class needs is to be discerned over the course of history. It might be replied that for the purposes of a strict-compliance theory, it is enough that upper-class needs might be gradually reduced by modifying educational institutions, in the broadest sense of the phrase, to make a representative member of each new upper-class generation less demanding in his needs than his forebears. But it is hard to see how this educational process could effectively obtain without the constant threat to the upper class of intolerable reductions in self-respect. After all, seeing that one's children are successfully and intentionally taught what one takes to be falsehoods, and that their basic needs and desires are systematically changed from one's own is never a small burden (cf. Rawls's discussion of self-respect and liberty of conscience in chapter 33). Thus, gradualism would be seen as at best a postponement of problems of intolerability.

I have tried to show that if Marxist social theory precludes a certain argument for a commitment to the immediate realization of the difference principle, it precludes the use of this argument in support of a gradualist commitment, as well. While this discussion of gradualism as a putative "way out" has been tied to reasoning from the strains of commitment, analogous considerations can readily be developed in connection with arguments we shall subsequently examine, which concern rationality, self-respect, and stability. In considering these arguments, rather than repeating my discussion of gradualism, I shall, on the whole, assume that gradualism does not remove conflicts between Rawls and Marxist social theory.

One further objection to my arguments about tolerability concerns supposed strains of pursuing something less than justice. I have assumed that members of an exploitive ruling class would oppose the changes that the difference principle requires, even if they had a sense of justice defined by Rawls's principles. It might be felt that this would produce a considerable burden of either self-hatred or self-deception, a burden so great that it would not, in fact, be in one's interests to resist the consequences of the difference principle, if on leaving the original position one turns out to be a member of an exploitive ruling class. The answer to this, I think, is that while the ruling class does, in a sense, practice considerable self-deception, this self-deception is of a peculiarly unburdensome kind.

In the following sense, the capacity for self-deception of an exploitive ruling class would be said by Marx to be practically infinite: The long-term nonmoral interests of a typical member of such a class often sharply conflict with the moral principles which he puts forward without conscious hypocrisy; and when this conflict obtains, no reasoning from those moral principles can, in a typical case, dissuade an exploiter from doing what his nonmoral interests demand. Thus, suppose a decision to speed up the pace of work without installing safety equipment will keep profits up at the cost of hundreds of workers' lives. According to Marx, a typical capitalist will make the decision that serves the needs of profit, in spite of an appeal to common principles of justice, even if that appeal is backed by the best arguments in the world. It should also be noted that the emotional strain associated with the instances of self-deception most of us have encountered will typically be lacking in such cases. In Marx's view, the unresponsiveness of members of an exploitive ruling class to arguments conflicting with their class interests is supported by falsehoods, e.g., "What's good for Business (or—what preserves feudal bonds) is good for everyone," which the immense variety of ideological institutions operating in the interests of the ruling class promote, and which everyone in the social circle of a typical member of that class acknowledges. Indeed, even if a revolution were to destroy the basic institutions that contribute to these falsehoods, the survival of bourgeois ideologues, and of bourgeois ideas among many people, including working people, together with the survival of exclusive networks of social acquaintance, would continue to insulate a member of the bourgeoisie from the truths on which the correct application of principles of justice depends. Thus, if one wants to speak of self-deception in situations like the one described (where the self gets so much help in its deception) it is not the sort of self-deception that imposes such strains as to make it preferable for a member of the exploitive ruling class to accept the objective fulfillment of his sense of justice.

I have sketched some reasons for rejecting the claim that the realization of Rawls's standard of social justice would be tolerable to a typical member of every income group. In particular I tried to show how a Rawlsian argument from a common interest in social cooperation conflicts with the conception of the best-off group in society as a ruling class. . . .

III
LIBERAL JUSTICE

Section B
The Utilitarian Tradition: Defenses and a Critique

8

On the Connection Between Justice and Utility

John Stuart Mill

In all ages of speculation one of the strongest obstacles to the reception of the doctrine that utility or happiness is the criterion of right and wrong has been drawn from the idea of justice. The powerful sentiment and apparently clear perception which that word recalls with a rapidity and certainty resembling an instinct have seemed to the majority of thinkers to point to an inherent quality in things; to show that the just must have an existence in nature as something absolute, generically distinct from every variety of the expedient and, in idea, opposed to it, though (as is commonly acknowledged) never, in the long run, disjoined from it in fact.

In the case of this, as of our other moral sentiments, there is no necessary connection between the question of its origin and that of its binding force. That a feeling is bestowed on us by nature does not necessarily legitimate all its promptings. The feeling of justice might be a peculiar instinct, and might yet require, like our other instincts, to be controlled and enlightened by a higher reason. If we have intellectual instincts leading us to judge in a particular way, as well as animal instincts that prompt us to act in a particular way, there is no necessity that the former should be more infallible in their sphere than the latter in theirs; it may as well happen that wrong judgments are occasionally suggested by those, as wrong actions by these. But though it is one thing to believe that we have natural feelings of justice, and another to acknowledge them as an ultimate criterion of conduct, these two opinions are very closely connected in point of fact. Mankind are always predisposed to believe that any subjective feeling, not otherwise accounted for, is a revelation of some objective reality. Our present object is to determine whether the

From *Utilitarianism*, Chapter V. First published 1863.

reality to which the feeling of justice corresponds is one which needs any such special revelation, whether the justice or injustice of an action is a thing intrinsically peculiar and distinct from all its other qualities or only a combination of certain of those qualities presented under a peculiar aspect. For the purpose of this inquiry it is practically important to consider whether the feeling itself, of justice and injustice, is *sui generis* like our sensations of color and taste or a derivative feeling formed by a combination of others. And this it is the more essential to examine, as people are in general willing enough to allow that objectively the dictates of justice coincide with a part of the field of general expediency; but inasmuch as the subjective mental feeling of justice is different from that which commonly attaches to simple expediency, and, except in the extreme cases of the latter, is far more imperative in its demands, people find it difficult to see in justice only a particular kind or branch of general utility, and think that its superior binding force requires a totally different origin.

To throw light upon this question, it is necessary to attempt to ascertain what is the distinguishing character of justice, or of injustice; what is the quality, or whether there is any quality, attributed in common to all modes of conduct designated as unjust (for justice, like many other moral attributes, is best defined by its opposite), and distinguishing them from such modes of conduct as are disapproved, but without having that particular epithet of disapprobation applied to them. If in everything which men are accustomed to characterize as just or unjust some one common attribute or collection of attributes is always present, we may judge whether this particular attribute or combination of attributes would be capable of gathering round it a sentiment of that peculiar character and intensity by virtue of the general laws of our emotional constitution, or whether the sentiment is inexplicable and requires to be regarded as a special provision of nature. If we find the former to be the case, we shall, in resolving this question, have resolved also the main problem; if the latter, we shall have to seek for some other mode of investigating it.

To find the common attributes of a variety of objects, it is necessary to begin by surveying the objects themselves in the concrete. Let us therefore advert successively to the various modes of action and arrangements of human affairs which are classed, by universal or widely spread opinion, as just or as unjust. The things well known to excite the sentiments associated with those names are of a very multifarious character. I shall pass them rapidly in review, without studying any particular arrangement.

In the first place, it is mostly considered unjust to deprive anyone of his personal liberty, his property, or any other thing which belongs to him by law. Here, therefore, is one instance of the application of the terms "just" and "unjust" in a perfectly definite sense, namely, that it is just to respect, unjust to violate, the *legal rights* of anyone. But this judgment admits of several exceptions, arising from the other forms in which the notions of justice and injustice present themselves. For example, the person who suffers the deprivation may (as the phrase is) have *forfeited* the rights which he is so deprived of—a case to which we shall return presently. But also—

Secondly, the legal rights of which he is deprived may be rights which *ought* not to have belonged to him; in other words, the law which confers on him these rights may be a bad law. When it is or when (which is the same thing for our purpose) it is supposed to be so, opinions will differ as to the justice or injustice of infringing it. Some maintain that no law, however bad, ought to be disobeyed by an individual citizen; that his opposition to it, if shown at all, should only be shown in endeavoring to get it altered by competent authority. This opinion (which condemns many of the most illustrious benefactors of mankind, and would often protect pernicious institutions against the only weapons which, in the state of things existing at the time, have any chance of succeeding against them) is defended by those who hold it on grounds of expediency, principally on that of the importance to the common interest of mankind, of maintaining inviolate the sentiment of submission to law. Other persons, again, hold the directly contrary opinion that any law, judged to be bad, may blamelessly be disobeyed, even though it be not judged to be unjust but only inexpedient, while others would confine the license of disobedience to the case of unjust laws; but, again, some say that all laws which are inexpedient are unjust, since every law imposes some restriction on the natural liberty of mankind, which restriction is an injustice unless legitimated by tending to their good. Among these diversities of opinion it seems to be universally admitted that there may be unjust laws, and that law, consequently, is not the ultimate criterion of justice, but may give to one person a benefit, or impose on another an evil, which justice condemns. When, however, a law is thought to be unjust, it seems always to be regarded as being so in the same way in which a breach of law is unjust; namely, by infringing somebody's right, which, as it cannot in this case be a legal right, receives a different appellation and is called a moral right. We may say, therefore, that a second case of injustice consists in taking or withholding from any person that to which he has a *moral right*.

Thirdly, it is universally considered just that each person should obtain that (whether good or evil) which he *deserves*, and unjust that he should obtain a good or be made to undergo an evil which he does not deserve. This is, perhaps, the clearest and most emphatic form in which the idea of justice is conceived by the general mind. As it involves the notion of desert, the question arises, what constitutes desert? Speaking in a general way, a person is understood to deserve good if he does right, evil if he does wrong; and in a more particular sense, to deserve good from those to whom he does or has done good, and evil from those to whom he does or has done evil. The precept of returning good for evil has never been regarded as a case of the fulfillment of justice, but as one in which the claims of justice are waived, in obedience to other considerations.

Fourthly, it is confessedly unjust to *break faith* with anyone: to violate an engagement, either express or implied, or disappoint expectations raised by our own conduct, at least if we have raised those expectations knowingly and voluntarily. Like the other obligations of justice already spoken of, this one is not regarded as absolute, but as capable of being overruled by a stronger obligation of justice on the other side, or by such conduct on the part of the person concerned as is deemed to absolve us from our obligation to him and to constitute a *forfeiture* of the benefit which he has been led to expect.

Fifthly, it is, by universal admission, inconsistent with justice to be *partial*—to show favor or preference to one person over another in matters to which favor and preference do not properly apply. Impartiality, however, does not seem to be regarded as a duty in itself, but rather as instrumental to some other duty; for it is admitted that favor and preference are not always censurable, and, indeed, the cases in which they are condemned are rather the exception than the rule. A person would be more likely to be blamed than applauded for giving his family or friends no superiority in good offices over strangers when he could do so without violating any other duty; and no one thinks it unjust to seek one person in preference to another as a friend, connection, or companion. Impartiality where rights are concerned is of course obligatory, but this is involved in the more general obligations of giving to everyone his right. A tribunal, for example, must be impartial because it is bound to award, without regard to any other consideration, a disputed object to the one of two parties who has the right to it. There are other cases in which impartiality means being solely influenced by desert, as with those who, in the capacity of judges, preceptors, or parents, administer reward and punishment as such. There are cases, again, in which it means being solely influenced by considerations for the public interest, as in making a selection among candidates for a government employment. Impartiality, in short, as an obligation of justice, may be said to mean being exclusively influenced by the considerations which it is supposed ought to influence the particular case in hand, and resisting solicitation of any motives which prompt to conduct different from what those considerations would dictate.

Nearly allied to the idea of impartiality is that of *equality*, which often enters as a component part both into the conception of justice and into the practice of it, and, in the eyes of many persons, constitutes its essence. But in this, still more than in any other case, the notion of justice varies in different persons, and always conforms in its variations to their notion of utility. Each person maintains that equality is the dictate of justice, except where he thinks that expediency requires inequality. The justice of giving equal protection to the rights of all is maintained by those who support the most outrageous inequality in the rights themselves. Even in slave countries it is theoretically admitted that the rights of the slave, such as they are, ought to be as sacred as those of the master, and that a tribunal which fails to enforce them with equal strictness is wanting in justice; while, at the same time, institutions which leave to the slave scarcely any rights to enforce are not deemed unjust because they are not deemed inexpedient. Those who think that utility requires distinctions of rank do not consider it unjust that riches and social privileges should be unequally dispensed; but those who think this inequality inexpedient think it unjust also. Whoever thinks that government is necessary sees no injustice in as much inequality as is constituted by giving to the magistrate powers not granted to other people. Even among those who hold leveling doctrines, there are differences of opinion about expediency. Some communists consider it unjust that the produce of the labor of the community should be shared on any other principle than that of exact equality; others think it just that those should receive most whose wants are greatest; while others hold that those who work harder, or who produce more, or whose services are more valuable to the community, may justly claim a larger quota in the division of the produce. And the sense of natural justice may be plausibly appealed to in behalf of every one of these opinions.

Among so many diverse applications of the term "justice," which yet is not regarded as ambiguous, it is a matter of some difficulty to seize the mental link which holds them together, and on which the moral sentiment adhering to the term essentially depends. Perhaps, in this embarrassment, some help may be derived from the history of the word, as indicated by its etymology.

In most if not all languages, the etymology of the word which corresponds to "just" points distinctly to an origin connected with the ordinances of law. *Justum* is a form of *jussum*, that which has been ordered. *Dikaion* comes directly from *dike*, a suit at law. *Recht*, from which came *right* and *righteous*, is synonymous with law. The courts of justice, the administration of justice, are the courts and the administration of law. *La justice*, in French, is the established term for judicature. I am not committing the fallacy, imputed with some show of truth to Horne Tooke, of assuming that a word must still continue to mean what it originally meant. Etymology is slight evidence of what the idea now signified is, but the very best evidence of how it sprang up. There can, I think, be no doubt that the *idée mère*, the primitive element, in the formation of the notion of justice was conformity to law. It constituted the entire idea among the Hebrews, up to the birth of Christianity; as might be expected in the case of a people whose laws attempted to embrace all subjects on which precepts were required, and who believed those laws to be a direct emanation from the Supreme Being. But other nations, and in particular the Greeks and Romans, who knew that their laws had been made originally, and still continued to be made, by men, were not afraid to admit that those men might make bad laws; might do, by law, the same things, and from the same motives, which if done by individuals without the sanction of law would be called unjust. And hence the sentiment of injustice came to be attached, not to all violations of law, but only to violations of such laws as *ought* to exist, including such as ought to exist but do not, and to laws themselves if supposed to be contrary to what ought to be law. In this manner the idea of law and of its injunctions was still predominant in the notion of justice, even when the laws actually in force ceased to be accepted as the standard of it.

It is true that mankind consider the idea of justice and its obligations as applicable to many things which neither are, nor is it desired that they should be, regulated by law. Nobody desires that laws should interfere with the whole detail of private life; yet everyone allows that in all daily conduct a person may and does show himself to be either just or unjust. But even here, the idea of the breach of what ought to be law still lingers in a modified shape. It would always give us pleasure, and chime in with our feelings of fitness, that acts which we deem unjust should be punished, though we do not always think it expedient that this should be done by the tribunals. We forego that gratification on account of incidental inconveniences. We should be glad to see just conduct enforced and injustice repressed, even in the minutest details, if we were not, with reason, afraid of trusting the magistrate with so unlimited an amount of power over individuals. When we think that a person is bound in justice to do a thing, it is an ordinary form of language to say that he ought to be compelled to do it. We should be gratified to see the obligation enforced by anybody who had the power. If we see that its enforcement by law would be inexpedient, we lament the impossibility, we consider the impunity given to injustice as an evil and strive to make amends for it by bringing a strong expression of our own and the public disapprobation to bear upon the offender. Thus the idea of legal constraint is still the generating idea of the notion of justice, though undergoing several transformations before that notion as it exists in an advanced state of society becomes complete.

The above is, I think, a true account, as far as it goes, of the origin and progressive growth of the idea of justice. But we must observe that it contains as yet nothing to distinguish that obligation from moral obligation in general. For the truth is that the idea of penal sanction, which is the essence of law, enters not only into the conception of injustice, but into that of any kind of wrong. We do not call anything wrong unless we mean to imply that a person ought to be punished in some way or other for doing it—if not by law, by the opinion of his fellow creatures; if not by opinion, by the reproaches of his own conscience. This seems the real turning point of the distinction between morality and simple expediency. It is a part of the notion of duty in every one of its forms that a person may rightfully be compelled to fulfill it. Duty is a thing which may be *exacted* from a person, as one exacts a debt. Unless we think that it may be exacted from him, we do not call it his duty. Reasons of prudence, or the interest of other people, may militate against actually exacting it, but the person himself, it is clearly understood, would not be entitled to complain. There are other things, on the contrary, which we wish that people should do, which we like or admire them for doing, perhaps dislike or despise them for not doing, but yet admit that they are not bound to do; it is not a case of moral obligation; we do not blame them; that is, we do not think that they are proper objects of punishment. How we come by these ideas of deserving and not deserving punishment will appear, perhaps, in the sequel; but I think there is no doubt that this distinction lies at the bottom of the notions of right and wrong; that we call any conduct wrong, or employ, instead, some other term of dislike or disparagement, according as we think that the person ought, or ought not, to be punished for it; and we say it would be right to do so and so, or merely that it would be desirable or laudable, according as we would wish to see the person whom it concerns compelled, or only persuaded and exhorted, to act in that manner.

Justice Correlated with Certain Rights

This, therefore, being the characteristic difference which marks off, not justice, but morality in general from the remaining provinces of expediency and worthiness, the character is still to be sought which distinguishes justice from other branches of morality. Now it is known that ethical writers divide moral duties into two classes, denoted by the ill-chosen expressions, duties of perfect and of imperfect obligation; the latter being those in which, though the act is obligatory, the particular occasions of performing it are left to our choice, as in the case of charity or beneficence, which we are indeed bound to practice but not toward any definite person, nor at any prescribed time. In the more precise language of philosophic jurists, duties of perfect obligation are those duties in virtue of which a correlative *right* resides in some person or persons; duties of imperfect obligation are those moral obligations which do not give birth to any right. I think it will be found that this distinction exactly coincides with that which exists between justice and the other obligations of morality. In our survey of the various popular acceptations of justice, the term appeared generally to involve the idea of a personal right—a claim on the part of one or more individuals, like that which the law gives when it confers a proprietary or other legal right. Whether the injustice consists in depriving a person of a possession, or in breaking faith with him, or in treating him worse than he deserves, or worse than other people who have no greater claims—in each case the supposition implies two things: a wrong done, and some assignable person who is wronged. Injustice may also be done by treating a person better than others; but the wrong in this case is to his competitors, who are also assignable persons. It seems to me that this feature in the case—a right in some person, correlative to the moral obligation—constitutes the specific difference between justice and generosity or beneficence. Justice implies something which it is not only right to do, and wrong not to do, but which some individual person can claim from us as his moral right. No one has a moral right to our generosity or beneficence because we are not morally bound to practice those virtues toward any given individual. And it will be found with respect to this as to every correct definition that the instances which seem to conflict with it are those which most confirm it. For if a moralist attempts, as some have done, to make out that mankind generally, though not any given individual, have a right to all the good we can do them, he at once, by that thesis, includes generosity and beneficence within the category of justice. He is obliged to say that our utmost exertions are *due* to our fellow creatures, thus assimilating them to a debt; or that nothing less can be a sufficient *return* for what society does for us, thus classing the case as one of gratitude; both of which are acknowledged cases of justice, and not of the virtue of beneficence; and whoever does not place the distinction between justice and morality in general, where we have now placed it, will be found to make no distinction between them at all, but to merge all morality in justice. . . . When we call anything a person's right, we mean that he has a valid claim on society to protect him in the possession of it, either by the force of law or by that of education and opinion. If he has what we consider a sufficient claim, on whatever account, to have something guaranteed to him by society, we say that he has a right to it. If we desire to prove that anything does not belong to him by right, we think this done as soon as it is admitted that society ought not to take measures for securing it to him, but should leave him to chance or to his own exertions. Thus a person is said to have a right to what he can earn in fair professional competition, because society ought not to allow any other person to hinder him from endeavoring to earn in that manner as much as he can. But he has not a right to three hundred a year, though he may happen to be earning it; because society is not called on to provide that he shall earn that sum. On the contrary, if he owns ten thousand pounds three-per-cent stock, he *has* a right to three hundred a year because society has come under an obligation to provide him with an income of that amount.

To have a right, then, is, I conceive, to have something which society ought to defend me in the possession of. If the objector goes on to ask why it ought, I can give him no other reason than general utility. If that expression does not seem to convey a sufficient feeling of the strength of the obligation, nor to account for the peculiar energy of the feeling, it is because there goes to the composition of the sentiment, not a rational only but also an animal element—the thirst for retaliation; and this thirst derives its intensity, as well as its moral justification, from the extraordinarily important and impressive kind of utility which is concerned. The interest involved is that of security, to everyone's feelings the most vital of all interests. All other earthly benefits are needed by one person, not needed by another; and many of them can, if necessary, be cheerfully foregone or replaced by something else; but security no human being can possibly do without; on it we depend for all our immunity from evil and for the whole value of all and every good, beyond the passing moment, since nothing but the gratification of the instant could be of any worth to us if we could be deprived of everything the next instant by whoever was momentarily stronger than ourselves. Now this most indispensable of all necessaries, after physical nutriment, cannot be had unless the machinery for providing it is kept unintermittedly in active play. Our notion, therefore, of the claim we have on our fellow creatures to join in making safe for us the very groundwork of our existence gathers feelings around it so much more intense than those concerned in any of the more common cases of utility that the difference in degree (as is often the case in psychology) becomes a real difference in kind. The claim assumes that character of absoluteness, that apparent infinity and incommensurability with all other considerations which constitute the distinction between the feeling of right and wrong and that of ordinary expediency and inexpediency. The feelings concerned are so powerful, and we count so positively on finding a responsive feeling in others (all being alike interested) that *ought* and *should* grow into *must*, and recognized indispensability becomes a moral necessity, analogous to physical, and often not inferior to it in binding force.

Justice and Utility

If the preceding analysis, or something resembling it, be not the correct account of the notion of justice—if justice be totally independent of utility, and be a standard *per se*, which the mind can recognize by simple introspection of itself—it is hard to understand why that internal oracle is so ambiguous, and why so many things appear either just or unjust, according to the light in which they are regarded.

We are continually informed that utility is an uncertain standard, which every different person interprets differently, and that there is no safety but in the immutable, ineffaceable, and unmistakable dictates of justice, which carry their evidence in themselves and are independent of the fluctuations of opinion. One would suppose from this that on questions of justice there could be no controversy; that, if we take that for our rule, its application to any given case could leave us in as little doubt as a mathematical demonstration. So far is this from being the fact that there is as much difference of opinion, and as much discussion, about what is just as about what is useful to society. Not only have different nations and individuals different notions of justice, but in the mind of one and the same individual, justice is not some one rule, principle, or maxim, but many which do not always coincide in their dictates, and, in choosing between which, he is guided either by some extraneous standard or by his own personal predilections. . . . [to take an] example from a subject already once referred to. In cooperative industrial association, is it just or not that talent or skill should give a title to superior remuneration? On the negative side of the question it is argued that whoever does the best he can deserves equally well, and ought not in justice to be put in a position of inferiority for no fault of his own; that superior abilities have already advantages more than enough, in the admiration they excite, the personal influence they command, and the internal sources of satisfaction attending them, without adding to these a superior share of the world's goods; and that society is bound in justice rather to make compensation to the less favored for this unmerited inequality of advantages than to aggravate it. On the contrary side it is contended that society receives more from the more efficient laborer; that, his services being more useful, society owes him a larger return for them; that a greater share of the joint result is actually his work, and not to allow his claim to it is a kind of robbery; that, if he is only to receive as much as others, he can only be justly required to produce as much, and to give a smaller amount of time and exertion, proportioned to his superior efficiency. Who shall decide between these appeals to conflicting principles of justice? Justice has in this case two sides to it, which it is impossible to bring into harmony, and the two disputants have chosen opposite sides; the one looks to what it is just that the individual should receive, the other to what it is just that the community should give. Each, from his own point of view, is unanswerable; and any choice between them, on grounds of justice, must be perfectly arbitrary. Social utility alone can decide the preference.

How many, again, and how irreconcilable are the standards of justice to which reference is made in discussing the repartition of taxation. One opinion is that payment to the state should be in numerical proportion to pecuniary means. Others think that justice dictates what they term graduated taxation—taking a higher percentage from those who have more to spare. In point of natural justice a strong case might be made for disregarding means altogether, and taking the same absolute sum (whenever it could be got) from everyone; as the subscribers to a mess or to a club all pay the same sum for the same privileges, whether they can all equally afford it or not. Since the protection (it might be said) of law and government is afforded to and is equally required by all, there is no injustice in making all buy it at the same price. It is reckoned justice, not injustice, that a dealer should charge to all customers the same price for the same article, not a price varying according to their means of payment. This doctrine, as applied to taxation, finds no advocates because it conflicts so strongly with man's feelings of humanity and of social expediency; but the principle of justice which it invokes is as true and as binding as those which can be appealed to against it. Accordingly it exerts a tacit influence on the line of defense employed for other modes of assessing taxation. People feel obliged to argue that the state does more for the rich man than for the poor, as a justification for its taking more from them, though this is in reality not true, for the rich would be far better able to protect themselves, in the absence of law or government, than the poor, and indeed would probably be successful in converting the poor into their slaves. Others, again, so far defer to the same conception of justice as to maintain that all should pay an equal capitation tax for the protection of their persons (these being of equal value to all), and an unequal tax for the protection of their property, which is unequal. To this others reply that the all of one man is as valuable to him as the all of another. From these confusions there is no other mode of extrication than the utilitarian.

Is, then, the difference between the just and the expedient a merely imaginary distinction? Have mankind been under a delusion in thinking that justice is a more sacred thing than policy, and that the latter ought only to be listened to after the former has been satisfied? By no means. The exposition we have given of the nature and origin of the sentiment recognizes a real distinction; and no one of those who profess the most sublime contempt for the consequences of actions as an element in their morality attaches more importance to the distinction than I do. While I dispute the pretensions of any theory which sets up an imaginary standard of justice not grounded on utility, I account the justice which is grounded on utility to be the chief part, and incomparably the most sacred and binding part, of all morality. Justice is a name for certain classes of moral rules which concern the essentials of human well-being more nearly, and are therefore of more absolute obligation, than any other rules for the guidance of life; and the notion which we have found to be of the essence of the idea of justice—that of a right residing in an individual—implies and testifies to this more binding obligation.

The moral rules which forbid mankind to hurt one another (in which we must never forget to include wrongful interference with each other's freedom) are more vital to human well-being than any maxims, however important, which only point out the best mode of managing some department of human affairs. They have also the peculiarity that they are the main element in determining the whole of the social feelings of mankind. It is their observance which alone preserves peace among human beings; if obedience to them were not the rule, and disobedience the exception, everyone would see in everyone else an enemy against whom he must be perpetually guarding himself. What is hardly less important, these are the precepts which mankind have the strongest and the most direct inducements for impressing upon one another. By merely giving to each other prudential instruction or exhortation, they may gain, or think they gain, nothing; in inculcating on each other the duty of positive beneficence, they have an unmistakable interest, but far less in degree; a person may possibly not need the benefits of others, but he always needs that they should not do him hurt. Thus the moralities which protect every individual from being harmed by others, either directly or by being hindered in his freedom of pursuing his own good, are at once those which he himself has most at heart and those which he has the strongest interest in publishing and enforcing by word and deed. It is by a person's observance of these that his fitness to exist as one of the fellowship of human beings is tested and decided; for on that depends his being a nuisance or not to those with whom he is in contact. Now it is these moralities primarily which compose the obligations of justice. The most marked cases of injustice, and those which give the tone to the feeling of repugnance which characterizes the sentiment, are acts of wrongful aggression or wrongful exercise of power over someone; the next are those which consist in wrongfully withholding from him something which is his due—in both cases inflicting on him a positive hurt, either in the form of direct suffering or of the privation of some good which he had reasonable ground, either of a physical or of a social kind, for counting upon.

The same powerful motives which command the observance of these primary moralities enjoin the punishment of those who violate them; and as the impulses of self-defense, of defense of others, and of vengeance are all called forth against such persons, retribution, or evil for evil, becomes closely connected with the sentiment of justice, and is universally included in the idea. Good for good is also one of the dictates of justice; and this, though its social utility is evident, and though it carries with it a natural human feeling, has not at first sight that obvious connection with hurt or injury which, existing in the most elementary cases of just and unjust, is the source of the characteristic intensity of the sentiment. But the connection, though less obvious, is not less real. He who accepts benefits and denies a return of them when needed inflicts a real hurt by disappointing one of the most natural and reasonable of expectations, and one which he must at least tacitly have encouraged, otherwise the benefits would seldom have been conferred. The important rank, among human evils and wrongs, of the disappointment of expectation is shown in the fact that it constitutes the principal criminality of two such highly immoral acts as a breach of friendship and a breach of promise. Few hurts which human beings can sustain are greater, and none wound more, than when that on which they habitually and with full assurance relied fails them in the hour of need; and few wrongs are greater than this mere withholding of good; none excite more resentment, either in the person suffering or in a sympathizing spectator. The principle, therefore, of giving to each what they deserve, that is, good for good as well as evil for evil, is not only included within the idea of justice as we have defined it, but is a proper object of that intensity of sentiment which places the just in human estimation above the simply expedient.

Most of the maxims of justice current in the world, and commonly appealed to in its transactions, are simply instrumental to carrying into effect the principles of justice which we have now spoken of. That a person is only responsible for what he has done voluntarily, or could voluntarily have avoided; that it is unjust to condemn any person unheard; that the punishment ought to be proportioned to the offense; and the like, are maxims intended to prevent the just principle of evil for evil from being perverted to the infliction of evil without that justification. The greater part of these common maxims have come into use from the practice of courts of justice, which have been naturally led to a more complete recognition and elaboration than was likely to suggest itself to others, of the rules necessary to enable them to fulfill their double function—of inflicting punishment when due, and of awarding to each person his right.

That first of judicial virtues, impartiality, is an obligation of justice, partly for the reason last mentioned, as being a necessary condition of the fulfillment of other obligations of justice. But this is not the only source of the exalted rank, among human obligations, of those maxims of equality and impartiality which, both in popular estimation and in that of the most enlightened, are included among the precepts of justice. In one point of view, they may be considered as corollaries from the principles already laid down. If it is a duty to do to each according to his deserts, returning good for good, as well as repressing evil by evil, it necessarily follows that we should treat all equally well (when no higher duty forbids) who have deserved equally well of *us*, and that society should treat all equally well who have deserved equally well of *it*, that is, who have deserved equally well absolutely. This is the highest abstract standard of social and distributive justice, toward which all institutions and the efforts of all virtuous citizens should be made in the utmost possible degree to converge. But this great moral duty rests upon a still deeper foundation, being a direct emanation from the first principle of morals, and not a mere logical corollary from secondary or derivative doctrines. It is involved in the very meaning of utility, or the greatest happiness principle. That principle is a mere form of words without rational signification unless one person's happiness, supposed equal in degree (with the proper allowance made for kind), is counted for exactly as much as another's. Those conditions being supplied, Bentham's dictum, "everybody to count for one, nobody for more than one," might be written under the principle of utility as an explanatory commentary.[1] The equal claim of everybody to happiness, in the estimation of the moralist and of the legislator, involves an equal claim to all the means of happiness except insofar as the inevitable conditions of human life and the general interest in which that of every individual is included set limits to the maxim; and those limits ought to be strictly construed. As every other maxim of justice, so this is by no means applied or held applicable universally; on the contrary, as I have already remarked, it bends to every person's ideas of social

[1]This implication, in the first principle of the utilitarian scheme, of perfect impartiality between persons is regarded by Mr. Herbert Spencer (in his *Social Statics*) as a disproof of the pretensions of utility to be a sufficient guide to right; since (he says) the principle of utility presupposes the anterior principle that everybody has an equal right to happiness. It may be more correctly described as supposing that equal amounts of happiness are equally desirable, whether felt by the same or different persons. This, however, is not a *pre*supposition, not a premise needful to support the principle of utility, but the very principle itself; for what is the principle of utility if it be not that "happiness" and "desirable" are synonymous terms? If there is any anterior principle implied, it can be no other than this, that the truths of arithmetic are applicable to the valuation of happiness, as of all other measurable quantities.

(Mr. Herbert Spencer, in a private communication on the subject of the preceding note, objects to being considered an opponent of utilitarianism and states that he regards happiness as the ultimate end of morality; but deems that end only partially attainable by empirical generalizations from the observed results of conduct, and completely attainable only by deducing, from the laws of life and the conditions of existence, what kinds of action necessarily tend to produce happiness, and what kinds to produce unhappiness. With the exception of the word "necessarily," I have no dissent to express from this doctrine; and (omitting that word) I am not aware that any modern advocate of utilitarianism is of a different opinion. Bentham, certainly, to whom in the *Social Statics* Mr. Spencer particularly referred, is, least of all writers, chargeable with unwillingness to deduce the effect of actions on happiness from the laws of human nature and the universal conditions of human life. The common charge against him is of relying too exclusively upon such deductions and declining altogether to be bound by the generalizations from specific experience which Mr. Spencer thinks that utilitarians generally confine themselves to. My own opinion (and, as I collect, Mr. Spencer's) is that in ethics, as in all other branches of scientific study, the concilience of the results of both these processes, each corroborating and verifying the other, is requisite to give to any general proposition the kind and degree of evidence which constitutes scientific proof.)

expediency. But in whatever case it is deemed applicable at all, it is held to be the dictate of justice. All persons are deemed to have a *right* to equality of treatment, except when some recognized social expediency requires the reverse. And hence all social inequalities which have ceased to be considered expedient assume the character, not of simple inexpediency, but of injustice, and appear so tyrannical that people are apt to wonder how they ever could have been tolerated—forgetful that they themselves, perhaps, tolerate other inequalities under an equally mistaken notion of expediency, the correction of which would make that which they approve seem quite as monstrous as what they have at last learned to condemn. The entire history of social improvement has been a series of transitions by which one custom or institution after another, from being a supposed primary necessity of social existence, has passed into the rank of a universally stigmatized injustice and tyranny. So it has been with the distinctions of slaves and freemen, nobles and serfs, patricians and plebeians; and so it will be, and in part already is, with the aristocracies of color, race, and sex.

It appears from what has been said that justice is a name for certain moral requirements which, regarded collectively, stand higher in the scale of social utility, and are therefore of more paramount obligation, than any others, though particular cases may occur in which some other social duty is so important as to overrule any one of the general maxims of justice. Thus, to save a life, it may not only be allowable, but a duty, to steal or take by force the necessary food or medicine, or to kidnap and compel to officiate the only qualified medical practitioner. In such cases, as we do not call anything justice which is not a virtue, we usually say, not that justice must give way to some other moral principle, but that what is just in ordinary cases is, by reason of that other principle, not just in the particular case. By this useful accommodation of language, the character of indefeasibility attributed to justice is kept up, and we are saved from the necessity of maintaining that there can be laudable injustice.

The considerations which have now been adduced resolve, I conceive, the only real difficulty in the utilitarian theory of morals. It has always been evident that all cases of justice are also cases of expediency; the difference is in the peculiar sentiment which attaches to the former, as contradistinguished from the latter. If this characteristic sentiment has been sufficiently accounted for; if there is no necessity to assume for it any peculiarity of origin; if it is simply the natural feeling of resentment, moralized by being made co-extensive with the demands of social good; and if this feeling not only does but ought to exist in all the classes of cases to which the idea of justice corresponds—that idea no longer presents itself as a stumbling block to the utilitarian ethics. Justice remains the appropriate name for certain social utilities which are vastly more important, and therefore more absolute and imperative, than any others are as a class (though not more so than others may be in particular cases); and which, therefore, ought to be, as well as naturally are, guarded by a sentiment, not only different in degree, but also in kind; distinguished from the milder feeling which attaches to the mere idea of promoting human pleasure or convenience at once by the more definite nature of its commands and by the sterner character of its sanctions.

9

Justice and Equality

R. M. Hare

There are several reasons why a philosopher of my persuasion should wish to write about justice. The first is the general one that ethical theory ought to be applied to practical issues, both for the sake of improving the theory and for any light it may shed on the practical issues, of which many of the most important involve questions of justice. This is shown by the frequency with which appeals are made to justice and fairness and related ideals when people are arguing about political or economic questions (about wages for example, or about schools policy or about relations between races or sexes). If we do not know what 'just' and 'fair' mean (and it looks as if we do not) and therefore do not know what would settle questions involving these concepts, then we are unlikely to be able to sort out these very difficult moral problems. I have also a particular interest in the topic: I hold a view about moral reasoning which has at least strong affinities with utilitarianism;[1] and there is commonly thought to be some kind of antagonism between justice and utility or, as it is sometimes called, expediency. I have therefore a special need to sort these questions out.

We must start by distinguishing between different kinds of justice, or between different senses or uses of the word 'just' (the distinction between these different ways of putting the matter need not now concern us). In distinguishing between different kinds of justice we shall have to make crucial use of a distinction between different levels of moral thinking which I have explained at length in other

From "Justice and Equality," *Justice and Economic Distribution*, edited by John Arthur and William Shaw (1978), pp. 116-131. Reprinted by permission of the author.
[1]See my 'Ethical Theory and Utilitarianism' (*ETU*) in *Contemporary British Philosophy 4*, ed. H. D. Lewis (London, 1976).

places.[2] It is perhaps simplest to distinguish three levels of thought, one ethical or meta-ethical and two moral or normative-ethical. At the meta-ethical level we try to establish the meanings of the moral words, and thus the formal properties of the moral concepts, including their logical properties. Without knowing these a theory of normative moral reasoning cannot begin. Then there are two levels of (normative) moral thinking which have often been in various ways distinguished. I have myself in the past called them 'level 2' and 'level 1'; but for ease of remembering I now think it best to give them names, and propose to call level 2 the *critical* level and level 1 the *intuitive* level. At the intuitive level we make use of *prima facie* moral principles of a fairly simple general sort, and do not question them but merely apply them to cases which we encounter. This level of thinking cannot be (as intuitionists commonly suppose) self-sustaining; there is a need for a critical level of thinking by which we select the *prima facie* principles for use at the intuitive level, settle conflicts between them, and give to the whole system of them a justification which intuition by itself can never provide. It will be one of the objects of this paper to distinguish those kinds of justice whose place is at the intuitive level and which are embodied in *prima facie* principles from those kinds which have a role in critical and indeed in meta-ethical thinking.

The principal result of meta-ethical enquiry in this field is to isolate a sense or kind of justice which has come to be known as 'formal justice'. Formal justice is a property of all moral principles (which is why Professor Rawls heads his chapter on this subject not 'Formal constraints of the concept of *just*' but 'Formal constraints of the concept of *right*',[3] and why his disciple David Richards is able to make a good attempt to found the whole of morality, and not merely a theory of justice, on a similar hypothetical-contract basis).[4] Formal justice is simply another name for the formal requirement of universality in moral principles on which, as I have explained in detail elsewhere,[5] golden-rule arguments are based. From the formal, logical properties of the moral words, and in particular from the logical prohibition of individual references in moral principles, it is possible to derive formal canons of moral argument, such as the rule that we are not allowed to discriminate morally between individuals unless there is some qualitative difference between them which is the ground for the discrimination; and the rule that the equal interests of different individuals have equal moral weight. Formal justice consists simply in the observance of these canons in our moral arguments; it is widely thought that this observance by itself is not enough to secure justice in some more substantial sense. As we shall see, one is not offending against the first rule if one says that extra privileges should be given to people just because they have white skins; and one is not offending against either rule if one says that one should take a cent from everybody and give it to the man with the biggest nose, provided that he benefits as much in total as they lose. The question is, How do we get from formal to substantial justice?

[2]See, e.g., my 'Principles', *Ar. Soc.* 72 (1972/3), 'Rules of War and Moral Reasoning', *Ph. and Pub. Aff.* 1 (1972) and *ETU.*
[3]Rawls, J., *A Theory of Justice* (Cambridge, Mass., 1971), p. 130.
[4]Richards, D. A. J., *A Theory of Reasons for Action* (Oxford, 1971).
[5]See my *Freedom and Reason*, pt. II (Oxford, 1963) and *ETU.*

This question arises because there are various kinds of material or substantial justice whose content cannot be established directly by appeal to the uses of moral words or the formal properties of moral concepts (we shall see later how much can be done indirectly by appeal to these formal properties *in conjunction with* other premises or postulates or presuppositions). There is a number of different kinds of substantial justice, and we can hardly do better than begin with Aristotle's classification of them,[6] since it is largely responsible for the different senses which the word 'just' still has in common use. This is a case where it is impossible to appeal to common use, at any rate of the word 'just' (the word 'fair' is better) in order to settle philosophical disputes, because the common use is itself the product of past philosophical theories. The expressions 'distributive' and 'retributive' justice go back to Aristotle,[7] and the word 'just' itself occupies the place (or places) that it does in our language largely because of its place in earlier philosophical discussions.

Aristotle first separated off a generic sense of the Greek word commonly translated 'just', a sense which had been used a lot by Plato: the sense in which justice is the whole of virtue in so far as it concerns our relations with other people.[8] The last qualification reminds us that this is not the most generic sense possible. Theognis had already used it to include the whole of virtue, full stop.[9] These very generic senses of the word, as applied to men and acts, have survived into modern English to confuse philosophers. One of the sources of confusion is that, in the less generic sense of 'just' to be discussed in most of this paper, the judgment that an act would be unjust is sometimes fairly easily overridden by other moral considerations ('unjust', we may say, 'but right as an act of mercy'; or 'unjust, but right because necessary in order to avert an appalling calamity'). It is much more difficult for judgments that an act is required by justice in the generic sense, in which 'unjust' is almost equivalent to 'not right', to be overridden in this way.

Adherents of the '*fiat justitia ruat caelum*'[10] school seldom make clear whether, when they say 'Let justice be done though the heavens fall', they are using a more or less generic sense of 'justice'; and they thus take advantage of its non-overridability in the more generic sense in order to claim unchallengeable sanctity for judgments made using one of the less generic senses. It must be right to do the just thing (whatever that may be) in the sense (if there still is one in English) in which 'just' *means* 'right'. In this sense, if it were right to cause the heavens to fall, and therefore just in the most generic sense, it would of course be right. But we might have to take into account, in deciding whether it would be right, the fact that the heavens would fall (that causing the heavens to fall would be one of the things we were doing if we did the action in question). On the other hand, if it were merely the just act in one of the less generic senses, we might hold that, though just, it was not right, because it would not be right to cause the heavens to fall merely in order to secure justice in

---

[6]*Nicomachean Ethics*, bk. V.
[7]ib. 1130 b 31, 1131 b 25.
[8]ib. 1130 a 8.
[9]Theognis 147; also attr. to Phocylides by Aristotle, ib. 1129 b 27.
[10]The earliest version of this tag is attr. by the *Oxford Dictionary of Quotations* to the Emperor Ferdinand I (1503–64).

this more limited sense; perhaps some concession to mercy, or even to common sense, would be in order.

This is an application of the 'split-level' structure of moral thinking sketched above. One of the theses I wish to maintain is that principles of justice in these less generic senses are all *prima facie* principles and therefore overridable. I shall later be giving a utilitarian account of justice which finds a place, at the intuitive level, for these *prima facie* principles of justice. At this level they have great importance and utility, but it is in accordance with utilitarianism, as indeed with common sense, to claim that they can on unusual occasions be overriden. Having said this, however, it is most important to stress that this does *not* involve conceding the overridability of either the generic kind of justice, which has its place at the critical level, or of formal justice, which operates at the metaethical level. These are preserved intact, and therefore defenders of the sanctity of justice ought to be content, since these are the core of justice as of morality. We may call to mind here Aristotle's[11] remarks about the 'better justice' or 'equity' which is required in order to rectify the crudities, giving rise to unacceptable results in particular cases, of a justice whose principles are, as they have to be, couched in general (i.e. simple) terms. The lawgiver who, according to Aristotle, 'would have' given a special prescription if he had been present at this particular case, and to whose prescription we must try to conform if we can, corresponds to the critical moral thinker, who operates under the constraints of formal justice and whose principles are not limited to simple general rules but can be specific enough to cover the peculiarities of unusual cases.

Retributive and Distributive Justice

After speaking briefly of generic justice, Aristotle goes on[12] to distinguish two main kinds of justice in the narrower or more particular sense in which it means 'fairness'. He calls these retributive and distributive justice. They have their place, respectively, in the fixing of penalties and rewards for bad and good actions, and in the distribution of goods and the opposite between the possible recipients. One of the most important questions is whether these two sorts of justice are reducible to a single sort. Rawls, for example, thinks that they are, and so do I. By using the expression 'justice as fairness', he implies that all justice can be reduced to kinds of distributive justice, which itself is founded on procedural justice (i.e. on the adoption of fair procedures) in distribution.[13]

We may (without attempting complete accuracy in exposition) explain how Rawls might effect this reduction as follows. The parties in his 'original position' are prevented by his 'veil of ignorance' from knowing what their own positions are in the world in which they are to live; so they are unable when adopting principles of

[11]ib. 1137 b 8.
[12]ib. 1130 a 14 ff.
[13]*A Theory of Justice*, p. 136.

justice to tailor them to suit their own individual interests. Impartiality (a very important constituent, at least, of justice) is thus secured. Therefore the principles which govern *both* the distribution of wealth and power and other good things *and* the assignment of rewards and penalties (and indeed all other matters which have to be regulated by principles of justice) will be impartial as between individuals, and in this sense just. In this way Rawls in effect reduces the justice of acts of retribution to justice in distributing between the affected parties the good and bad effects of a system of retributions, and reduces this distributive justice in turn to the adoption of a just procedure for selecting the system of retributions to be used.

This can be illustrated by considering the case of a criminal facing a judge (a case which has been thought to give trouble to me too, though I dealt with it adequately, on the lines which I am about to repeat here, in my book *Freedom and Reason*).[14] A Rawlsian judge, when sentencing the criminal, could defend himself against the charge of injustice or unfairness by saying that he was faithfully observing the principles of justice which would be adopted in the original position, whose conditions are procedurally fair. What these principles would be requires, no doubt, a great deal of discussion, in the course of which I might find myself in disagreement with Rawls. But my own view on how the judge should justify his action is, in its formal properties, very like his. On my view likewise, the judge can say that, when he asks himself what universal principles he is prepared to adopt for situations exactly like the one he is in, and considers examples of such logically possible situations in which *he* occupies, successively, the positions of judge, and of criminal, and of all those who are affected by the administration and enforcement of the law under which he is sentencing the criminal, including, of course, potential victims of possible future crimes—he can say that when he asks himself this, he has no hesitation in accepting the principle which bids him impose such and such a sentence in accordance with the law.

I am assuming that the judge is justifying himself at the critical level. If he were content with justifying himself at the intuitive level, his task would be easier, because, we hope, he, like most of us, has intuitions about the proper administration of justice in the courts, embodying *prima facie* principles of a sort whose inculcation in judges and in the rest of us has a high social utility. I say this while recognizing that *some* judges have intuitions about these matters which have a high social *dis*utility. The question of what intuitions judges ought to have about retributive justice is a matter for *critical* moral thinking.

On both Rawls' view and mine retributive justice has thus been reduced to distributive; on Rawls' view the principles of justice adopted are those which *distribute* fairly between those affected the good and the evil consequences of having or not having certain enforced criminal laws; on my own view likewise it is the impartiality secured by the requirement to universalize one's prescriptions which makes the judge say what he says, and here too it is an impartiality in distributing good and evil consequences between the affected parties. For the judge to let off the rapist would not be *fair* to all those who would be raped if the law were not enforced. I conclude that retributive justice can be reduced to distributive, and that therefore we shall

[14]Pp. 115-7, 124.

have done what is required of us if we can give an adequate account of the latter.

What is common to Rawls' method and my own is the recognition that to get solutions to particular questions about what is just or unjust, we have to have a way of selecting principles of justice to answer such questions, and that to ask them in default of such principles is senseless. And we both recognize that the method for selecting the principles has to be founded on what he calls 'the formal constraints of the concept of right'. This measure of agreement can extend to the method of selecting principles of distributive justice as well as retributive. Neither Rawls nor I need be put off our stride by an objector who says that we have not addressed ourselves to the question of what acts are just, but have divagated on to the quite different question of how to select principles of justice. The point is that the first question cannot be answered without answering the second. Most of the apparently intractable conflicts about justice and rights that plague the world have been generated by taking certain answers to the first question as obvious and requiring no argument. We shall resolve these conflicts only by asking what arguments are available for the principles by which questions about the justice of individual acts are to be answered. In short, we need to ascend from intuitive to critical thinking; as I have argued in my review of his book, Rawls is to be reproached with not *completing* the ascent.[15]

Nozick, however, seems hardly to have begun it.[16] Neither Rawls nor I have anything to fear from him, so long as we stick to the formal part of our systems which we in effect share. When it comes to the application of this formal method to produce substantial principles of justice, I might find myself in disagreement with Rawls, because he relies much too much on his own intuitions which are open to question. Nozick's intuitions differ from Rawls', and sometimes differ from, sometimes agree with mine. This sort of question is simply not to be settled by appeal to intuitions, and it is time that the whole controversy ascended to a more serious, critical level. At this level, the answer which both Rawls and I should give to Nozick is that whatever sort of principles of justice we are after, whether structural principles, as Rawls thinks, or historical principles, as Nozick maintains, they have to be supported by critical thinking, of which Nozick seems hardly to see the necessity. This point is quite independent of the structural-historical disagreement.

For example, if Nozick thinks that it is just for people to retain whatever property they have acquired by voluntary exchange which benefited all parties, starting from a position of equality but perhaps ending up with a position of gross inequality, and if Rawls, by contrast, thinks that such inequality should be rectified in order to make the position of the least advantaged in society as good as possible, how are we to decide between them? Not by intuition, because there seems to be a deadlock between their intuitions. Rawls has a procedure, which *need* not appeal to intuition, for justifying distributions; this would give him the game, if he were to base the procedure on firm logical grounds, and if he followed it correctly. Actually he does not so base it, and mixes up so many intuitions in the argument that the conclusions he reaches are not such as the procedure really justifies. But Nozick has no procedure at all: only a variety of considerations of different sorts, all in the end

[15]*Ph. Q.* 23 (1973), repr. in *Reading Rawls*, ed. N. Daniels (Oxford, 1975).
[16]Nozick, R. D., *Anarchy, State and Utopia* (New York, 1974).

based on intuition. Sometimes he seems to be telling us what arrangements in society would be arrived at if bargaining took place in accordance with games-theory between mutually disinterested parties; sometimes what arrangements would maximize the welfare of members of society; and sometimes what arrangements would strike them as fair. He does not often warn us when he is switching from one of these grounds to another; and he does little to convince us by argument that the arrangements so selected would be in accordance with justice. He hopes that we will think what he thinks; but Rawls at least thinks otherwise.

Formal Justice and Substantial Equality

How then do we get from formal to substantial justice? We have had an example of how this is done in the sphere of retributive justice; but how is this method to be extended to cover distributive justice as a whole, and its relation, if any, to equality in distribution? The difficulty of using formal justice in order to establish principles of substantial justice can indeed be illustrated very well by asking whether, and in what sense, justice demands equality in distribution. The complaint is often made that a certain distribution is unfair or unjust because unequal; so it looks, at least, as if the substantial principle that goods ought to be distributed equally in default of reasons to the contrary forms part of some people's conception of justice. Yet, it is argued, this substantial principle cannot be established simply on the basis of the formal notions we have mentioned. The following kind of schematic example is often adduced: consider two possible distributions of a given finite stock of goods, in one of which the goods are distributed equally, and in the other of which a few of the recipients have nearly all the goods, and the rest have what little remains. It is claimed with some plausibility that the second distribution is unfair, and the first fair. But it might also be claimed that impartiality and formal justice alone will not establish that we ought to distribute the goods equally.

There are two reasons which might be given for this second claim, the first of them a bad one, the other more cogent. The bad reason rests on an underestimate of the powers of golden-rule arguments. It is objected, for example, that people with white skins, if they claimed privileges in distribution purely on the ground of skin-colour, would not be offending against the formal principle of impartiality or universalizability, because no individual reference need enter into the principle to which they are appealing. Thus the principle that blacks ought to be subservient to whites is impartial as between *individuals;* any individual whatever who has the bad luck to find himself with a black skin or the good luck to find himself with a white skin is impartially placed by the principle in the appropriate social rank. This move receives a brief answer in my *Freedom and Reason*,[17] and a much fuller one in a forthcoming paper.[18] If the whites are faced with the decision, not merely of whether to frame this principle, but of whether to prescribe its adoption universally

---

[17]Pp. 106f.

[18]'Relevance', in a volume in honor of R. Brandt, W. Frankena and C. Stevenson, eds. A. Goldman and J. Kim (Reidel, forthcoming).

in all cases, including hypothetical ones in which their own skins turn black, they will at once reject it.

The other, more cogent-sounding argument is often used as an argument against utilitarians by those who think that justice has a lot to do with equality. It could also, at first sight, be used as an argument against the adequacy of formal justice or impartiality as a basis for distributive justice. That the argument could be leveled against both these methods is no accident; as I have tried to show elsewhere,[19] utilitarianism of a certain sort is the embodiment of—the method of moral reasoning which fulfills in practice—the requirement of universalizability or formal justice. Having shown that neither of these methods can produce a direct justification for equal distribution, I shall then show that both can produce indirect justifications, which depend, not on a priori reasoning alone, but on likely assumptions about what the world and the people in it are like.

The argument is this. Formal impartiality only requires us to treat everybody's interest as of equal weight. Imagine, then, a situation in which utilities are equally distributed. (There is a complication here which we can for the moment avoid by choosing a suitable example. Shortly I shall be mentioning the so-called principle of diminishing marginal utility, and shall indeed be making important use of it. But for now let us take a case in which it does not operate, so that we can, for ease of illustration, treat money as a linear measure of utility.) Suppose that we can vary the equal distribution that we started with by taking a dollar each away from everybody in the town, and that the loss of purchasing power is so small that they hardly notice it, and therefore the utility enjoyed by each is not much diminished. However, when we give the resulting large sum to one man, he is able to buy himself a holiday in Acapulco, which gives him so much pleasure that his access of utility is equal to the sum of the small losses suffered by all the others. Many would say that this redistribution was unfair. But we were, in the required sense, being impartial between the equal interests of all the parties; we were treating an equal access or loss of utility to any party as of equal value or disvalue. For, on our suppositions, the taking away of a dollar from one of the unfortunate parties deprived him of just as much utility as the addition of that dollar gave to the fortunate one. But if we are completely impartial, we have to regard *who has* that dollar or that access of utility as irrelevant. So there will be nothing to choose, from an impartial point of view, between our original equal distribution and our later highly unequal one, in which everybody else is deprived of a dollar in order to give one person a holiday in Acapulco. And that is why people say that formal impartiality alone is not enough to secure social justice, nor even to secure impartiality itself in some more substantial sense.

What is needed, in the opinion of these people, is some principle which says that it is unjust to give a person more when he already has more than the others—some sort of egalitarian principle. Egalitarian principles are only one possible kind of principles of distributive justice; and it is so far an open question whether they are to be preferred to alternative inegalitarian principles. It is fairly clear as a matter of history that different principles of justice have been accepted in different societies.

[19]See note 2 above.

As Aristotle says, 'everybody agrees that the just distribution is one in accordance with desert of some kind; but they do not call desert the same thing, but the democrats say it is being a free citizen, the oligarchs being rich, others good lineage, and the aristocrats virtue'.[20] It is not difficult to think of some societies in which it would be thought unjust for one man to have privileges not possessed by all men, and of others in which it would be thought unjust for a slave to have privileges which a free man would take for granted, or for a commoner to have the sort of house which a nobleman could aspire to. Even Aristotle's democrats did not think that slaves, but only citizens, had equal rights; and Plato complains of democracy that it 'bestows equality of a sort on equals and unequals alike'.[21] We have to ask, therefore, whether there are any reasons for preferring one of these attitudes to another.

At this point some philosophers will be ready to step in with their intuitions, and tell us that some distributions or ways of achieving distributions are *obviously* more just than others, or that *everyone will agree on reflection* that they are. These philosophers appeal to our intuitions or prejudices in support of the most widely divergent methods or patterns of distribution. But this is a way of arguing which should be abjured by anybody who wishes to have rational grounds for his moral judgments. Intuitions prove nothing; general consensus proves nothing; both have been used to support conclusions which *our* intuitions and our consensus may well find outrageous. We want arguments, and in this field seldom get them.

However, it is too early to despair of finding some. The utilitarian, and the formalist like me, still have some moves to make. I am supposing that we have already made the major move suggested above, and have ruled out discrimination on grounds of skin colour and the like, in so far as such discrimination could not be accepted by all for cases where they were the ones discriminated against. I am supposing that our society has absorbed this move, and contains no racists, sexists or in general discriminators, but does still contain economic men who do not think it wrong, in pursuit of Nozickian economic liberty, to get what they can, even if the resulting distribution is grotesquely unequal. Has the egalitarian any moves to make against them, and are they moves which can be supported by appeal to formal justice, in conjunction with the empirical facts?

Two Arguments for Equal Distribution

He has two. The first is based on that good old prop of egalitarian policies, the diminishing marginal utility, within the ranges that matter, of money and of nearly all goods. Almost always, if money or goods are taken away from someone who has a lot of them already, and given to someone who has little, total utility is increased, other things being equal. As we shall see, they hardly ever are equal; but the principle is all right. Its ground is that the poor man will get more utility out of what he is given than the rich man from whom it is taken would have got. A

---

[20]ib. 1131 a 25.
[21]*Republic* 558 c.

millionaire minds less about the gain or loss of a dollar than I do, and I than a pauper.

It must be noted that this is not an *a priori* principle. It is an empirical fact (if it is) that people are so disposed. The most important thing I have to say in this paper is that when we are, as we now are, trying to establish *prima facie* principles of distributive justice, it is enough if they can be justified in the world as it actually is, among people as they actually are. It is a wholly illegitimate argument against formalists or utilitarians that states of society or of the people in it could be *conceived of* in which gross inequalities could be justified by formal or utilitarian arguments. We are seeking principles for practical use in the world as it is. The same applies when we ask what qualifications are required to the principles.

Diminishing marginal utility is the firmest support for policies of progressive taxation of the rich and other egalitarian measures. However, as I said above, other things are seldom equal, and there are severe empirical, practical restraints on the equality that can sensibly be imposed by governments. To mention just a few of these hackneyed other things: the removal of incentives to effort may diminish the total stock of goods to be divided up; abrupt confiscation or even very steep progressive taxation may antagonize the victims so much that a whole class turns from a useful element in society to a hostile and dangerous one; or, even if that does not happen, it may merely become demoralized and either lose all enterprise and readiness to take business risks, or else just emigrate if it can. Perhaps one main cause of what is called the English sickness is the alienation of the middle class. It is an empirical question, just when egalitarian measures get to the stage of having these effects; and serious political argument on this subject should concentrate on such empirical questions, instead of indulging in the rhetoric of equal (or for that matter of unequal) rights. Rights are the offspring of *prima facie*, intuitive principles, and I have nothing against them; but the question is, What *prima facie* principles ought we to adopt? What intuitions ought we to have? On these questions the rhetoric of rights sheds no light whatever, any more than do appeals to intuition (i.e. to prejudice, i.e. to the *prima facie* principles, good or bad, which our upbringings happen to have implanted in us). The worth of intuitions is to be known by their fruits; as in the case of the principles to be followed by judges in administering the law, the best principles are those with the highest acceptance-utility, i.e. those whose general acceptance maximizes the furtherance of the interests, in sum, of all the affected parties, treating all those interests as of equal weight, i.e. impartially, i.e. with formal justice.

We have seen that, given the empirical assumption of diminishing marginal utility, such a method provides a justification for moderately egalitarian policies. The justification is strengthened by a second move that the egalitarian can make. This is to point out that inequality itself has a tendency to produce envy, which is a disagreeable state of mind and leads people to do disagreeable things. It makes no difference to the argument whether the envy is a good or a bad quality, nor whether it is justified or unjustified—any more than it makes a difference whether the alienation of the middle class which I mentioned above is to be condemned or excused. These states of mind are facts, and moral judgments have to be made in the light of the facts as they are. We have to take account of the actual state of the world and of the people in it. We can very easily think of societies which are highly unequal, but in which the more fortunate members have contrived to find some real or metaphorical opium or some Platonic noble lie[22] to keep the people quiet, so that the people feel no envy of privileges which we should consider outrageous. Imagine, for example, a society consisting of happy slave-owners and of happy slaves, all of whom know their places and do not have ideas above their station. Since there is *ex hypothesi* no envy, this source of disutility does not exist, and the whole argument from envy collapses.

It is salutary to remember this. It may make us stop looking for purely formal, *a priori* reasons for demanding equality, and look instead at the actual conditions which obtain in particular societies. To make the investigation more concrete, albeit oversimplified, let us ask what would have to be the case before we ought to be ready to push this happy slaveowning society into a revolution—peaceful or violent—which would turn the slaves into free and moderately equal wage-earners. I shall be able only to sketch my answer to this question, without doing nearly enough to justify it.

Arguments For and Against
Egalitarian Revolutions

First of all, as with all moral questions, we should have to ask what would be the actual consequences of what we were doing—which is the same as to ask what we should be *doing*, so that accusations of 'consequentialism'[23] need not be taken very seriously. Suppose, to simplify matters outrageously, that we can actually predict the consequences of the revolution and what will happen during its course. We can then consider two societies (one actual and one possible) and a possible process of transition from one to the other. And we have to ask whether the transition from one to the other will, all in all, promote the interest of all those affected more than to stay as they are, or rather, to develop as they would develop if the revolution did not occur. The question can be divided into questions about the process of transition and questions about the relative merits of the actual society (including its probably subsequent 'natural' development) and the possible society which would be produced by the revolution.

We have supposed that the slaves in the existing society feel no envy, and that therefore the disutility of envy cannot be used as an argument for change. If there *were* envy, as in actual cases is probable, this argument *could* be employed; but let us see what can be done without it. We have the fact that there is gross inequality in the actual society and much greater equality in the possible one. The principle of diminishing marginal utility will therefore support the change, provided that its effects are not outweighed by a reduction in total utility resulting from the change and the way it comes about. But we have to be sure that this condition is fulfilled.

[22]ib. 414 b.
[23]See, e.g., Anscombe, G. E. M., 'Modern Moral Philosophy', *Philosophy* 33 (1958) and Williams, B. A. O., in Smart, J. J. C. and Williams, B. A. O., *Utilitarianism: For and Against* (Cambridge, Eng., 1973), p. 82.

Suppose, for example, that the actual society is a happy bucolic one and is likely to remain so, but that the transition to the possible society initiates the growth of an industrial economy in which everybody has to engage in a rat-race and is far less happy. We might in that case pronounce the actual society better. In general it is not self-evident that the access of what is called wealth makes people happier, although they nearly always think that it will.

Let us suppose, however, that we are satisfied that the people in the possible society will be better off all round than in the actual. There is also the point that there will be more generations to enjoy the new regime than suffer in the transition from the old. At least, this is what revolutionaries often say; and we have set them at liberty to say it by assuming, contrary to what is likely to be the case, that the future state of society is predictable. In actual fact, revolutions usually produce states of society very different from, and in most cases worse than, what their authors expected—which does not always stop them being better than what went before, once things have settled down. However, let us waive these difficulties and suppose that the future state of society can be predicted, and that it is markedly better than the existing state, because a greater equality of distribution has, owing to diminishing marginal utility, resulted in greater total utility.

Let us also suppose that the more enterprising economic structure which results leads to increased production without causing a rat-race. There will then be more wealth to go round and the revolution will have additional justification. Other benefits of the same general kind may also be adduced; and what is perhaps the greatest benefit of all, namely liberty itself. That people like having this is an empirical fact; it may not be a fact universally, but it is at least *likely* that by freeing slaves we shall *pro tanto* promote their interests. Philosophers who ask for *a priori* arguments for liberty or equality often talk as if empirical facts like this were totally irrelevant to the question. Genuine egalitarians and liberals ought to abjure the aid of these philosophers, because they have taken away the main ground for such views, namely the fact that people are as they are.

The arguments so far adduced support the call for a revolution. They will have to be balanced against the disutilities which will probably be caused by the process of transition. If heads roll, that is contrary to the interests of their owners; and no doubt the economy will be disrupted at least temporarily, and the new rulers, whoever they are, may infringe liberty just as much as the old, and possibly in an even more arbitrary manner. Few revolutions are pleasant while they are going on. But if the revolution can be more or less smooth or even peaceful, it may well be that (given the arguments already adduced about the desirability of the future society thereby achieved) revolution can have a utilitarian justification, and therefore a justification on grounds of formal impartiality between people's interests. But it is likely to be better for all if the same changes can be achieved less abruptly by an evolutionary process, and those who try to persuade us that this is not so are often merely giving way to impatience and showing a curious indifference to the interests of those for whom they purport to be concerned.

The argument in favour of change from a slave-owning society to a wage-earning one has been extremely superficial, and has served only to illustrate the lines on which a utilitarian or a formalist might argue. If we considered instead the transition from a capitalist society to a socialist one, the same forms of argument would have to be employed, but might not yield the same result. Even if the introduction of a fully socialist economy would promote greater equality, or more equal liberties (and I can see no reason for supposing this, but rather the reverse; for socialism tends to produce very great inequalities of *power*), it needs to be argued what the consequences would be, and then an assessment has to be made of the relative benefits and harms accruing from leaving matters alone and from having various sorts of bloody or bloodless change. Here again the rhetoric of rights will provide nothing but inflammatory material for agitators on both sides. It is designed to lead to, not to resolve, conflicts.

Remarks About Methods

But we must now leave this argument and attend to a methodological point which has become pressing. We have not, in the last few pages, been arguing about what state of society would be just, but about what state of society would best promote the interests of its members. All the arguments have been utilitarian. Where then does justice come in? It is likely to come into the propaganda of revolutionaries, as I have already hinted. But so far as I can see it has no direct bearing on the question of what would be the better society. It has, however, an important indirect bearing which I shall now try to explain. Our *prima facie* moral principles and intuitions are, as I have already said, the products of our upbringings; and it is a very important question *what* principles and intuitions it is best to bring up people to have. I have been arguing on the assumption that this question is to be decided by looking at the consequences for society, and the effects on the interests of people in society, of inculcating different principles. We are looking for the set of principles with the highest acceptance-utility.

Will these include principles of justice? The answer is obviously 'Yes', if we think that society and the people in it are better off with *some* principles of justice than without any. A 'land without justice' (to use the title of Milovan Djilas' book)[24] is almost bound to be an unhappy one. But what are the principles to be? Are we, for example, to inculcate the principle that it is just for people to perform the duties of their station and not envy those of higher social rank? Or the principle that all inequalities of any sort are unjust and ought to be removed? For my part, I would think that neither of these principles has a very high acceptance-utility. It may be that the principle with the highest acceptance-utility is one which makes just reward vary (but not immoderately) with desert, and assesses desert according to service to the interests of one's fellow-men. It would have to be supplemented by a principle securing equality of opportunity. But it is a partly empirical question what principles would have the highest acceptance-utility, and in any case beyond the scope of this paper. If some such principle is adopted and inculcated, people will *call* breaches of it

[24]Djilas, M., *Land without Justice* (London, 1958).

unjust. Will they *be* unjust? Only in the sense that they will be contrary to a *prima facie* principle of distributive justice which we ought to adopt (not because it is itself a just principle, but because it is the best principle). The only sense that can be given to the question of whether it is a just principle (apart from the purely circular or tautological question of whether the principle obeys itself), is by asking whether the procedure by which we have selected the principle satisfies the logical requirements of critical moral thinking, i.e. is *formally* just. We might add that the adoption of such a formally just procedure and of the principles it selects is just in the *generic* sense mentioned at the beginning of this paper: it is the right thing to do; we morally ought to do it. The reason is that critical thinking, because it follows the requirements of formal justice based on the logical properties of the moral concepts, especially 'ought' and 'right', can therefore not fail, if pursued correctly in the light of the empirical facts, to lead to principles of justice which are in accord with morality. But because the requirements are all formal, they do not by themselves determine the content of the principles of justice. We have to do the thinking.

What principles of justice are best to try to inculcate will depend on the circumstances of particular societies, and especially on psychological facts about their members. One of these facts is their readiness to accept the principles themselves. There might be a principle of justice which it would be highly desirable to inculcate, but which we have no chance of successfully inculcating. The best principles for a society to *have* are, as I said, those with the highest acceptance-utility. But the best principles to *try to inculcate* will not necessarily be these, if these are impossible to inculcate. Imagine that in our happy slave-society both slaves and slave-owners are obstinately conservative and know their places, and that the attempt to get the slaves to have revolutionary or egalitarian thoughts will result only in a very few of them becoming discontented, and probably going to the gallows as a result, and the vast majority merely becoming unsettled and therefore more unhappy. Then we ought not to try to inculcate such an egalitarian principle. On the other hand, if, as is much more likely, the principle stood a good chance of catching on, and the revolution was likely to be as advantageous as we have supposed, then we ought. The difference lies in the dispositions of the inhabitants. I am not saying that the probability of being accepted is the same thing as acceptance-utility; only that the rationality of trying to inculcate a principle (like the rationality of trying to do anything else) varies with the likelihood of success. In this sense the advisability of trying to inculcate principles of justice (though not their merit) is relative to the states of mind of those who, it is hoped, will hold them.

It is important to be clear about the extent to which what I am advocating is a kind of relativism. It is certainly not relativistic in any strong sense. Relativism is the doctrine that the truth of some moral statement depends on whether people accept it. A typical example would be the thesis that if in a certain society people think that they ought to get their male children circumcised, then they ought to get them circumcised, full stop. Needless to say, I am not supporting any such doctrine, which is usually the result of confusion, and against which there are well-known arguments. It is, however, nearly always the case that among the facts relevant to a moral decision are facts about people's thoughts or dispositions. For example, if I am wondering whether I ought to take my wife for a holiday in Acapulco, it is relevant to ask whether she would like it. What I have been saying is to be assimilated to this last example. If we take as given certain dispositions in the members of society (namely dispositions not to accept a certain principle of justice however hard we work at propagating it) then we have to decide whether, in the light of these facts, we ought to propagate it. What principles of justice we ought to propagate will vary with the probable effects of propagating them. The answer to this 'ought'-question is not relative to what we, who are asking it, think about the matter; it is to be arrived at by moral thought on the basis of the facts of the situation. But among these facts are facts about the dispositions of people in the society in question.

The moral I wish to draw from the whole argument is that ethical reasoning *can* provide us with a way of conducting political arguments about justice and rights rationally and with hope of agreement; that such rational arguments have to rest on an understanding of the concepts being used, *and* of the facts of our actual situation. The key question is 'What principles of justice, what attitudes towards the distribution of goods, what ascriptions of rights, are such that their acceptance is in the general interest?' I advocate the asking of this question as a substitute for one which is much more commonly asked, namely 'What rights do I have?' For people who ask this latter question will, being human, nearly always answer that they have just those rights, whatever they are, which will promote a distribution of goods which is in the interest of their own social group. The rhetoric of rights, which is engendered by this question, is a recipe for class war, and civil war. In pursuit of these rights, people will, because they have convinced themselves that justice demands it, inflict almost any harms on the rest of society and on themselves. To live at peace, we need principles such as critical thinking can provide, based on formal justice and on the facts of the actual world in which we have to live. It is possible for all to practise this critical thinking in cooperation, if only they would learn how; for all share the same moral concepts with the same logic, if they could but understand them and follow it.

10

Utilitarianism and the
Distinction Between Persons

John Rawls

There are many forms of utilitarianism, and the development of the theory has continued in recent years. I shall not survey these forms here, nor take account of the numerous refinements found in contemporary discussions. My aim is to work out a theory of justice that represents an alternative to utilitarian thought generally and so to all of these different versions of it. I believe that the contrast between the contract view and utilitarianism remains essentially the same in all these cases. Therefore I shall compare justice as fairness with familiar variants of intuitionism, perfectionism, and utilitarianism in order to bring out the underlying differences in the simplest way. With this end in mind, the kind of utilitarianism I shall describe here is the strict classical doctrine which receives perhaps its clearest and most accessible formulation in Sidgwick. The main idea is that society is rightly ordered, and therefore just, when its major institutions are arranged so as to achieve the greatest net balance of satisfaction summed over all the individuals belonging to it.[1]

From *A Theory of Justice* (1971), pp. 22–27. Reprinted by permission of the publishers from *A Theory of Justice* by John Rawls, Cambridge, Mass.: The Belknap Press of Harvard University Press, Copyright © 1971 by the President and Fellows of Harvard College.

[1] I shall take Henry Sidgwick's *The Methods of Ethics*, 7th ed. (London, 1907), as summarizing the development of utilitarian moral theory. Book III of his *Principles of Political Economy* (London, 1883) applies this doctrine to questions of economic and social justice, and is a precursor of A. C. Pigou, *The Economics of Welfare* (London, Macmillan, 1920). Sidgwick's *Outlines of the History of Ethics*, 5th ed. (London, 1902), contains a brief history of the utilitarian tradition. We may follow him in assuming, somewhat arbitrarily, that it begins with Shaftesbury's *An Inquiry Concerning Virtue and Merit* (1711) and Hutcheson's *An Inquiry Concerning Moral Good and Evil* (1725). Hutcheson seems to have been the first to state clearly the principle of utility. He says in *Inquiry*, sec. III, §8, that "that action is best, which procures the greatest happiness for the greatest numbers; and that, worst, which, in like manner, occasions misery." Other major

We may note first that there is, indeed, a way of thinking of society which makes it easy to suppose that the most rational conception of justice is utilitarian. For consider: each man in realizing his own interests is certainly free to balance his own losses against his own gains. We may impose a sacrifice on ourselves now for the sake of a greater advantage later. A person quite properly acts, at least when others are not affected, to achieve his own greatest good, to advance his rational ends as far as possible. Now why should not a society act on precisely the same principle applied to the group and therefore regard that which is rational for one man as right for an association of men? Just as the well-being of a person is constructed from the series of satisfactions that are experienced at different moments in the course of his life, so in very much the same way the well-being of society is to be constructed from the fulfillment of the systems of desires of the many individuals who belong to it. Since the principle for an individual is to advance as far as possible his own welfare, his own system of desires, the principle for society is to advance as far as possible the welfare of the group, to realize to the greatest extent the comprehensive system of desire arrived at from the desires of its members. Just as an individual balances present and future gains against present and future losses, so a society may balance satisfactions and dissatisfactions among different individuals. And so by these reflections one reaches the principle of utility in a natural way: a society is properly arranged when its institutions maximize the net balance of satisfaction. The principle of choice for an association of men is interpreted as an extension of the principle of choice for one man. Social justice is the principle of rational prudence applied to an aggregative conception of the welfare of the group.[2] . . .

eighteenth century works are Hume's *A Treatise of Human Nature* (1739), and *An Enquiry Concerning the Principles of Morals* (1751); Adam Smith's *A Theory of the Moral Sentiments* (1759); and Bentham's *The Principles of Morals and Legislation* (1789). To these we must add the writings of J. S. Mill represented by *Utilitarianism* (1863) and F. Y. Edgeworth's *Mathematical Psychics* (London, 1888).

The discussion of utilitarianism has taken a different turn in recent years by focusing on what we may call the coordination problem and related questions of publicity. This development stems from the essays of R. F. Harrod, "Utilitarianism Revised," *Mind*, vol. 45 (1936); J. D. Mabbott, "Punishment" *Mind*, vol. 48 (1939); Jonathan Harrison, "Utilitarianism, Universalisation, and Our Duty to Be Just," *Proceedings of the Aristotelian Society*, vol. 53 (1952-53): and J. O. Urmson, "The Interpretation of the Philosophy of J. S. Mill," *Philosophical Quarterly*, vol. 3 (1953). See also J. J. C. Smart, "Extreme and Restricted Utilitarianism," *Philosophical Quarterly*, vol. 6 (1956), and his *An Outline of a System of Utilitarian Ethics* (Cambridge, The University Press, 1961). For an account of these matters, see David Lyons, *Forms and Limits of Utilitarianism* (Oxford, The Clarendon Press, 1965); and Allan Gibbard, "Utilitarianisms and Coordination" (dissertation, Harvard University, 1971). The problems raised by these works, as important as they are, I shall leave aside as not bearing directly on the more elementary question of distribution which I wish to discuss.

Finally, we should note here the essays of J. C. Harsanyi, in particular, "Cardinal Utility in Welfare Economics and in the Theory of Risk-Taking," *Journal of Political Economy*, 1953, and "Cardinal Welfare, Individualistic Ethics, and Interpersonal Comparisons of Utility," *Journal of Political Economy*, 1955; and R. B. Brandt, "Some Merits of One Form of Rule-Utilitarianism," *University of Colorado Studies* (Boulder, Colorado, 1967). See below §§27-28.

[2]On this point see also D. P. Gauthier, *Practical Reasoning* (Oxford, Clarendon Press, 1963), pp. 126f. The text elaborates the suggestion found in "Constitutional Liberty and the Concept of

This idea is made all the more attractive by a further consideration. The two main concepts of ethics are those of the right and the good; the concept of a morally worthy person is, I believe, derived from them. The structure of an ethical theory is, then, largely determined by how it defines and connects these two basic notions. Now it seems that the simplest way of relating them is taken by teleological theories: the good is defined independently from the right, and then the right is defined as that which maximizes the good.[3] More precisely, those institutions and acts are right which of the available alternatives, produce the most good, or at least as much good as any of the other institutions and acts open as real possibilities (a rider needed when the maximal class is not a singleton). Teleological theories have a deep intuitive appeal since they seem to embody the idea of rationality. It is natural to think that rationality is maximizing something and that in morals it must be maximizing the good. Indeed, it is tempting to suppose that it is self-evident that things should be arranged so as to lead to the most good.

It is essential to keep in mind that in a teleological theory the good is defined independently from the right. This means two things. First, the theory accounts for our considered judgments as to which things are good (our judgments of value) as a separate class of judgments intuitively distinguishable by common sense, and then proposes the hypothesis that the right is maximizing the good as already specified. Second, the theory enables one to judge the goodness of things without referring to what is right. For example, if pleasure is said to be the sole good, then presumably pleasures can be recognized and ranked in value by criteria that do not presuppose any standards of right, or what we would normally think of as such. Whereas if the distribution of goods is also counted as a good, perhaps a higher order one, and the theory directs us to produce the most good (including the good of distribution among others), we no longer have a teleological view in the classical sense. The problem of distribution falls under the concept of right as one intuitively understands it, and so the theory lacks an independent definition of the good. The clarity and simplicity of classical teleological theories derive largely from the fact that they factor our moral judgments into two classes, the one being characterized separately while the other is then connected with it by a maximizing principle.

Teleological doctrines differ, pretty clearly, according to how the conception of the good is specified. If it is taken as the realization of human excellence in the various forms of culture, we have what may be called perfectionism. This notion is found in Aristotle and Nietzsche, among others. If the good is defined as pleasure, we have hedonism; if as happiness, eudaimonism, and so

Justice," *Nomos VI: Justice*, ed. C. J. Friedrich and J. W. Chapman (New York, Atherton Press, 1963), pp. 124f, which in turn is related to the idea of justice as a higher-order administrative decision. See "Justice as Fairness," *Philosophical Review*, 1958, pp. 185–187. . . . That the principle of social integration is distinct from the principle of personal integration is stated by R. B. Perry, *General Theory of Value* (New York, Longmans, Green, and Company, 1926), pp. 674–677. He attributes the error of overlooking this fact to Emile Durkheim and others with similar views. Perry's conception of social integration is that brought about by a shared and dominant benevolent purpose. . . .

[3]Here I adopt W. K. Frankena's definition of teleological theories in *Ethics* (Englewood Cliffs, N. J., Prentice Hall, Inc., 1963), p. 13.

on. I shall understand the principle of utility in its classical form as defining the good as the satisfaction of desire, or perhaps better, as the satisfaction of rational desire. This accords with the view in all essentials and provides, I believe, a fair interpretation of it. The appropriate terms of social cooperation are settled by whatever in the circumstances will achieve the greatest sum of satisfaction of the rational desires of individuals. It is impossible to deny the initial plausibility and attractiveness of this conception.

The striking feature of the utilitarian view of justice is that it does not matter, except indirectly, how this sum of satisfactions is distributed among individuals any more than it matters, except indirectly, how one man distributes his satisfactions over time. The correct distribution in either case is that which yields the maximum fulfillment. Society must allocate its means of satisfaction whatever these are, rights and duties, opportunities and privileges, and various forms of wealth, so as to achieve this maximum if it can. But in itself no distribution of satisfaction is better than another except that the more equal distribution is to be preferred to break ties.[4] It is true that certain common sense precepts of justice, particularly those which concern the protection of liberties and rights, or which express the claims of desert, seem to contradict this contention. But from a utilitarian standpoint the explanation of these precepts and of their seemingly stringent character is that they are those precepts which experience shows should be strictly respected and departed from only under exceptional circumstances if the sum of advantages is to be maximized.[5] Yet, as with all other precepts, those of justice are derivative from the one end of attaining the greatest balance of satisfaction. Thus there is no reason in principle why the greater gains of some should not compensate for the lesser losses of others; or more importantly, why the violation of the liberty of a few might not be made right by the greater good shared by many. It simply happens that under most conditions, at least in a reasonably advanced stage of civilization, the greatest sum of advantages is not attained in this way. No doubt the strictness of common sense precepts of justice has a certain usefulness in limiting men's propensities to injustice and to socially injurious actions, but the utilitarian believes that to affirm this strictness as a first principle of morals is a mistake. For just as it is rational for one man to maximize the fulfillment of his system of desires, it is right for a society to maximize the net balance of satisfaction taken over all of its members.

The most natural way, then, of arriving at utilitarianism (although not, of course, the only way of doing so) is to adopt for society as a whole the principle of rational choice for one man. Once this is recognized, the place of the impartial spectator and the emphasis on sympathy in the history of utilitarian thought is readily understood. For it is by the conception of the impartial spectator and the use of sympathetic identification in guiding our imagination that the principle for one man is applied to society. It is this spectator who is conceived as carrying out the required organization of the desires of all persons into one coherent system of desire; it is by this construction that many persons are fused into one. Endowed with

[4]On this point see Sidgwick, *The Methods of Ethics*, pp. 416f.
[5]See J. S. Mill, *Utilitarianism*, ch. V, last two parts.

ideal powers of sympathy and imagination, the impartial spectator is the perfectly rational individual who identifies with and experiences the desires of others as if these desires were his own. In this way he ascertains the intensity of these desires and assigns them their appropriate weight in the one system of desire the satisfaction of which the ideal legislator then tries to maximize by adjusting the rules of the social system. On this conception of society separate individuals are thought of as so many different lines along which rights and duties are to be assigned and scarce means of satisfaction allocated in accordance with rules so as to give the greatest fulfillment of wants. The nature of the decision made by the ideal legislator is not, therefore, materially different from that of an entrepreneur deciding how to maximize his profit by producing this or that commodity, or that of a consumer deciding how to maximize his satisfaction by the purchase of this or that collection of goods. In each case there is a single person whose system of desires determines the best allocation of limited means. The correct decision is essentially a question of efficient administration. This view of social cooperation is the consequence of extending to society the principle of choice for one man, and then, to make this extension work, conflating all persons into one through the imaginative acts of the impartial sympathetic spectator. Utilitarianism does not take seriously the distinction between persons.

IV
LIBERTARIAN JUSTICE: DEFENSES
AND A CRITIQUE

11
Liberty, Equality, and Merit
F. A. Hayek

> *I have no respect for the passion for equality, which*
> *seems to me merely idealizing envy.*
> Oliver Wendell Holmes, Jr.

The great aim of the struggle for liberty has been equality before the law. This equality under the rules which the state enforces may be supplemented by a similar equality of the rules that men voluntarily obey in their relations with one another. This extension of the principle of equality to the rules of moral and social conduct is the chief expression of what is commonly called the democratic spirit— and probably that aspect of it that does most to make inoffensive the inequalities that liberty necessarily produces.

Equality of the general rules of law and conduct, however, is the only kind of equality conducive to liberty and the only equality which we can secure without destroying liberty. Not only has liberty nothing to do with any other sort of equality, but it is even bound to produce inequality in many respects. This is the necessary result and part of the justification of individual liberty: if the result of individual liberty did not demonstrate that some manners of living are more successful than others, much of the case for it would vanish.

It is neither because it assumes that people are in fact equal nor because it attempts to make them equal that the argument for liberty demands that government treat them equally. This argument not only recognizes that individuals are very different but in a great measure rests on that assumption. It insists that these individual differences provide no justification for government to treat them differently. And it objects to the differences in treatment by the state that would be necessary if persons who are in fact very different were to be assured equal positions in life.

From *The Constitution of Liberty* (1960), pp. 85–100. Reprinted by permission of the author and The University of Chicago Press.

Modern advocates of a more far-reaching material equality usually deny that their demands are based on any assumption of the factual equality of all men.[1] It is nevertheless still widely believed that this is the main justification for such demands. Nothing, however, is more damaging to the demand for equal treatment than to base it on so obviously untrue an assumption as that of the factual equality of all men. To rest the case for equal treatment of national or racial minorities on the assertion that they do not differ from other men is implicitly to admit that factual inequality would justify unequal treatment; and the proof that some differences do, in fact, exist would not be long in forthcoming. It is of the essence of the demand for equality before the law that people should be treated alike in spite of the fact that they are different.

The Importance of Individual Differences

The boundless variety of human nature—the wide range of differences in individual capacities and potentialities—is one of the most distinctive facts about the human species. Its evolution has made it probably the most variable among all kinds of creatures. It has been well said that "biology, with variability as its cornerstone, confers on every human individual a unique set of attributes which give him a dignity he could not otherwise possess. Every newborn baby is an unknown quantity so far as potentialities are concerned because there are many thousands of unknown interrelated genes and gene-patterns which contribute to his makeup. As a result of nature and nurture the newborn infant may become one of the greatest of men or women ever to have lived. In every case he or she has the making of a distinctive individual. . . . If the differences are not very important, then freedom is not very important and the idea of individual worth is not very important."[2] The writer justly adds that the widely held uniformity theory of human nature," which on the surface appears to accord with democracy . . . would in time undermine the very basic ideals of freedom and individual worth and render life as we know it meaningless."[3]

It has been the fashion in modern times to minimize the importance of congenital differences between men and to ascribe all the important differences to the influence of environment.[4] However important the latter may be, we must not overlook the fact that individuals are very different from the outset. The importance of individual differences would hardly be less if all people were brought up in very

[1]See, e.g., R. H. Tawney, *Equality* (London, 1931), p. 47.

[2]Roger J. Williams, *Free and Unequal: The Biological Basis of Individual Liberty* (Austin: University of Texas Press, 1953), pp. 23 and 70; cf. also J. B. S. Haldane, *The Inequality of Man* (London, 1932), and P. B. Medawar, *The Uniqueness of the Individual* (London, 1957).

[3]Williams, *op. cit.*, p. 152.

[4]See the description of this fashionable view in H. M. Kallen's article "Behaviorism," *E.S.S.*, II, 498: "At birth human infants, regardless of their heredity, are as equal as Fords."

similar environments. As a statement of fact, it just is not true that "all men are born equal." We may continue to use this hallowed phrase to express the ideal that legally and morally all men ought to be treated alike. But if we want to understand what this ideal of equality can or should mean, the first requirement is that we free ourselves from the belief in factual equality.

From the fact that people are very different it follows that, if we treat them equally, the result must be inequality in their actual position,[5] and that the only way to place them in an equal position would be to treat them differently. Equality before the law and material equality are therefore not only different but are in conflict with each other; and we can achieve either the one or the other, but not both at the same time. The equality before the law which freedom requires leads to material inequality. Our argument will be that, though where the state must use coercion for other reasons, it should treat all people alike, the desire of making people more alike in their condition cannot be accepted in a free society as a justification for further and discriminatory coercion.

We do not object to equality as such. It merely happens to be the case that a demand for equality is the professed motive of most of those who desire to impose upon society a preconceived pattern of distribution. Our objection is against all attempts to impress upon society a deliberately chosen pattern of distribution, whether it be an order of equality or of inequality. We shall indeed see that many of those who demand an extension of equality do not really demand equality but a distribution that conforms more closely to human conceptions of individual merit and that their desires are as irreconcilable with freedom as the more strictly egalitarian demands.

If one objects to the use of coercion in order to bring about a more even or a more just distribution, this does not mean that one does not regard these as desirable. But if we wish to preserve a free society, it is essential that we recognize that the desirability of a particular object is not sufficient justification for the use of coercion. One may well feel attracted to a community in which there are no extreme contrasts between rich and poor and may welcome the fact that the general increase in wealth seems gradually to reduce those differences. I fully share these feelings and certainly regard the degree of social equality that the United States has achieved as wholly admirable.

There also seems no reason why these widely felt preferences should not guide policy in some respects. Wherever there is a legitimate need for government action and we have to choose between different methods of satisfying such a need, those that incidentally also reduce inequality may well be preferable. If, for example, in the law of intestate succession one kind of provision will be more conducive to equality than another, this may be a strong argument in its favor. It is a different matter, however, if it is demanded that, in order to produce substantive equality, we should abandon the basic postulate of a free society, namely, the limitation of all coercion by equal law. Against this we shall hold that economic inequality is not one of the evils which justify our resorting to discriminatory coercion or privilege as a remedy.

[5]Cf. Plato *Laws* vi. 757A: "To unequals equals become unequal."

Nature and Nurture

Our contention rests on two basic propositions which probably need only be stated to win fairly general assent. The first of them is an expression of the belief in a certain similarity of all human beings: it is the proposition that no man or group of men possesses the capacity to determine conclusively the potentialities of other human beings and that we should certainly never trust anyone invariably to exercise such a capacity. However great the differences between men may be, we have no ground for believing that they will ever be so great as to enable one man's mind in a particular instance to comprehend fully all that another responsible man's mind is capable of.

The second basic proposition is that the acquisition by any member of the community of additional capacities to do things which may be valuable must always be regarded as a gain for that community. It is true that particular people may be worse off because of the superior ability of some new competitor in their field; but any such additional ability in the community is likely to benefit the majority. This implies that the desirability of increasing the abilities and opportunities of any individual does not depend on whether the same can also be done for others— provided, of course, that others are not thereby deprived of the opportunity of acquiring the same or other abilities which might have been accessible to them had they not been secured by that individual.

Egalitarians generally regard differently those differences in individual capacities which are inborn and those which are due to the influences of environment, or those which are the result of "nature" and those which are the result of "nurture." Neither, be it said at once, has anything to do with moral merit.[6] Though either may greatly affect the value which an individual has for his fellows, no more credit belongs to him for having been born with desirable qualities than for having grown up under favorable circumstances. The distinction between the two is important only because the former advantages are due to circumstances clearly beyond human control, while the latter are due to factors which we might be able to alter. The important question is whether there is a case for so changing our institutions as to eliminate as much as possible those advantages due to environment. Are we to agree that "all inequalities that rest on birth and inherited property ought to be abolished and none remain unless it is an effect of superior talent and industry"?[7]

The fact that certain advantages rest on human arrangements does not necessarily mean that we could provide the same advantages for all or that, if they are given to some, somebody else is thereby deprived of them. The most important factors to be considered in this connection are the family, inheritance, and

---

[6]Cf. F. H. Knight, *Freedom and Reform* (New York, 1947), p. 151: "There is no visible reason why anyone is more or less entitled to the earnings of inherited personal capacities than to those of inherited property in any other form"; and the discussion in W. Roepke, *Mass und Mitte* (Erlenbach and Zurich, 1950), pp. 65–75.

[7]This is the position of R. H. Tawney as summarized by J. P. Plamenatz, "Equality of Opportunity," in *Aspects of Human Equality*, ed. L. Bryson and others (New York, 1956), p. 100.

education, and it is against the inequality which they produce that criticism is mainly directed. They are, however, not the only important factors of environment. Geographic conditions such as climate and landscape, not to speak of local and sectional differences in cultural and moral traditions, are scarcely less important. We can, however, consider here only the three factors whose effects are most commonly impugned.

So far as the family is concerned, there exists a curious contrast between the esteem most people profess for the institution and their dislike of the fact that being born into a particular family should confer on a person special advantages. It seems to be widely believed that, while useful qualities which a person acquires because of his native gifts under conditions which are the same for all are socially beneficial, the same qualities become somehow undesirable if they are the result of environmental advantages not available to others. Yet it is difficult to see why the same useful quality which is welcomed when it is the result of a person's natural endowment should be less valuable when it is the product of such circumstances as intelligent parents or a good home.

The value which most people attach to the institution of the family rests on the belief that, as a rule, parents can do more to prepare their children for a satisfactory life than anyone else. This means not only that the benefits which particular people derive from their family environment will be different but also that these benefits may operate cumulatively through several generations. What reason can there be for believing that a desirable quality in a person is less valuable to society if it has been the result of family background than if it has not? There is, indeed, good reason to think that there are some socially valuable qualities which will be rarely acquired in a single generation but which will generally be formed only by the continuous efforts of two or three. This means simply that there are parts of the cultural heritage of a society that are more effectively transmitted through the family. Granted this, it would be unreasonable to deny that a society is likely to get a better elite if ascent is not limited to one generation, if individuals are not deliberately made to start from the same level, and if children are not deprived of the chance to benefit from the better education and material environment which their parents may be able to provide. To admit this is merely to recognize that belonging to a particular family is part of the individual personality, that society is made up as much of families as of individuals, and that the transmission of the heritage of civilization within the family is as important a tool in man's striving toward better things as is the heredity of beneficial physical attributes.

Many people who agree that the family is desirable as an instrument for the transmission of morals, tastes, and knowledge still question the desirability of the transmission of material property. Yet there can be little doubt that, in order that the former may be possible, some continuity of standards, of the external forms of life, is essential, and that this will be achieved only if it is possible to transmit not only immaterial but also material advantages. There is, of course, neither greater merit nor any greater injustice involved in some people being born to wealthy parents than there is in others being born to kind or intelligent parents. The fact is that it is no less of an advantage to the community if at least some children can start with the advantages which at any given time only wealthy homes can offer than if some children inherit great intelligence or are taught better morals at home.

We are not concerned here with the chief argument for private inheritance, namely, that it seems essential as a means to preserve the dispersal in the control of capital and as an inducement for its accumulation. Rather, our concern here is whether the fact that it confers unmerited benefits on some is a valid argument against the institution. It is unquestionably one of the institutional causes of inequality. In the present context we need not inquire whether liberty demands unlimited freedom of bequest. Our problem here is merely whether people ought to be free to pass on to children or others such material possessions as will cause substantial inequality.

Once we agree that it is desirable to harness the natural instincts of parents to equip the new generation as well as they can, there seems no sensible ground for limiting this to nonmaterial benefits. The family's function of passing on standards and traditions is closely tied up with the possibility of transmitting material goods. And it is difficult to see how it would serve the true interest of society to limit the gain in material conditions to one generation.

There is also another consideration which, though it may appear somewhat cynical, strongly suggests that if we wish to make the best use of the natural partiality of parents for their children, we ought not to preclude the transmission of property. It seems certain that among the many ways in which those who have gained power and influence might provide for their children, the bequest of a fortune is socially by far the cheapest. Without this outlet, these men would look for other ways of providing for their children, such as placing them in positions which might bring them the income and the prestige that a fortune would have done; and this would cause a waste of resources and an injustice much greater than is caused by the inheritance of property. Such is the case with all societies in which inheritance of property does not exist, including the communist. Those who dislike the inequalities caused by inheritance should therefore recognize that, men being what they are, it is the least of evils, even from their point of view.

Equality of Opportunity

Though inheritance used to be the most widely criticized source of inequality, it is today probably no longer so. Egalitarian agitation now tends to concentrate on the unequal advantages due to differences in education. There is a growing tendency to express the desire to secure equality of conditions in the claim that the best education we have learned to provide for some should be made gratuitously available for all and that, if this is not possible, one should not be allowed to get a better education than the rest merely because one's parents are able to pay for it, but only those and all those who can pass a uniform test of ability should be admitted to the benefits of the limited resources of higher education.

The problem of educational policy raises too many issues to allow of their being discussed incidentally under the general heading of equality. . . . For the present we shall only point out that enforced equality in this field can hardly avoid preventing some from getting the education they otherwise might. Whatever we might do, there is no way of preventing those advantages which only some can have, and which it is desirable that some should have, from going to people who neither individually merit them nor will make as good a use of them as some other person might have done. Such a problem cannot be satisfactorily solved by the exclusive and coercive powers of the state.

It is instructive at this point to glance briefly at the change that the ideal of equality has undergone in this field in modern times. A hundred years ago, at the height of the classical liberal movement, the demand was generally expressed by the phrase *la carrière ouverte aux talents*. It was a demand that all manmade obstacles to the rise of some should be removed, that all privileges of individuals should be abolished, and that what the state contributed to the chance of improving one's conditions should be the same for all. That so long as people were different and grew up in different families this could not assure an equal start was fairly generally accepted. It was understood that the duty of government was not to ensure that everybody had the same prospect of reaching a given position but merely to make available to all on equal terms those facilities which in their nature depended on government action. That the results were bound to be different, not only because the individuals were different, but also because only a small part of the relevant circumstances depended on government action, was taken for granted.

This conception that all should be allowed to try has been largely replaced by the altogether different conception that all must be assured an equal start and the same prospects. This means little less than that the government, instead of providing the same circumstances for all, should aim at controlling all conditions relevant to a particular individual's prospects and so adjust them to his capacities as to assure him of the same prospects as everybody else. Such deliberate adaptation of opportunities to individual aims and capacities would, of course, be the opposite of freedom. Nor could it be justified as a means of making the best use of all available knowledge except on the assumption that government knows best how individual capacities can be used.

When we inquire into the justification of these demands, we find that they rest on the discontent that the success of some people often produces in those that are less successful, or, to put it bluntly, on envy. The modern tendency to gratify this passion and to disguise it in the respectable garment of social justice is developing into a serious threat to freedom. Recently an attempt was made to base these demands on the argument that it ought to be the aim of politics to remove all sources of discontent.[8] This would, of course, necessarily mean that it is the responsibility of government to see that nobody is healthier or possesses a happier temperament, a better-suited spouse or more prospering children, than anybody else. If really all unfulfilled desires have a claim on the community, individual responsibility is at an end. However human, envy is certainly not one of the sources of discontent that a free society can eliminate. It is probably one of the essential conditions for the preservation of such a society that we do not countenance envy, not sanction its

[8]C. A. R. Crosland, *The Future of Socialism* (London, 1956), p. 205.

demands by camouflaging it as social justice, but treat it, in the words of John Stuart Mill, as "the most antisocial and evil of all passions."[9]

The Conflict Between Merit and Value

While most of the strictly egalitarian demands are based on nothing better than envy, we must recognize that much that on the surface appears as a demand for greater equality is in fact a demand for a juster distribution of the good things of this world and springs therefore from much more creditable motives. Most people will object not to the bare fact of inequality but to the fact that the differences in reward do not correspond to any recognizable differences in the merits of those who receive them. The answer commonly given to this is that a free society on the whole achieves this kind of justice.[10] This, however, is an indefensible contention if by justice is meant proportionality of reward to moral merit. Any attempt to found the case for freedom on this argument is very damaging to it, since it concedes that material rewards ought to be made to correspond to recognizable merit and then opposes the conclusion that most people will draw from this by an assertion which is untrue. The proper answer is that in a free system it is neither desirable nor practicable that material rewards should be made generally to correspond to what men recognize as merit and that it is an essential characteristic of a free society that an individual's position should not necessarily depend on the views that his fellows hold about the merit he has acquired.

This contention may appear at first so strange and even shocking that I will ask the reader to suspend judgment until I have further explained the distinction between value and merit.[11] The difficulty in making the point clear is due to the fact

[9] J. S. Mill, *On Liberty*, ed. R. B. McCallum (Oxford, 1946), p. 70.

[10] Cf. W. B. Gallie, "Liberal Morality and Socialist Morality," in *Philosophy, Politics, and Society*, ed. P. Laslett (Oxford, 1956), pp. 123–25. The author represents it as the essence of "liberal morality" that it claims that rewards are equal to merit in a free society. This was the position of some nineteenth-century liberals which often weakened their argument. A characteristic example is W. G. Sumner, who argued (*What Social Classes Owe to Each Other*, reprinted in *Freeman*, VI [Los Angeles, n.d.], 141) that if all "have equal chances so far as chances are provided or limited by society," this will "produce inequal results—that is, results which shall be proportioned to the merits of individuals." This is true only if "merit" is used in the sense in which we have used "value," without any moral connotations, but certainly not if it is meant to suggest proportionality to any endeavor to do the good or right thing, or to any subjective effort to conform to an ideal standard.

But, as we shall presently see, Mr. Gallie is right that, in the Aristotelian terms he uses, liberalism aims at commutative justice and socialism at distributive justice. But, like most socialists, he does not see that distributive justice is irreconcilable with freedom in the choice of one's activities: it is the justice of a hierarchic organization, not of a free society.

[11] Although I believe that this distinction between merit and value is the same as that which Aristotle and Thomas Aquinas had in mind when they distinguished "distributive justice" from "commutative justice," I prefer not to tie up the discussion with all the difficulties and confusions which in the course of time have become associated with these traditional concepts. That what we call here "reward according to merit" corresponds to the Aristotelian

that the term "merit," which is the only one available to describe what I mean, is also used in a wider and vaguer sense. It will be used here exclusively to describe the attributes of conduct that make it deserving of praise, that is, the moral character of the action and not the value of the achievement.[12]

As we have seen throughout our discussion, the value that the performance or capacity of a person has to his fellows has no necessary connection with its ascertainable merit in this sense. The inborn as well as the acquired gifts of a person clearly have a value to his fellows which does not depend on any credit due to him for possessing them. There is little a man can do to alter the fact that his special talents are very common or exceedingly rare. A good mind or a fine voice, a beautiful face or a skillful hand, and a ready wit or an attractive personality are in a large measure as independent of a person's efforts as the opportunities or the experiences he has had. In all these instances the value which a person's capacities or services have for us and for which he is recompensed has little relation to anything that we can call moral merit or deserts. Our problem is whether it is desirable that people should enjoy advantages in proportion to the benefits which their fellows derive from their activities or whether the distribution of these advantages should be based on other men's views of their merits.

Reward according to merit must in practice mean reward according to assessable merit, merit that other people can recognize and agree upon and not merit merely in the sight of some higher power. Assessable merit in this sense presupposes that we can ascertain that a man has done what some accepted rule of conduct demanded of him and that this has cost him some pain and effort. Whether this has been the case cannot be judged by the result: merit is not a matter of the objective outcome but of subjective effort. The attempt to achieve a valuable result may be highly meritorious but a complete failure, and full success may be entirely the result of accident and thus without merit. If we know that a man has done his best, we will often wish to see him rewarded irrespective of the result; and if we know that a most valuable achievement is almost entirely due to luck or favorable circumstances, we will give little credit to the author.

We may wish that we were able to draw this distinction in every instance. In fact, we can do so only rarely with any degree of assurance. It is possible only where we possess all the knowledge which was at the disposal of the acting person,

distributive justice seems clear. The difficult concept is that of "commutative justice," and to speak of justice in this sense seems always to cause a little confusion. Cf. M. Solomon, *Der Begriff der Gerechtigkeit bei Aristoteles* (Leiden, 1937); and for a survey of the extensive literature G. del Vecchio, *Die Gerechtigkeit* (2d ed.; Basel, 1950).

[12]The terminological difficulties arise from the fact that we use the word merit also in an objective sense and will speak of the "merit" of an idea, a book, or a picture, irrespective of the merit acquired by the person who has created them. Sometimes the word is also used to describe what we regard as the "true" value of some achievement as distinguished from its market value. Yet even a human achievement which has the greatest value or merit in this sense is not necessarily proof of moral merit on the part of him to whom it is due. It seems that our use has the sanction of philosophical tradition. Cf., for instance, D. Hume, *Treatise*, II, 252: "The external performance has no merit. We must look within to find the moral quality. . . . The ultimate object of our praise and approbation is the motive, that produc'd them."

including a knowledge of his skill and confidence, his state of mind and his feelings, his capacity for attention, his energy and persistence, etc. The possibility of a true judgment of merit thus depends on the presence of precisely those conditions whose general absence is the main argument for liberty. It is because we want people to use knowledge which we do not possess that we let them decide for themselves. But insofar as we want them to be free to use capacities and knowledge of facts which we do not have, we are not in a position to judge the merit of their achievements. To decide on merit presupposes that we can judge whether people have made such use of their opportunities as they ought to have made and how much effort of will or self-denial this has cost them; it presupposes also that we can distinguish between that part of their achievement which is due to circumstances within their control and that part which is not.

Principles of Remuneration and Freedom of Choice

The incompatibility of reward according to merit with freedom to choose one's pursuit is most evident in those areas where the uncertainty of the outcome is particularly great and our individual estimates of the chances of various kinds of effort very different.[13] In those speculative efforts which we call "research" or "exploration," or in economic activities which we commonly describe as "speculation," we cannot expect to attract those best qualified for them unless we give the successful ones all the credit or gain, though many others may have striven as meritoriously. For the same reason that nobody can know beforehand who will be the successful ones, nobody can say who has earned greater merit. It would clearly not serve our purpose if we let all who have honestly striven share in the prize. Moreover, to do so would make it necessary that somebody have the right to decide who is to be allowed to strive for it. If in their pursuit of uncertain goals people are to use their own knowledge and capacities, they must be guided, not by what other people think they ought to do, but by the value others attach to the result at which they aim.

What is so obviously true about those undertakings which we commonly regard as risky is scarcely less true of any chosen object we decide to pursue. Any such decision is beset with uncertainty, and if the choice is to be as wise as it is humanly possible to make it, the alternative results anticipated must be labeled according to their value. If the remuneration did not correspond to the value that the product of a man's efforts has for his fellows, he would have no basis for deciding whether the pursuit of a given object is worth the effort and risk. He would necessarily have to be told what to do, and some other person's estimate of what was

[13]Cf. the important essay by A. A. Alchian, "Uncertainty, Evolution, and Economic Theory," *J.P.E.*, LVIII (1950), esp. 213–14, Sec. II, headed "Success Is Based on Results, Not Motivation." It probably is also no accident that the American economist who has done most to advance our understanding of a free society, F. H. Knight, began his professional career with a study of *Risk, Uncertainty, and Profit*. Cf. also B. de Jouvenel, *Power* (London, 1948), p. 298.

the best use of his capacities would have to determine both his duties and his remuneration.[14]

The fact is, of course, that we do not wish people to earn a maximum of merit but to achieve a maximum of usefulness at a minimum of pain and sacrifice and therefore a minimum of merit. Not only would it be impossible for us to reward all merit justly, but it would not even be desirable that people should aim chiefly at earning a maximum of merit. Any attempt to induce them to do this would necessarily result in people being rewarded differently for the same service. And it is only the value of the result that we can judge with any degree of confidence, not the different degrees of effort and care that it has cost different people to achieve it.

The prizes that a free society offers for the result serve to tell those who strive for them how much effort they are worth. However, the same prizes will go to all those who produce the same result, regardless of effort. What is true here of the remuneration for the same services rendered by different people is even more true of the relative remuneration for different services requiring different gifts and capacities: they will have little relation to merit. The market will generally offer for services of any kind the value they will have for those who benefit from them; but it will rarely be known whether it was necessary to offer so much in order to obtain these services, and often, no doubt, the community could have had them for much less. The pianist who was reported not long ago to have said that he would perform even if he had to pay for the privilege probably described the position of many who earn large incomes from activities which are also their chief pleasure.

The Consequences of Distribution According to Merit

Though most people regard as very natural the claim that nobody should be rewarded more than he deserves for his pain and effort, it is nevertheless based on a colossal presumption. It presumes that we are able to judge in every individual instance how well people use the different opportunities and talents given to them and how meritorious their achievements are in the light of all the circumstances which have made them possible. It presumes that some human beings are in a position to determine conclusively what a person is worth and are entitled to determine what he may achieve. It presumes, then, what the argument for liberty specifically rejects: that we can and do know all that guides a person's action.

[14]It is often maintained that justice requires that remuneration be proportional to the unpleasantness of the job and that for this reason the street cleaner or the sewage worker ought to be paid more than the doctor or office worker. This, indeed, would seem to be the consequence of the principle of remuneration according to merit (or "distributive justice"). In a market such a result would come about only if all people were equally skillful in all jobs so that those who could earn as much as others in the more pleasant occupations would have to be paid more to undertake the distasteful ones. In the actual world those unpleasant jobs provide those whose usefulness in the more attractive jobs is small an opportunity to earn more than they could elsewhere. That persons who have little to offer their fellows should be able to earn an income similar to that of the rest only at a much greater sacrifice is inevitable in any arrangement under which the individual is allowed to choose his own sphere of usefulness.

A society in which the position of the individuals was made to correspond to human ideas of moral merit would therefore be the exact opposite of a free society. It would be a society in which people were rewarded for duty performed instead of for success, in which every move of every individual was guided by what other people thought he ought to do, and in which the individual was thus relieved of the responsibility and the risk of decision. But if nobody's knowledge is sufficient to guide all human action, there is also no human being who is competent to reward all efforts according to merit.

In our individual conduct we generally act on the assumption that it is the value of a person's performance and not his merit that determines our obligation to him. Whatever may be true in more intimate relations, in the ordinary business of life we do not feel that, because a man has rendered us a service at a great sacrifice, our debt to him is determined by this, so long as we could have had the same service provided with ease by somebody else. In our dealings with other men we feel that we are doing justice if we recompense value rendered with equal value, without inquiring what it might have cost the particular individual to supply us with these services. What determines our responsibility is the advantage we derive from what others offer us, not their merit in providing it. We also expect in our dealings with others to be remunerated not according to our subjective merit but according to what our services are worth to them. Indeed, so long as we think in terms of our relations to particular people, we are generally quite aware that the mark of the free man is to be dependent for his livelihood not on other people's views of his merit but solely on what he has to offer them. It is only when we think of our position or our income as determined by "society" as a whole that we demand reward according to merit.

Though moral value or merit is a species of value, not all value is moral value, and most of our judgments of value are not moral judgments. That this must be so in a free society is a point of cardinal importance; and the failure to distinguish between value and merit has been the source of serious confusion. We do not necessarily admire all activities whose product we value; and in most instances where we value what we get, we are in no position to assess the merit of those who have provided it for us. If a man's ability in a given field is more valuable after thirty years' work than it was earlier, this is independent of whether these thirty years were most profitable and enjoyable or whether they were a time of unceasing sacrifice and worry. If the pursuit of a hobby produces a special skill or an accidental invention turns out to be extremely useful to others, the fact that there is little merit in it does not make it any less valuable than if the result had been produced by painful effort.

This difference between value and merit is not peculiar to any one type of society—it would exist anywhere. We might, of course, attempt to make rewards correspond to merit instead of value, but we are not likely to succeed in this. In attempting it, we would destroy the incentives which enable people to decide for themselves what they should do. Moreover, it is more than doubtful whether even a fairly successful attempt to make rewards correspond to merit would produce a more attractive or even a tolerable social order. A society in which it was generally presumed that a high income was proof of merit and a low income of the lack of it, in which it was universally believed that position and remuneration corresponded to merit, in which there was no other road to success than the approval of one's conduct by the majority of one's fellows, would probably be much more unbearable to the unsuccessful ones than one in which it was frankly recognized that there was no necessary connection between merit and success.[15]

It would probably contribute more to human happiness if, instead of trying to make remuneration correspond to merit, we made clearer how uncertain is the connection between value and merit. We are probably all much too ready to ascribe personal merit where there is, in fact, only superior value. The possession by an individual or a group of a superior civilization or education certainly represents an important value and constitutes an asset for the community to which they belong; but it usually constitutes little merit. Popularity and esteem do not depend more on merit than does financial success. It is, in fact, largely because we are so used to assuming an often nonexistent merit wherever we find value that we balk when, in particular instances, the discrepancy is too large to be ignored.

There is every reason why we ought to endeavor to honor special merit where it has gone without adequate reward. But the problem of rewarding action of outstanding merit which we wish to be widely known as an example is different from that of the incentives on which the ordinary functioning of society rests. A free society produces institutions in which, for those who prefer it, a man's advancement depends on the judgment of some superior or of the majority of his fellows. Indeed, as organizations grow larger and more complex, the task of ascertaining the individual's contribution will become more difficult; and it will become increasingly necessary that, for many, merit in the eyes of the managers rather than the ascertainable value of the contribution should determine the rewards. So long as this does not produce a situation in which a single comprehensive scale of merit is imposed upon the whole society, so long as a multiplicity of organizations compete with one another in offering different prospects, this is not merely compatible with freedom but extends the range of choice open to the individual.

Freedom and Distributive Justice

Justice, like liberty and coercion, is a concept which, for the sake of clarity, ought to be confined to the deliberate treatment of men by other men. It is an aspect of the intentional determination of those conditions of people's lives that are subject

[15]Cf. Crosland, op. cit., p. 235: "Even if all the failures could be convinced that they had an equal chance, their discontent would still not be assuaged; indeed it might actually be intensified. When opportunities are known to be unequal, and the selection clearly biased toward wealth or lineage, people can comfort themselves for failure by saying that they never had a proper chance—the system was unfair, the scales too heavily weighted against them. But if the selection is obviously by merit, this source of comfort disappears, and failure induces a total sense of inferiority, with no excuse or consolation; and this, by a natural quirk of human nature, actually increases the envy and resentment at the success of others." Cf. also chap. xxiv, at n. 8. I have not yet seen Michael Young, *The Rise of the Meritocracy* (London, 1958), which, judging from reviews, appears to bring out these problems very clearly.

to such control. Insofar as we want the efforts of individuals to be guided by their own views about prospects and chances, the results of the individual's efforts are necessarily unpredictable, and the question as to whether the resulting distribution of incomes is just has no meaning.[16] Justice does require that those conditions of people's lives that are determined by government be provided equally for all. But equality of those conditions must lead to inequality of results. Neither the equal provision of particular public facilities nor the equal treatment of different partners in our voluntary dealings with one another will secure reward that is proportional to merit. Reward for merit is reward for obeying the wishes of others in what we do, not compensation for the benefits we have conferred upon them by doing what we thought best.

It is, in fact, one of the objections against attempts by government to fix income scales that the state must attempt to be just in all it does. Once the principle of reward according to merit is accepted as the just foundation for the distribution of incomes, justice would require that all who desire it should be rewarded according to that principle. Soon it would also be demanded that the same principle be applied to all and that incomes not in proportion to recognizable merit not be tolerated. Even an attempt merely to distinguish between those incomes or gains which are "earned" and those which are not will set up a principle which the state will have to try to apply but cannot in fact apply generally.[17] And every such attempt at deliberate control of some remunerations is bound to create further demands for new controls. The principle of distributive justice, once introduced, would not be fulfilled until the whole of society was organized in accordance with it. This would produce a kind of society which in all essential respects would be the opposite of a free society—a society in which authority decided what the individual was to do and how he was to do it.

[16]See the interesting discussion in R. G. Collingwood, "Economics as a Philosophical Science," *Ethics*, Vol. XXXVI (1926), who concludes (p. 174): "A just price, a just wage, a just rate of interest, is a contradiction in terms. The question what a person ought to get in return for his goods and labor is a question absolutely devoid of meaning. The only valid questions are what he *can* get in return for his goods or labor, and whether he ought to sell them at all."

[17]It is, of course, possible to give the distinction between "earned" and "unearned" incomes, gains, or increments a fairly precise legal meaning, but it then rapidly ceases to correspond to the moral distinction which provides its justification. Any serious attempt to apply the moral distinction in practice soon meets the same insuperable difficulties as any attempt to assess subjective merit. How little these difficulties are generally understood by philosophers (except in rare instances, as that quoted in the preceding note) is well illustrated by a discussion in L. S. Stebbing, *Thinking to Some Purpose* ("Pelican Books" [London, 1939]), p. 184, in which, as an illustration of a distinction which is clear but not sharp, she chooses that between "legitimate" and "excess" profits and asserts: "The distinction is clear between 'excess profits' (or 'profiteering') and 'legitimate profits,' although it is not a sharp distinction."

12

The Distribution of Income

Milton Friedman

A central element in the development of a collectivist sentiment in this century, at least in Western countries, has been a belief in equality of income as a social goal and a willingness to use the arm of the state to promote it. Two very different questions must be asked in evaluating this egalitarian sentiment and the egalitarian measures it has produced. The first is normative and ethical: what is the justification for state intervention to promote equality? The second is positive and scientific: what has been the effect of the measures actually taken?

The Ethics of Distribution

The ethical principle that would directly justify the distribution of income in a free market society is, "To each according to what he and the instruments he owns produces." The operation of even this principle implicitly depends on state action. Property rights are matters of law and social convention. As we have seen, their definition and enforcement is one of the primary functions of the state. The final distribution of income and wealth under the full operation of this principle may well depend markedly on the rules of property adopted.

What is the relation between this principle and another that seems ethically appealing, namely, equality of treatment? In part, the two principles are not contradictory. Payment in accordance with product may be necessary to achieve true equality of treatment. Given individuals whom we are prepared to regard as

From *Capitalism and Freedom* (1962), pp. 161–172. Reprinted by permission of the author and The University of Chicago Press.

alike in ability and initial resources, if some have a greater taste for leisure and others for marketable goods, inequality of return through the market is necessary to achieve equality of total return or equality of treatment. One man may prefer a routine job with much time off for basking in the sun to a more exacting job paying a higher salary; another man may prefer the opposite. If both were paid equally in money, their incomes in a more fundamental sense would be unequal. Similarly, equal treatment requires that an individual be paid more for a dirty, unattractive job than for a pleasant rewarding one. Much observed inequality is of this kind. Differences of money income offset differences in other characteristics of the occupation or trade. In the jargon of economists, they are "equalizing differences" required to make the whole of the "net advantages," pecuniary and nonpecuniary, the same.

Another kind of inequality arising through the operation of the market is also required, in a somewhat more subtle sense, to produce equality of treatment, or to put it differently, to satisfy men's tastes. It can be illustrated most simply by a lottery. Consider a group of individuals who initially have equal endowments and who all agree voluntarily to enter a lottery with very unequal prizes. The resultant inequality of income is surely required to permit the individuals in question to make the most of their initial equality. Redistribution of the income after the event is equivalent to denying them the opportunity to enter the lottery. This case is far more important in practice than would appear by taking the notion of a "lottery" literally. Individuals choose occupations, investments, and the like partly in accordance with their taste for uncertainty. The girl who tries to become a movie actress rather than a civil servant is deliberately choosing to enter a lottery, so is the individual who invests in penny uranium stocks rather than government bonds. Insurance is a way of expressing a taste for certainty. Even these examples do not indicate fully the extent to which actual inequality may be the result of arrangements designed to satisfy men's tastes. The very arrangements for paying and hiring people are affected by such preferences. If all potential movie actresses had a great dislike of uncertainty, there would tend to develop "cooperatives" of movie actresses, the members of which agreed in advance to share income receipts more or less evenly, thereby in effect providing themselves insurance through the pooling of risks. If such a preference were widespread, large diversified corporations combining risky and nonrisky ventures would become the rule. The wildcat oil prospector, the private proprietorship, the small partnership, would all become rare.

Indeed, this is one way to interpret governmental measures to redistribute income through progressive taxes and the like. It can be argued that for one reason or another, costs of administration perhaps, the market cannot produce the range of lotteries or the kind of lottery desired by the members of the community, and that progressive taxation is, as it were, a government enterprise to do so. I have no doubt that this view contains an element of truth. At the same time, it can hardly justify present taxation, if only because the taxes are imposed *after* it is already largely known who have drawn the prizes and who the blanks in the lottery of life, and the taxes are voted mostly by those who think they have drawn the blanks. One might, along these lines, justify one generation's voting the tax schedules to be applied to an as yet unborn generation. Any such procedure would, I conjecture, yield income tax schedules much less highly graduated than present schedules are, at least on paper.

Though much of the inequality of income produced by payment in accordance with product reflects "equalizing" differences or the satisfaction of men's tastes for uncertainty, a large part reflects initial differences in endowment, both of human capacities and of property. This is the part that raises the really difficult ethical issue.

It is widely argued that it is essential to distinguish between inequality in personal endowments and in property, and between inequalities arising from inherited wealth and from acquired wealth. Inequality resulting from differences in personal capacities, or from differences in wealth accumulated by the individual in question, are considered appropriate, or at least not so clearly inappropriate as differences resulting from inherited wealth.

This distinction is untenable. Is there any greater ethical justification for the high returns to the individual who inherits from his parents a peculiar voice for which there is a great demand than for the high returns to the individual who inherits property? The sons of Russian commissars surely have a higher expectation of income—perhaps also of liquidation—than the sons of peasants. Is this any more or less justifiable than the higher income expectation of the son of an American millionaire? We can look at this same question in another way. A parent who has wealth that he wishes to pass on to his child can do so in different ways. He can use a given sum of money to finance his child's training as, say, a certified public accountant, or to set him up in business, or to set up a trust fund yielding him a property income. In any of these cases, the child will have a higher income than he otherwise would. But in the first case, his income will be regarded as coming from human capacities; in the second, from profits; in the third, from inherited wealth. Is there any basis for distinguishing among these categories of receipts on ethical grounds? Finally, it seems illogical to say that a man is entitled to what he has produced by personal capacities or to the produce of the wealth he has accumulated, but that he is not entitled to pass any wealth on to his children; to say that a man may use his income for riotous living but may not give it to his heirs. Surely, the latter is one way to use what he has produced.

The fact that these arguments against the so-called capitalist ethic are invalid does not of course demonstrate that the capitalist ethic is an acceptable one. I find it difficult to justify either accepting or rejecting it, or to justify any alternative principle. I am led to the view that it cannot in and of itself be regarded as an ethical principle; that it must be regarded as instrumental or a corollary of some other principle such as freedom.

Some hypothetical examples may illustrate the fundamental difficulty. Suppose there are four Robinson Crusoes, independently marooned on four islands in the same neighborhood. One happened to land on a large and fruitful island which enables him to live easily and well. The others happened to land on tiny and rather barren islands from which they can barely scratch a living. One day, they discover the existence of one another. Of course, it would be generous of the Crusoe on the large island if he invited the others to join him and share its wealth. But suppose he does not. Would the other three be justified in joining forces and compelling him to share his wealth with them? Many a reader will be tempted to say yes. But before yielding to this temptation, consider precisely the same situation in different guise. Suppose you and three friends are walking along the street and you happen to spy and retrieve a $20 bill on the pavement. It would be generous of you, of course, if you were to divide it equally with them, or at least blow them to a drink. But suppose you do not. Would the other three be justified in joining forces and compelling you to share the $20 equally with them? I suspect most readers will be tempted to say no. And on further reflection, they may even conclude that the generous course of action is not itself clearly the "right" one. Are we prepared to urge on ourselves or our fellows that any person whose wealth exceeds the average of all persons in the world should immediately dispose of the excess by distributing it equally to all the rest of the world's inhabitants? We may admire and praise such action when undertaken by a few. But a universal "potlatch" would make a civilized world impossible.

In any event, two wrongs do not make a right. The unwillingness of the rich Robinson Crusoe or the lucky finder of the $20 bill to share his wealth does not justify the use of coercion by the others. Can we justify being judges in our own case, deciding on our own when we are entitled to use force to extract what we regard as our due from others? Or what we regard as not their due? Most differences of status or position or wealth can be regarded as the product of chance at a far enough remove. The man who is hard-working and thrifty is to be regarded as "deserving"; yet these qualities owe much to the genes he was fortunate (or unfortunate?) enough to inherit.

Despite the lip service that we all pay to "merit" as compared to "chance," we are generally much readier to accept inequalities arising from chance than those clearly attributable to merit. The college professor whose colleague wins a sweepstake will envy him but is unlikely to bear him any malice or to feel unjustly treated. Let the colleague receive a trivial raise that makes his salary higher than the professor's own, and the professor is far more likely to feel aggrieved. After all, the goddess of chance, as of justice, is blind. The salary raise was a deliberate judgment of relative merit.

The Instrumental Role of Distribution According to Product

The operative function of payment in accordance with product in a market society is not primarily distributive, but allocative. As was pointed out . . ., the central principle of a market economy is cooperation through voluntary exchange. Individuals cooperate with others because they can in this way satisfy their own wants more effectively. But unless an individual receives the whole of what he adds to the product, he will enter into exchanges on the basis of what he can receive rather than what he can produce. Exchanges will not take place that would have been mutually beneficial if each party received what he contributed to the aggregate product. Payment in accordance with product is therefore necessary in order that resources be used most effectively, at least under a system depending on voluntary cooperation. Given sufficient knowledge, it might be that compulsion could be substituted for the incentive of reward, though I doubt that it could. One can shuffle inanimate objects around; one can compel individuals to be at certain places at certain times; but one can hardly compel individuals to put forward their best efforts. Put another way, the substitution of compulsion for cooperation changes the amount of resources available.

Though the essential function of payment in accordance with product in a market society is to enable resources to be allocated efficiently without compulsion, it is unlikely to be tolerated unless it is also regarded as yielding distributive justice. No society can be stable unless there is a basic core of value judgments that are unthinkingly accepted by the great bulk of its members. Some key institutions must be accepted as "absolutes," not simply as instrumental. I believe that payment in accordance with product has been, and, in large measure, still is, one of these accepted value judgments or institutions.

One can demonstrate this by examining the grounds on which the internal opponents of the capitalist system have attacked the distribution of income resulting from it. It is a distinguishing feature of the core of central values of a society that it is accepted alike by its members, whether they regard themselves as proponents or as opponents of the system of organization of the society. Even the severest internal critics of capitalism have implicitly accepted payment in accordance with product as ethically fair.

The most far-reaching criticism has come from the Marxists. Marx argued that labor was exploited. Why? Because labor produced the whole of the product but got only part of it: the rest is Marx's "surplus value." Even if the statements of fact implicit in this assertion were accepted, the value judgment follows only if one accepts the capitalist ethic. Labor is "exploited" only if labor is entitled to what it produces. If one accepts instead the socialist premise, "to each according to his need, from each according to his ability"—whatever that may mean—it is necessary to compare what labor produces, not with what it gets but with its "ability," and to compare what labor gets, not with what it produces but with its "need."

Of course, the Marxist argument is invalid on other grounds as well: There is, first, the confusion between the total product of all cooperating resources and the amount added to product—in the economist's jargon, marginal product. Even more striking, there is an unstated change in the meaning of "labor" in passing from the premise to the conclusion. Marx recognized the role of capital in producing the product but regarded capital as embodied labor. Hence, written out in full, the premises of the Marxist syllogism would run: "Present and past labor produce the whole of the product. Present labor gets only part of the product." The logical conclusion is presumably "Past labor is exploited," and the inference for action is that past labor should get more of the product, though it is by no means clear how, unless it be in elegant tombstones.

The achievement of allocation of resources without compulsion is the major instrumental role in the marketplace of distribution in accordance with product. But it is not the only instrumental role of the resulting inequality. We have noted [earlier] the role that inequality plays in providing independent foci of power to offset the centralization of political power, as well as the role that it plays in promoting civil freedom by providing "patrons" to finance the dissemination of unpopular or simply novel ideas. In addition, in the economic sphere, it provides "patrons" to finance experimentation and the development of new products—to buy the first experimental automobiles and television sets, let alone impressionist paintings. Finally, it enables distribution to occur impersonally without the need for "authority"—a special facet of the general role of the market in effecting cooperation and coordination without coercion.

Facts of Income Distribution

A capitalist system involving payment in accordance with product can be, and in practice is, characterized by considerable inequality of income and wealth. This fact is frequently misinterpreted to mean that capitalism and free enterprise produce wider inequality than alternative systems and, as a corollary, that the extension and development of capitalism has meant increased inequality. This misinterpretation is fostered by the misleading character of most published figures on the distribution of income, in particular their failure to distinguish short-run from long-run inequality. Let us look at some of the broader facts about the distribution of income.

One of the most striking facts which runs counter to many people's expectation has to do with the sources of income. The more capitalistic a country is, the smaller the fraction of income paid for the use of what is generally regarded as capital, and the larger the fraction paid for human services. In underdeveloped countries like India, Egypt, and so on, something like half of total income is property income. In the United States, roughly one-fifth is property income. And in other advanced capitalist countries, the proportion is not very different. Of course, these countries have much more capital than the primitive countries but they are even richer in the productive capacity of their residents; hence, the larger income from property is a smaller fraction of the total. The great achievement of capitalism has not been the accumulation of property, it has been the opportunities it has offered to men and women to extend and develop and improve their capacities. Yet the enemies of capitalism are fond of castigating it as materialist, and its friends all too often apologize for capitalism's materialism as a necessary cost of progress.

Another striking fact, contrary to popular conception, is that capitalism leads to less inequality than alternative systems of organization and that the development of capitalism has greatly lessened the extent of inequality. Comparisons over space and time alike confirm this view. There is surely drastically less inequality in Western capitalist societies like the Scandinavian countries, France, Britain, and the United States, than in a status society like India or a backward country like Egypt. Comparison with communist countries like Russia is more difficult because of paucity and unreliability of evidence. But if inequality is measured by differences in levels of living between the privileged and other classes, such inequality may well be decidedly less in capitalist than in communist countries. Among the Western countries alone, inequality appears to be less, in any meaningful sense, the more highly capitalist the country is: less in Britain than in France, less in the United States than in Britain—though these comparisons are rendered difficult by the problem of allowing for the intrinsic heterogeneity of populations; for a fair comparison, for example, one should perhaps compare the United States, not with the United Kingdom alone but with the United Kingdom plus the West Indies plus its African possessions.

With respect to changes over time, the economic progress achieved in the capitalist societies has been accompanied by a drastic diminution in inequality. As late as 1848, John Stuart Mill could write, "Hitherto [1848] it is questionable if all the mechanical inventions yet made have lightened the day's toil of any human being. They have enabled a greater population to live the same life of drudgery and imprisonment, and an increased number of manufacturers and others to make fortunes. They have increased the comforts of the middle classes. But they have not yet begun to effect those great changes in human destiny, which it is in their nature and in their futurity to accomplish."[1] This statement was probably not correct even for Mill's day, but certainly no one could write this today about the advanced capitalist countries. It is still true about the rest of the world.

The chief characteristic of progress and development over the past century is that it has freed the masses from backbreaking toil and has made available to them products and services that were formerly the monopoly of the upper classes, without in any corresponding way expanding the products and services available to the wealthy. Medicine aside, the advances in technology have for the most part simply made available to the masses of the people luxuries that were always available in one form or another to the truly wealthy. Modern plumbing, central heating, automobiles, television, radio, to cite just a few examples, provide conveniences to the masses equivalent to those that the wealthy could always get by the use of servants, entertainers, and so on.

Detailed statistical evidence on these phenomena, in the form of meaningful and comparable distributions of income, is hard to come by, though such studies as have been made confirm the broad conclusions just outlined. Such statistical data, however, can be extremely misleading. They cannot segregate differences in income that are equalizing from those that are not. For example, the short working life of a baseball player means that the annual income during his active years must be much higher than in alternative pursuits open to him to make it equally attractive financially. But such a difference affects the figures in exactly the same way as any other difference in income. The income unit for which the figures are given is also of great importance. A distribution for individual income recipients always shows very much greater apparent inequality than a distribution for family units: many of the individuals are housewives working part-time or receiving a small amount of property income, or other family members in a similar position. Is the distribution that is relevant for families one in which the families are classified by

[1]Principles of Political Economy (Ashley edition; London: Longmans, Green & Co., 1909), p. 751.

total family income? Or by income per person? Or per equivalent unit? This is no mere quibble. I believe that the changing distribution of families by number of children is the most important single factor that has reduced inequality of levels of living in this country during the past half century. It has been far more important than graduated inheritance and income taxes. The really low levels of living were the joint product of relatively low family incomes and relatively large numbers of children. The average number of children has declined and, even more important, this decline has been accompanied and largely produced by a virtual elimination of the very large family. As a result, families now tend to differ much less with respect to number of children. Yet this change would not be reflected in a distribution of families by the size of total family income.

A major problem in interpreting evidence on the distribution of income is the need to distinguish two basically different kinds of inequality: temporary, short-run differences in income, and differences in long-run income status. Consider two societies that have the same distribution of annual income. In one there is great mobility and change so that the position of particular families in the income hierarchy varies widely from year to year. In the other, there is great rigidity so that each family stays in the same position year after year. Clearly, in any meaningful sense, the second would be the more unequal society. The one kind of inequality is a sign of dynamic change, social mobility, equality of opportunity; the other, of a status society. The confusion of these two kinds of inequality is particularly important, precisely because competitive free-enterprise capitalism tends to substitute the one for the other. Noncapitalist societies tend to have wider inequality than capitalist, even as measured by annual income; in addition, inequality in them tends to be permanent, whereas capitalism undermines status and introduces social mobility.

13
Distributive Justice
Robert Nozick

The minimal state is the most extensive state that can be justified. Any state more extensive violates people's rights. Yet many persons have put forth reasons purporting to justify a more extensive state. It is impossible within the compass of this book to examine all the reasons that have been put forth. Therefore, I shall focus upon those generally acknowledged to be most weighty and influential, to see precisely wherein they fail. In this chapter we consider the claim that a more extensive state is justified, because [it is] necessary (or the best instrument) to achieve distributive justice; in the next chapter we shall take up diverse other claims.

The term "distributive justice" is not a neutral one. Hearing the term "distribution," most people presume that some thing or mechanism uses some principle or criterion to give out a supply of things. Into this process of distributing shares some error may have crept. So it is an open question, at least, whether *re*distribution should take place; whether we should do again what has already been done once, though poorly. However, we are not in the position of children who have been given portions of pie by someone who now makes last minute adjustments to rectify careless cutting. There is no *central* distribution, no person or group entitled to control all the resources, jointly deciding how they are to be doled out. What each person gets, he gets from others who give to him in exchange for something, or as a gift. In a free society, diverse persons control different resources, and new holdings arise out of the voluntary exchanges and actions of persons. There is no more a distributing or distribution of shares than there is a distributing of mates in a society in which persons choose whom they shall marry. The total result is the product of many individual decisions which the different individuals involved are entitled to

From *Anarchy, State, and Utopia* (1974), pp. 149–164, 167–182. © 1974 by Basic Books, Inc., Publishers, New York. Reprinted by permission of Basic Books, Inc., Publishers.

make. Some uses of the term "distribution," it is true, do not imply a previous distributing appropriately judged by some criterion (for example, "probability distribution"); nevertheless, despite the title of this chapter, it would be best to use a terminology that clearly is neutral. We shall speak of people's holdings; a principle of justice in holdings describes (part of) what justice tells us (requires) about holdings. I shall state first what I take to be the correct view about justice in holdings, and then turn to the discussion of alternate views.

The Entitlement Theory

The subject of justice in holdings consists of three major topics. The first is the *original acquisition of holdings*, the appropriation of unheld things. This includes the issues of how unheld things may come to be held, the process, or processes, by which unheld things may come to be held, the things that may come to be held by these processes, the extent of what comes to be held by a particular process, and so on. We shall refer to the complicated truth about this topic, which we shall not formulate here, as the principle of justice in acquisition. The second topic concerns the *transfer of holdings* from one person to another. By what processes may a person transfer holdings to another? How may a person acquire a holding from another who holds it? Under this topic come general descriptions of voluntary exchange, and gift and (on the other hand) fraud, as well as reference to particular conventional details fixed upon in a given society. The complicated truth about this subject (with placeholders for conventional details) we shall call the principle of justice in transfer. (And we shall suppose it also includes principles governing how a person may divest himself of a holding, passing it into an unheld state.)

If the world were wholly just, the following inductive definition would exhaustively cover the subject of justice in holdings.

1. A person who acquires a holding in accordance with the principle of justice in acquisition is entitled to that holding.
2. A person who acquires a holding in accordance with the principle of justice in transfer, from someone else entitled to the holding, is entitled to the holding.
3. No one is entitled to a holding except by (repeated) applications of 1 and 2.

The complete principle of distributive justice would say simply that a distribution is just if everyone is entitled to the holdings they possess under the distribution.

A distribution is just if it arises from another just distribution by legitimate means. The legitimate means of moving from one distribution to another are specified by the principle of justice in transfer. The legitimate first "moves" are specified by the principle of justice in acquisition.[1] Whatever arises from a just

---

[1] Applications of the principle of justice in acquisition may also occur as part of the move from one distribution to another. You may find an unheld thing now and appropriate it. Acquisitions also are to be understood as included when, to simplify, I speak only of transitions by transfers.

situation by just steps is itself just. The means of change specified by the principle of justice in transfer preserve justice. As correct rules of inference are truth-preserving, and any conclusion deduced via repeated application of such rules from only true premises is itself true, so the means of transition from one situation to another specified by the principle of justice in transfer are justice-preserving, and any situation actually arising from repeated transitions in accordance with the principle from a just situation is itself just. The parallel between justice-preserving transformations and truth-preserving transformations illuminates where it fails as well as where it holds. That a conclusion could have been deduced by truth-preserving means from premises that are true suffices to show its truth. That from a just situation a situation *could* have arisen via justice-preserving means does *not* suffice to show its justice. The fact that a thief's victims voluntarily *could* have presented him with gifts does not entitle the thief to his ill-gotten gains. Justice in holdings is historical; it depends upon what actually has happened. We shall return to this point later.

Not all actual situations are generated in accordance with the two principles of justice in holdings: the principle of justice in acquisition and the principle of justice in transfer. Some people steal from others, or defraud them, or enslave them, seizing their product and preventing them from living as they choose, or forcibly exclude others from competing in exchanges. None of these are permissible modes of transition from one situation to another. And some persons acquire holdings by means not sanctioned by the principle of justice in acquisition. The existence of past injustice (previous violations of the first two principles of justice in holdings) raises the third major topic under justice in holdings: the rectification of injustice in holdings. If past injustice has shaped present holdings in various ways, some identifiable and some not, what now, if anything, ought to be done to rectify these injustices? What obligations do the performers of injustice have toward those whose position is worse than it would have been had the injustice not been done? Or, than it would have been had compensation been paid promptly? How, if at all, do things change if the beneficiaries and those made worse off are not the direct parties in the act of injustice, but, for example, their descendants? Is an injustice done to someone whose holding was itself based upon an unrectified injustice? How far back must one go in wiping clean the historical slate of injustices? What may victims of injustice permissibly do in order to rectify the injustices being done to them, including the many injustices done by persons acting through their government? I do not know of a thorough or theoretically sophisticated treatment of such issues. Idealizing greatly, let us suppose theoretical investigation will produce a principle of rectification. This principle uses historical information about previous situations and injustices done in them (as defined by the first two principles of justice and rights against interference), and information about the actual course of events that flowed from these injustices, until the present, and it yields a description (or descriptions) of holdings in the society. The principle of rectification presumably will make use of its best estimate of subjunctive information about what would have occurred (or a probability distribution over what might have occurred, using the expected value) if the injustice had not taken place. If the actual description of holdings turns out not to be one of the descriptions yielded by the principle, then one of the descriptions yielded must be realized.[2]

The general outlines of the theory of justice in holdings are that the holdings of a person are just if he is entitled to them by the principles of justice in acquisition and transfer, or by the principle of rectification of injustice (as specified by the first two principles). If each person's holdings are just, then the total set (distribution) of holdings is just. To turn these general outlines into a specific theory we would have to specify the details of each of the three principles of justice in holdings: the principle of acquisition of holdings, the principle of transfer of holdings, and the principle of rectification of violations of the first two principles. I shall not attempt that task here. (Locke's principle of justice in acquisition is discussed below.)

Historical Principles and
End-Result Principles

The general outlines of the entitlement theory illuminate the nature and defects of other conceptions of distributive justice. The entitlement theory of justice in distribution is *historical*; whether a distribution is just depends upon how it came about. In contrast, *current time-slice principles* of justice hold that the justice of a distribution is determined by how things are distributed (who has what) as judged by some *structural* principle(s) of just distribution. A utilitarian who judges between any two distributions by seeing which has the greater sum of utility and, if the sums tie, applies some fixed equality criterion to choose the more equal distribution, would hold a current time-slice principle of justice. As would someone who had a fixed schedule of trade-offs between the sum of happiness and equality. According to a current time-slice principle, all that needs to be looked at, in judging the justice of a distribution, is who ends up with what; in comparing any two distributions one need look only at the matrix presenting the distributions. No further information need be fed into a principle of justice. It is a consequence of such principles of justice that any two structurally identical distributions are equally just. (Two distributions are structurally identical if they present the same profile, but perhaps have different persons occupying the particular slots. My having ten and your having five, and my having five and your having ten are structurally identical distributions.) Welfare economics is the theory of current time-slice principles of justice. The subject is conceived as operating on matrices representing only current information about distribution. This, as well as some of the usual conditions (for example, the choice of

---

[2]If the principle of rectification of violations of the first two principles yields more than one description of holdings, then some choice must be made as to which of these is to be realized. Perhaps the sort of considerations about distributive justice and equality that I argue against play a legitimate role in *this* subsidiary choice. Similarly, there may be room for such considerations in deciding which otherwise arbitrary features a statute will embody, when such features are unavoidable because other considerations do not specify a precise line; yet a line must be drawn.

distribution is invariant under relabeling of columns), guarantees that welfare economics will be a current time-slice theory, with all of its inadequacies.

Most persons do not accept current time-slice principles as constituting the whole story about distributive shares. They think it relevant in assessing the justice of a situation to consider not only the distribution it embodies, but also how that distribution came about. If some persons are in prison for murder or war crimes, we do not say that to assess the justice of the distribution in the society we must look only at what this person has, and that person has, and that person has, . . . at the current time. We think it relevant to ask whether someone did something so that he *deserved* to be punished, deserved to have a lower share. Most will agree to the relevance of further information with regard to punishments and penalties. Consider also desired things. One traditional socialist view is that workers are entitled to the product and full fruits of their labor; they have earned it; a distribution is unjust if it does not give the workers what they are entitled to. Such entitlements are based upon some past history. No socialist holding this view would find it comforting to be told that because the actual distribution *A* happens to coincide structurally with the one he desires *D*, *A* therefore is no less just than *D*; it differs only in that the "parasitic" owners of capital receive under *A* what the workers are entitled to under *D*, and the workers receive under *A* what the owners are entitled to under *D*, namely very little. This socialist rightly, in my view, holds onto the notions of earning, producing, entitlement, desert, and so forth, and he rejects current time-slice principles that look only to the structure of the resulting set of holdings. (The set of holdings resulting from what? Isn't it implausible that how holdings are produced and come to exist has no effect at all on who should hold what?) His mistake lies in his view of what entitlements arise out of what sorts of productive processes.

We construe the position we discuss too narrowly by speaking of *current* time-slice principles. Nothing is changed if structural principles operate upon a time sequence of current time-slice profiles and, for example, give someone more now to counterbalance the less he has had earlier. A utilitarian or an egalitarian or any mixture of the two over time will inherit the difficulties of his more myopic comrades. He is not helped by the fact that *some* of the information others consider relevant in assessing a distribution is reflected, unrecoverably, in past matrices. Henceforth, we shall refer to such unhistorical principles of distributive justice, including the current time-slice principles, as *end-result principles* or *end-state principles*.

In contrast to end-result principles of justice, *historical principles* of justice hold that past circumstances or actions of people can create differential entitlements or differential deserts to things. An injustice can be worked by moving from one distribution to another structurally identical one, for the second, in profile the same, may violate people's entitlements or deserts; it may not fit the actual history.

Patterning

The entitlement principles of justice in holdings that we have sketched are historical principles of justice. To better understand their precise character, we shall distinguish them from another subclass of the historical principles. Consider, as an example, the principle of distribution according to moral merit. This principle requires that total distributive shares vary directly with moral merit; no person should have a greater share than anyone whose moral merit is greater. (If moral merit could be not merely ordered but measured on an interval or ratio scale, stronger principles could be formulated.) Or consider the principle that results by substituting "usefulness to society" for "moral merit" in the previous principle. Or instead of "distribute according to moral merit," or "distribute according to usefulness to society," we might consider "distribute according to the weighted sum of moral merit, usefulness to society, and need," with the weights of the different dimensions equal. Let us call a principle of distribution patterned if it specifies that a distribution is to vary along with some natural dimension, weighted sum of natural dimensions, or lexicographic ordering of natural dimensions. And let us say a distribution is patterned if it accords with some patterned principle. (I speak of natural dimensions, admittedly without a general criterion for them, because for any set of holdings some artificial dimensions can be gimmicked up to vary along with the distribution of the set.) The principle of distribution in accordance with moral merit is a patterned historical principle, which specifies a patterned distribution. "Distribute according to I.Q." is a patterned principle that looks to information not contained in distributional matrices. It is not historical, however, in that it does not look to any past actions creating differential entitlements to evaluate a distribution; it requires only distributional matrices whose columns are labeled by I.Q. scores. The distribution in a society, however, may be composed of such simple patterned distributions, without itself being simply patterned. Different sectors may operate different patterns, or some combination of patterns may operate in different proportions across a society. A distribution composed in this manner, from a small number of patterned distributions, we also shall term "patterned." And we extend the use of "pattern" to include the overall designs put forth by combinations of end-state principles.

Almost every suggested principle of distributive justice is patterned: to each according to his moral merit, or needs, or marginal product, or how hard he tries, or the weighted sum of the foregoing, and so on. The principle of entitlement we have sketched is *not* patterned.[3] There is no one natural dimension or weighted sum or combination of a small number of natural dimensions that yields the

[3]One might try to squeeze a patterned conception of distributive justice into the framework of the entitlement conception, by formulating a gimmicky obligatory "principle of transfer" that would lead to the pattern. For example, the principle that if one has more than the mean income one must transfer everything one holds above the mean to persons below the mean so as to bring them up to (but not over) the mean. We can formulate a criterion for a "principle of transfer" to rule out such obligatory transfers, or we can say that no correct principle of transfer, no principle of transfer in a free society will be like this. The former is probably the better course, though the latter also is true.

Alternatively, one might think to make the entitlement conception instantiate a pattern, by using matrix entries that express the relative strength of a person's entitlements as measured by some real-valued function. But even if the limitation to natural dimensions failed to exclude this function, the resulting edifice would *not* capture our system of entitlements to *particular* things.

distributions generated in accordance with the principle of entitlement. The set of holdings that results when some persons receive their marginal products, others win at gambling, others receive a share of their mate's income, others receive gifts from foundations, others receive interest on loans, others receive gifts from admirers, others receive returns on investment, others make for themselves much of what they have, others find things, and so on, will not be patterned. Heavy strands of patterns will run through it; significant portions of the variance in holdings will be accounted for by pattern-variables. If most people most of the time choose to transfer some of their entitlements to others only in exchange for something from them, then a large part of what many people hold will vary with what they held that others wanted. More details are provided by the theory of marginal productivity. But gifts to relatives, charitable donations, bequests to children, and the like, are not best conceived, in the first instance, in this manner. Ignoring the strands of pattern, let us suppose for the moment that a distribution actually arrived at by the operation of the principle of entitlement is random with respect to any pattern. Though the resulting set of holdings will be unpatterned, it will not be incomprehensible, for it can be seen as arising from the operation of a small number of principles. These principles specify how an initial distribution may arise (the principle of acquisition of holdings) and how distributions may be transformed into others (the principle of transfer of holdings). The process whereby the set of holdings is generated will be intelligible, though the set of holdings itself that results from this process will be unpatterned.

The writings of F. A. Hayek focus less than is usually done upon what patterning distributive justice requires. Hayek argues that we cannot know enough about each person's situation to distribute to each according to his moral merit (but would justice demand we do so if we did have this knowledge?); and he goes on to say, "our objection is against all attempts to impress upon society a deliberately chosen pattern of distribution, whether it be an order of equality or of inequality."[4] However, Hayek concludes that in a free society there will be distribution in accordance with value rather than moral merit; that is, in accordance with the perceived value of a person's actions and services to others. Despite his rejection of a patterned conception of distributive justice, Hayek himself suggests a pattern he thinks justifiable: distribution in accordance with the perceived benefits given to others, leaving room for the complaint that a free society does not realize exactly this pattern. Stating this patterned strand of a free capitalist society more precisely, we get "To each according to how much he benefits others who have the resources for benefiting those who benefit them." This will seem arbitrary unless some acceptable initial set of holdings is specified, or unless it is held that the operation of the system over time washes out any significant effects from the initial set of holdings. As an example of the latter, if almost anyone would have bought a car from Henry Ford, the supposition that it was an arbitrary matter who held the money then (and so bought) would not place Henry Ford's earnings under a cloud. In any event, *his* coming to hold it is not arbitrary. Distribution according to benefits to others *is* a major patterned strand in a free capitalist society, as Hayek correctly

[4]F. A. Hayek, *The Constitution of Liberty* (Chicago: University of Chicago Press, 1960), p. 87.

points out, but it is only a strand and does not constitute the whole pattern of a system of entitlements (namely, inheritance, gifts for arbitrary reasons, charity, and so on) or a standard that one should insist society fit. Will people tolerate for long a system yielding distributions that they believe are unpatterned?[5] No doubt people will not long accept a distribution they believe is *unjust*. People want their society to be and to look just. But must the look of justice reside in a resulting pattern rather than in the underlying generating principles? We are in no position to conclude that the inhabitants of a society embodying an entitlement conception of justice in holdings will find it unacceptable. Still, it must be granted that were people's reasons for transferring some of their holdings to others always irrational or arbitrary, we would find this disturbing. (Suppose people always determined what holdings they would transfer, and to whom, by using a random device.) We feel more comfortable upholding the justice of an entitlement system if most of the transfers under it are done for reasons. This does not mean necessarily that all deserve what holdings they receive. It means only that there is a purpose or point to someone's transferring a holding to one person rather than to another; that usually we can see what the transferrer thinks he's gaining, what cause he thinks he's serving, what goals he thinks he's helping to achieve, and so forth. Since in a capitalist society people often transfer holdings to others in accordance with how much they perceive these others benefiting them, the fabric constituted by the individual transactions and transfers is largely reasonable and intelligible.[6] (Gifts to loved ones, bequests to children, charity to the needy also are nonarbitrary components of the fabric.) In stressing the large strand of distribution in accordance with benefit to others, Hayek shows the point of many transfers, and so shows that the system of transfer of entitlements is not just spinning its gears aimlessly. The system of entitlements is defensible when constituted by the individual aims of individual transactions. No overarching aim is needed, no distributional pattern is required.

To think that the task of a theory of distributive justice is to fill in the blank in "to each according to his _____" is to be predisposed to search for a pattern; and the separate treatment of "from each according to his _____" treats production

---

[5]This question does not imply that they will tolerate any and every patterned distribution. In discussing Hayek's views, Irving Kristol has recently speculated that people will not long tolerate a system that yields distributions patterned in accordance with value rather than merit. ("'When Virtue Loses All Her Loveliness'—Some Reflections on Capitalism and 'The Free Society,'" *The Public Interest*, Fall 1970, pp. 3–15.) Kristol, following some remarks of Hayek, equates the merit system with justice. Since some case can be made for the external standard of distribution in accordance with benefit to others, we ask about a weaker (and therefore more plausible) hypothesis.

[6]We certainly benefit because great economic incentives operate to get others to spend much time and energy to figure out how to serve us by providing things we will want to pay for. It is not mere paradox mongering to wonder whether capitalism should be criticized for most rewarding and hence encouraging, not individualists like Thoreau who go about their own lives, but people who are occupied with serving others and winning them as customers. But to defend capitalism one need not think businessmen are the finest human types. (I do not mean to join here the general maligning of businessmen, either.) Those who think the finest should acquire the most can try to convince their fellows to transfer resources in accordance with *that* principle.

and distribution as two separate and independent issues. On an entitlement view these are *not* two separate questions. Whoever makes something, having bought or contracted for all other held resources used in the process (transferring some of his holdings for these cooperating factors), is entitled to it. The situation is *not* one of something's getting made, and there being an open question of who is to get it. Things come into the world already attached to people having entitlements over them. From the point of view of the historical entitlement conception of justice in holdings, those who start afresh to complete "to each according to his _____" treat objects as if they appeared from nowhere, out of nothing. A complete theory of justice might cover this limit case as well; perhaps here is a use for the usual conceptions of distributive justice.[7]

So entrenched are maxims of the usual form that perhaps we should present the entitlement conception as a competitor. Ignoring acquisition and rectification, we might say:

> From each according to what he chooses to do, to each according to what he makes for himself (perhaps with the contracted aid of others) and what others choose to do for him and choose to give him of what they've been given previously (under this maxim) and haven't yet expended or transferred.

This, the discerning reader will have noticed, has its defects as a slogan. So as a summary and great simplification (and not as a maxim with any independent meaning) we have:

> *From each as they choose, to each as they are chosen.*

How Liberty Upsets Patterns

It is not clear how those holding alternative conceptions of distributive justice can reject the entitlement conception of justice in holdings. For suppose a distribution favored by one of these nonentitlement conceptions is realized. Let us suppose it is your favorite one and let us call this distribution D_1; perhaps everyone has an equal share, perhaps shares vary in accordance with some dimension you treasure. Now suppose that Wilt Chamberlain is greatly in demand by basketball teams, being a great gate attraction. (Also suppose contracts run only for a year, with players being free agents.) He signs the following sort of contract with a team: In each home game, twenty-five cents from the price of each ticket of admission goes to him. (We ignore the question of whether he is "gouging" the owners, letting them look out for themselves.) The season starts, and people cheerfully attend his team's games; they buy their tickets, each time dropping a separate twenty-five cents of

---

[7]Varying situations continuously from that limit situation to our own would force us to make explicit the underlying rationale of entitlements and to consider whether entitlement considerations lexicographically precede the considerations of the usual theories of distributive justice, so that the *slightest* strand of entitlement outweighs the considerations of the usual theories of distributive justice.

their admission price into a special box with Chamberlain's name on it. They are excited about seeing him play; it is worth the total admission price to them. Let us suppose that in one season one million persons attend his home games, and Wilt Chamberlain winds up with $250,000, a much larger sum than the average income and larger even than anyone else has. Is he entitled to this income? Is this new distribution D_2, unjust? If so, why? There is *no* question about whether each of the people was entitled to the control over the resources they held in D_1, because that was the distribution (your favorite) that (for the purposes of argument) we assumed was acceptable. Each of these persons *chose* to give twenty-five cents of their money to Chamberlain. They could have spent it on going to the movies, or on candy bars, or on copies of *Dissent* magazine, or of *Monthly Review*. But they all, at least one million of them, converged on giving it to Wilt Chamberlain in exchange for watching him play basketball. If D_1 was a just distribution, and people voluntarily moved from it to D_2 transferring parts of their shares they were given under D_1 (what was it for if not to do something with?), isn't D_2 also just? If people were entitled to dispose of the resources to which they were entitled (under D_1), didn't this include their being entitled to give it to, or exchange it with, Wilt Chamberlain? Can anyone else complain on grounds of justice? Each other person already has his legitimate share under D_1. Under D_1, there is nothing that anyone has that anyone else has a claim of justice against. After someone transfers something to Wilt Chamberlain, third parties *still* have their legitimate shares; *their* shares are not changed. By what process could such a transfer among two persons give rise to a legitimate claim of distributive justice on a portion of what was transferred, by a third party who had no claim of justice on any holding of the others *before* the transfer?[8] To cut off objections irrelevant here, we might imagine the exchanges occurring in a socialist society, after hours: After playing whatever basketball he does in his daily work, or doing whatever other daily work he does, Wilt Chamberlain decides to put in *overtime* to earn additional money. (First his work quota is set; he works time over that.) Or imagine it is a skilled juggler people like to see, who puts on shows after hours.

Why might someone work overtime in a society in which it is assumed their needs are satisfied? Perhaps because they care about things other than needs. I like to write in books that I read, and to have easy access to books for browsing at odd

[8]Might not a transfer have instrumental effects on a third party, changing his feasible options? (But what if the two parties to the transfer independently had used their holdings in this fashion?) I discuss this question below, but note here that this question concedes the point for distributions of ultimate intrinsic noninstrumental goods (pure utility experiences, so to speak) that are transferable. It also might be objected that the transfer might make a third party more envious because it worsens his position relative to someone else. I find it incomprehensible how this can be thought to involve a claim of justice. . . .

Here and elsewhere in this chapter, a theory which incorporates elements of pure procedural justice might find what I say acceptable, *if* kept in its proper place; that is, if background institutions exist to ensure the satisfaction of certain conditions on distributive shares. But if these institutions are not themselves the sum or invisible-hand result of people's voluntary (nonaggressive) actions, the constraints they impose require justification. At no point does *our* argument assume any background institutions more extensive than those of the minimal night-watchman state, a state limited to protecting persons against murder, assault, theft, fraud, and so forth.

hours. It would be very pleasant and convenient to have the resources of Widener Library in my back yard. No society, I assume, will provide such resources close to each person who would like them as part of his regular allotment (under D_1). Thus, persons either must do without some extra things that they want, or be allowed to do something extra to get some of these things. On what basis could the inequalities that would eventuate be forbidden? Notice also that small factories would spring up in a socialist society, unless forbidden. I melt down some of my personal possessions (under D_1) and build a machine out of the material. I offer you, and others, a philosophy lecture once a week in exchange for your cranking the handle on my machine, whose products I exchange for yet other things, and so on. (The raw materials used by the machine are given to me by others who possess them under D_1, in exchange for hearing lectures.) Each person might participate to gain things over and above their allotment under D_1. Some persons even might want to leave their job in socialist industry and work full time in this private sector. [In any case] I wish merely to note how private property even in means of production would occur in a socialist society that did not forbid people to use as they wished some of the resources they are given under the socialist distribution D_1.[9] The socialist society would have to forbid capitalist acts between consenting adults.

The general point illustrated by the Wilt Chamberlain example and the example of the entrepreneur in a socialist society is that no end-state principle or distributional patterned principle of justice can be continuously realized without continuous interference with people's lives. Any favored pattern would be transformed into one unfavored by the principle, by people choosing to act in various ways; for example, by people exchanging goods and services with other people, or giving things to other people, things the transferrers are entitled to under the favored distributional pattern. To maintain a pattern one must either continually interfere to stop people from transferring resources as they wish to, or continually (or periodically) interfere to take from some persons resources that others for some reason chose to transfer to them. (But if some time limit is to be set on how long people may keep resources others voluntarily transfer to them, why let

[9] See the selection from John Henry MacKay's novel, The Anarchists, reprinted in Leonard Krimmerman and Lewis Perry, eds., Patterns of Anarchy (New York: Doubleday Anchor Books, 1966), in which an individualist anarchist presses upon a communist anarchist the following question: "Would you, in the system of society which you call 'free Communism' prevent individuals from exchanging their labor among themselves by means of their own medium of exchange? And further: Would you prevent them from occupying land for the purpose of personal use?" The novel continues: "[the] question was not to be escaped. If he answered 'Yes!' he admitted that society had the right of control over the individual and threw overboard the autonomy of the individual which he had always zealously defended; if, on the other hand, he answered 'No!' he admitted the right of private property which he had just denied so emphatically. . . . Then he answered, 'In Anarchy any number of men must have the right of forming a voluntary association, and so realizing their ideas in practice. Nor can I understand how anyone could justly be driven from the land and house which he uses and occupies . . . every serious man must declare himself: for Socialism, and thereby for force and against liberty, or for Anarchism, and thereby for liberty and against force.'" In contrast, we find Noam Chomsky writing, "Any consistent anarchist must oppose private ownership of the means of production," "the consistent anarchist then . . . will be a socialist . . . of a particular sort." Introduction to Daniel Guerin, Anarchism: From Theory to Practice (New York: Monthly Review Press, 1970), pages xiii, xv.

them keep these resources for *any* period of time? Why not have immediate confiscation?) It might be objected that all persons voluntarily will choose to refrain from actions which would upset the pattern. This presupposes unrealistically (1) that all will most want to maintain the pattern (are those who don't, to be "reeducated" or forced to undergo "self-criticism"?), (2) that each can gather enough information about his own actions and the ongoing activities of others to discover which of his actions will upset the pattern, and (3) that diverse and far-flung persons can coordinate their actions to dovetail into the pattern. Compare the manner in which the market is neutral among persons' desires, as it reflects and transmits widely scattered information via prices, and coordinates persons' activities.

It puts things perhaps a bit too strongly to say that every patterned (or end-state) principle is liable to be thwarted by the voluntary actions of the individual parties transferring some of their shares they receive under the principle. For perhaps some *very* weak patterns are not so thwarted.[10] Any distributional pattern with any egalitarian component is overturnable by the voluntary actions of individual persons over time; as is every patterned condition with sufficient content so as actually to have been proposed as presenting the central core of distributive justice. Still, given the possibility that some weak conditions or patterns may not be unstable in this way, it would be better to formulate an explicit description of the kind of interesting and contentful patterns under discussion, and to prove a theorem about their instability. Since the weaker the patterning, the more likely it is that the entitlement system itself satisfies it, a plausible conjecture is that any patterning either is unstable or is satisfied by the entitlement system. . . .

Redistribution and Property Rights

Apparently, patterned principles allow people to choose to expend upon themselves, but not upon others, those resources they are entitled to (or rather, receive) under some favored distributional pattern D_1. For if each of several persons chooses to expend some of his D_1 resources upon one other person, then that other person will receive more than his D_1 share, disturbing the favored distributional pattern. Maintaining a distributional pattern is individualism with a vengeance!

---

[10]Is the patterned principle stable that requires merely that a distribution be Pareto-optimal? One person might give another a gift or bequest that the second could exchange with a third to their mutual benefit. Before the second makes this exchange, there is not Pareto-optimality. Is a stable pattern presented by a principle choosing that among the Pareto-optimal positions that satisfies some further condition C? It may seem that there cannot be a counterexample, for won't any voluntary exchange made away from a situation show that the first situation wasn't Pareto-optimal? (Ignore the implausibility of this last claim for the case of bequests.) But principles are to be satisfied over time, during which new possibilities arise. A distribution that at one time satisfies the criterion of Pareto-optimality might not do so when some new possibilities arise (Wilt Chamberlain grows up and starts playing basketball); and though people's activities will tend to move them to a new Pareto-optimal position, *this* new one need not satisfy the contentful condition C. Continual interference will be needed to insure the continual satisfaction of C. (The theoretical possibility of a pattern's being maintained by some invisible-hand process that brings it back to an equilibrium that fits the pattern when deviations occur should be investigated.)

Patterned distributional principles do not give people what entitlement principles do, only better distributed. For they do not give the right to choose what to do with what one has; they do not give the right to choose to pursue an end involving (intrinsically, or as a means) the enhancement of another's position. To such views, families are disturbing; for within a family occur transfers that upset the favored distributional pattern. Either families themselves become units to which distribution takes place, the column occupiers (on what rationale?), or loving behavior is forbidden. We should note in passing the ambivalent position of radicals toward the family. Its loving relationships are seen as a model to be emulated and extended across the whole society, at the same time that it is denounced as a suffocating institution to be broken and condemned as a focus of parochial concerns that interfere with achieving radical goals. Need we say that it is not appropriate to enforce across the wider society the relationships of love and care appropriate within a family, relationships which are voluntarily undertaken?[11] Incidentally, love is an interesting instance of another relationship that is historical, in that (like justice) it depends upon what actually occurred. An adult may come to love another because of the other's characteristics; but it is the other person, and not the characteristics, that is loved.[12] The love is not transferable to someone else with the same characteristics, even to one who "scores" higher for these characteristics. And the love endures through changes of the characteristics that gave rise to it. One loves the particular person one actually encountered. Why love is historical, attaching to persons in this way and not to characteristics, is an interesting and puzzling question.

Proponents of patterned principles of distributive justice focus upon criteria for determining who is to receive holdings; they consider the reasons for which someone should have something, and also the total picture of holdings. Whether or not it is better to give than to receive, proponents of patterned principles ignore giving altogether. In considering the distribution of goods, income, and so forth, their theories are theories of recipient justice; they completely ignore any right a person might have to give something to someone. Even in exchanges where each party is simultaneously giver and recipient, patterned principles of justice focus only upon the recipient role and its supposed rights. Thus discussions tend to focus on whether people (should) have a right to inherit, rather than on whether people (should) have a right to bequeath or on whether persons who have a right to hold also have a right to choose that others hold in their place. I lack a good explanation of

[11]One indication of the stringency of Rawls's difference principle, which we attend to in the second part of this chapter, is its inappropriateness as a governing principle even within a family of individuals who love one another. Should a family devote its resources to maximizing the position of its least well off and least talented child, holding back the other children or using resources for their education and development only if they will follow a policy through their lifetimes of maximizing the position of their least fortunate sibling? Surely not. How then can this even be considered as the appropriate policy for enforcement in the wider society? (I discuss below what I think would be Rawls's reply: that some principles apply at the macro level which do not apply to micro situations.)

[12]See Gregory Vlastos, "The Individual as an Object of Love in Plato" in his *Platonic Studies* (Princeton: Princeton University Press, 1973), pp. 3–34.

why the usual theories of distributive justice are so recipient oriented; ignoring givers and transferrers and their rights is of a piece with ignoring producers and their entitlements. But why is it *all* ignored?

Patterned principles of distributive justice necessitate *re*distributive activities. The likelihood is small that any actual freely-arrived-at set of holdings fits a given pattern; and the likelihood is nil that it will continue to fit the pattern as people exchange and give. From the point of view of an entitlement theory, redistribution is a serious matter indeed, involving, as it does, the violation of people's rights. (An exception is those takings that fall under the principle of the rectification of injustices.) From other points of view, also, it is serious.

Taxation of earnings from labor is on a par with forced labor.[13] Some persons find this claim obviously true: taking the earnings of *n* hours labor is like taking *n* hours from the person; it is like forcing the person to work *n* hours for another's purpose. Others find the claim absurd. But even these, *if* they object to forced labor, would oppose forcing unemployed hippies to work for the benefit of the needy.[14] And they would also object to forcing each person to work five extra hours each week for the benefit of the needy. But a system that takes five hours' wages in taxes does not seem to them like one that forces someone to work five hours, since it offers the person forced a wider range of choice in activities than does taxation in kind with the particular labor specified. (But we can imagine a gradation of systems of forced labor, from one that specifies a particular activity, to one that gives a choice among two activities, to . . . ; and so on up.) Furthermore, people envisage a system with something like a proportional tax on everything above the amount necessary for basic needs. Some think this does not force someone to work extra hours, since there is no fixed number of extra hours he is forced to work, and since he can avoid the tax entirely by earning only enough to cover his basic needs. This is a very uncharacteristic view of forcing for those who *also* think people are forced to do something *whenever* the alternatives they face are considerably worse. However, *neither* view is correct. The fact that others intentionally intervene, in violation of a side constraint against aggression, to threaten force to limit the alternatives, in this case to paying taxes or (presumably the worse alternative) bare subsistence, makes the taxation system one of forced labor and distinguishes it from other cases of limited choices which are not forcings.[15]

The man who chooses to work longer to gain an income more than

---

[13]I am unsure as to whether the arguments I present below show that such taxation merely *is* forced labor; so that "is on a par with" means "is one kind of." Or alternatively, whether the arguments emphasize the great similarities between such taxation and forced labor, to show it is plausible and illuminating to view such taxation in the light of forced labor. This latter approach would remind one of how John Wisdom conceives of the claims of metaphysicians.

[14]Nothing hangs on the fact that here and elsewhere I speak loosely of *needs*, since I go on, each time, to reject the criterion of justice which includes it. If, however, something did depend upon the notion, one would want to examine it more carefully. For a skeptical view, see Kenneth Minogue, *The Liberal Mind* (New York: Random House, 1963), pp. 103–112.

[15]Further details which this statement should include are contained in my essay "Coercion," in *Philosophy, Science, and Method*, ed. S. Morgenbesser, P. Suppes, and M. White (New York: St. Martin, 1969).

sufficient for his basic needs prefers some extra goods or services to the leisure and activities he could perform during the possible nonworking hours; whereas the man who chooses not to work the extra time prefers the leisure activities to the extra goods or services he could acquire by working more. Given this, if it would be illegitimate for a tax system to seize some of a man's leisure (forced labor) for the purpose of serving the needy, how can it be legitimate for a tax system to seize some of a man's goods for that purpose? Why should we treat the man whose happiness requires certain material goods or services differently from the man whose preferences and desires make such goods unnecessary for his happiness? Why should the man who prefers seeing a movie (and who has to earn money for a ticket) be open to the required call to aid the needy, while the person who prefers looking at a sunset (and hence need earn no extra money) is not? Indeed, isn't it surprising that redistributionists choose to ignore the man whose pleasures are so easily attainable without extra labor, while adding yet another burden to the poor unfortunate who must work for his pleasures? If anything, one would have expected the reverse. Why is the person with the nonmaterial or nonconsumption desire allowed to proceed unimpeded to his most favored feasible alternative, whereas the man whose pleasures or desires involve material things and who must work for extra money (thereby serving whomever considers his activities valuable enough to pay him) is constrained in what he can realize? Perhaps there is no difference in principle. And perhaps some think the answer concerns merely administrative convenience. (These questions and issues will not disturb those who think that forced labor to serve the needy or to realize some favored end-state pattern is acceptable.) In a fuller discussion we would have (and want) to extend our argument to include interest, entrepreneurial profits, and so on. Those who doubt that this extension can be carried through, and who draw the line here at taxation of income from labor, will have to state rather complicated patterned *historical* principles of distributive justice, since end-state principles would not distinguish *sources* of income in any way. It is enough for now to get away from end-state principles and to make clear how various patterned principles are dependent upon particular views about the sources or the illegitimacy or the lesser legitimacy of profits, interest, and so on; which particular views may well be mistaken.

What sort of right over others does a legally institutionalized end-state pattern give one? The central core of the notion of a property right in X, relative to which other parts of the notion are to be explained, is the right to determine what shall be done with X; the right to choose which of the constrained set of options concerning X shall be realized or attempted.[16] The constraints are set by other principles or laws operating in the society; in our theory, by the Lockean rights people possess (under the minimal state). My property rights in my knife allow me to leave it where I will, but not in your chest. I may choose which of the acceptable options involving the knife is to be realized. This notion of property helps us to understand why earlier theorists spoke of people as having property in themselves and their labor. They viewed each person as having a right to decide what would

[16]On the themes in this and the next paragraph, see the writings of Armen Alchian.

become of himself and what he would do, and as having a right to reap the benefits of what he did.

This right of selecting the alternative to be realized from the constrained set of alternatives may be held by an *individual* or by a *group* with some procedure for reaching a joint decision; or the right may be passed back and forth, so that one year I decide what's to become of X, and the next year you do (with the alternative of destruction, perhaps, being excluded). Or, during the same time period, some types of decisions about X may be made by me, and others by you. And so on. We lack an adequate, fruitful, analytical apparatus for classifying the *types* of constraints on the set of the options among which choices are to be made, and the *types* of ways decision powers can be held, divided, and amalgamated. A *theory* of property would, among other things, contain such a classification of constraints and decision modes, and from a small number of principles would follow a host of interesting statements about the *consequences* and effects of certain combinations of constraints and modes of decision.

When end-result principles of distributive justice are built into the legal structure of a society, they (as do most patterned principles) give each citizen an enforceable claim to some portion of the total social product; that is, to some portion of the sum total of the individually and jointly made products. This total product is produced by individuals laboring, using means of production others have saved to bring into existence, by people organizing production or creating means to produce new things or things in a new way. It is on this batch of individual activities that patterned distributional principles give each individual an enforceable claim. Each person has a claim to the activities and the products of other persons, independently of whether the other persons enter into particular relationships that give rise to these claims, and independently of whether they voluntarily take these claims upon themselves, in charity or in exchange for something.

Whether it is done through taxation on wages or on wages over a certain amount, or through seizure of profits, or through there being a big *social pot* so that it's not clear what's coming from where and what's going where, patterned principles of distributive justice involve appropriating the actions of other persons. Seizing the results of someone's labor is equivalent to seizing hours from him and directing him to carry on various activities. If people force you to do certain work, or unrewarded work, for a certain period of time, they decide what you are to do and what purposes your work is to serve apart from your decisions. This process whereby they take this decision from you makes them a *part owner* of you; it gives them a property right in you. Just as having such partial control and power of decision, by right, over an animal or inanimate object would be to have a property right in it.

End-state and most patterned principles of distributive justice institute (partial) ownership by others of people and their actions and labor. These principles involve a shift from the classical liberals' notion of self-ownership to a notion of (partial) property rights in *other* people.

Considerations such as these confront end-state and other patterned conceptions of justice with the question of whether the actions necessary to achieve the selected pattern don't themselves violate moral side constraints. Any view holding that there are moral side constraints on actions, that not all moral considerations can be built into end states that are to be achieved . . . must face the possibility that some of its goals are not achievable by any morally permissible available means. An entitlement theorist will face such conflicts in a society that deviates from the principles of justice for the generation of holdings, if and only if the only actions available to realize the principles themselves violate some moral constraints. Since deviation from the first two principles of justice (in acquisition and transfer) will involve other persons' direct and aggressive intervention to violate rights, and since moral constraints will not exclude defensive or retributive action in such cases, the entitlement theorist's problem rarely will be pressing. And whatever difficulties he has in applying the principle of rectification to persons who did not themselves violate the first two principles are difficulties in balancing the conflicting considerations so as correctly to formulate the complex principle of rectification itself; he will not violate moral side constraints by applying the principle. Proponents of patterned conceptions of justice, however, often will face head-on clashes (and poignant ones if they cherish each party to the clash) between moral side constraints on how individuals may be treated and their patterned conception of justice that presents an end state or other pattern that *must* be realized.

May a person emigrate from a nation that has institutionalized some end-state or patterned distributional principle? For some principles (for example, Hayek's) emigration presents no theoretical problem. But for others it is a tricky matter. Consider a nation having a compulsory scheme of minimal social provision to aid the neediest (or one organized so as to maximize the position of the worst-off group); no one may opt out of participating in it. (None may say, "Don't compel me to contribute to others and don't provide for me via this compulsory mechanism if I am in need.") Everyone above a certain level is forced to contribute to aid the needy. But if emigration from the country were allowed, anyone could choose to move to another country that did not have compulsory social provision but otherwise was (as much as possible) identical. In such a case, the person's *only* motive for leaving would be to avoid participating in the compulsory scheme of social provision. And if he does leave, the needy in his initial country will receive no (compelled) help from him. What rationale yields the result that the person be permitted to emigrate, yet forbidden to stay and opt out of the compulsory scheme of social provision? If providing for the needy is of overriding importance, this does militate against allowing internal opting out; but it also speaks against allowing external emigration. (Would it also support, to some extent, the kidnapping of persons living in a place without compulsory social provision, who could be forced to make a contribution to the needy in your community?) Perhaps the crucial component of the position that allows emigration solely to avoid certain arrangements, while not allowing anyone internally to opt out of them, is a concern for fraternal feelings within the country. "We don't want anyone here who doesn't contribute, who doesn't care enough about the others to contribute." That concern, in this case, would have to be tied to the view that forced aiding tends to produce fraternal feelings between the aided and the aider (or perhaps merely to the view that the knowledge that someone or other voluntarily is not aiding produces unfraternal feelings).

Locke's Theory of Acquisition

Before we turn to consider other theories of justice in detail, we must introduce an additional bit of complexity into the structure of the entitlement theory. This is best approached by considering Locke's attempt to specify a principle of justice in acquisition. Locke views property rights in an unowned object as originating through someone's mixing his labor with it. This gives rise to many questions. What are the boundaries of what labor is mixed with? If a private astronaut clears a place on Mars, has he mixed his labor with (so that he comes to own) the whole planet, the whole uninhabited universe, or just a particular plot? Which plot does an act bring under ownership? The minimal (possibly disconnected) area such that an act decreases entropy in that area, and not elsewhere? Can virgin land (for the purposes of ecological investigation by high-flying airplane) come under ownership by a Lockean process? Building a fence around a territory presumably would make one the owner of only the fence (and the land immediately underneath it).

Why does mixing one's labor with something make one the owner of it? Perhaps because one owns one's labor, and so one comes to own a previously unowned thing that becomes permeated with what one owns. Ownership seeps over into the rest. But why isn't mixing what I own with what I don't own a way of losing what I own rather than a way of gaining what I don't? If I own a can of tomato juice and spill it in the sea so that its molecules (made radioactive, so I can check this) mingle evenly throughout the sea, do I thereby come to own the sea, or have I foolishly dissipated my tomato juice? Perhaps the idea, instead, is that laboring on something improves it and makes it more valuable; and anyone is entitled to own a thing whose value he has created. (Reinforcing this, perhaps, is the view that laboring is unpleasant. If some people made things effortlessly, as the cartoon characters in *The Yellow Submarine* trail flowers in their wake, would they have lesser claim to their own products whose making didn't *cost* them anything?) Ignore the fact that laboring on something may make it less valuable (spraying pink enamel paint on a piece of driftwood that you have found). Why should one's entitlement extend to the whole object rather than just to the *added value* one's labor has produced? (Such reference to value might also serve to delimit the extent of ownership; for example, substitute "increases the value of" for "decreases entropy in" in the above entropy criterion.) No workable or coherent value-added property scheme has yet been devised, and any such scheme presumably would fall to objections (similar to those) that fell the theory of Henry George.

It will be implausible to view improving an object as giving full ownership to it, if the stock of unowned objects that might be improved is limited. For an object's coming under one person's ownership changes the situation of all others.

Whereas previously they were at liberty (in Hohfeld's sense) to use the object, they now no longer are. This change in the situation of others (by removing their liberty to act on a previously unowned object) need not worsen their situation. If I appropriate a grain of sand from Coney Island, no one else may now do as they will with *that* grain of sand. But there are plenty of other grains of sand left for them to do the same with. Or if not grains of sand, then other things. Alternatively, the things I do with the grain of sand I appropriate might improve the position of others, counterbalancing their loss of the liberty to use that grain. The crucial point is whether appropriation of an unowned object worsens the situation of others.

Locke's proviso that there be "enough and as good left in common for others" . . . is meant to ensure that the situation of others is not worsened. (If this proviso is met is there any motivation for his further condition of nonwaste?) It is often said that this proviso once held but now no longer does. But there appears to be an argument for the conclusion that if the proviso no longer holds, then it cannot ever have held so as to yield permanent and inheritable property rights. Consider the first person Z for whom there is not enough and as good left to appropriate. The last person Y to appropriate left Z without his previous liberty to act on an object, and so worsened Z's situation. So Y's appropriation is not allowed under Locke's proviso. Therefore the next to last person X to appropriate left Y in a worse position, for X's act ended permissible appropriation. Therefore X's appropriation wasn't permissible. But then the appropriator two from last, W, ended permissible appropriation and so, since it worsened X's position, W's appropriation wasn't permissible. And so on back to the first person A to appropriate a permanent property right.

This argument, however, proceeds too quickly. Someone may be made worse off by another's appropriation in two ways: first, by losing the opportunity to improve his situation by a particular appropriation or any one; and second, by no longer being able to use freely (without appropriation) what he previously could. A *stringent* requirement that another not be made worse off by an appropriation would exclude the first way if nothing else counterbalances the diminution in opportunity, as well as the second. A *weaker* requirement would exclude the second way, though not the first. With the weaker requirement, we cannot zip back so quickly from Z to A, as in the above argument; for though person Z can no longer *appropriate*, there may remain some for him to *use* as before. In this case Y's appropriation would not violate the weaker Lockean condition. (With less remaining that people are at liberty to use, users might face more inconvenience, crowding, and so on; in that way the situation of others might be worsened, unless appropriation stopped far short of such a point.) It is arguable that no one legitimately can complain if the weaker provision is satisfied. However, since this is less clear than in the case of the more stringent proviso, Locke may have intended this stringent proviso by "enough and as good" remaining, and perhaps he meant the nonwaste condition to delay the end point from which the argument zips back.

Is the situation of persons who are unable to appropriate (there being no more accessible and useful unowned objects) worsened by a system allowing appropriation and permanent property? Here enter the various familiar social considerations favoring private property: it increases the social product by putting means of production in the hands of those who can use them most efficiently (profitably); experimentation is encouraged, because with separate persons controlling resources, there is no one person or small group whom someone with a new idea must convince to try it out; private property enables people to decide on the pattern and types of risks they wish to bear, leading to specialized types of risk bearing; private property protects future persons by leading some to hold back resources from current consumption for future markets; it provides alternate sources of employment for unpopular persons who don't have to convince any one person or small group to hire them, and so on. These considerations enter a Lockean theory to support the claim that appropriation of private property satisfies the intent behind the "enough and as good left over" proviso, *not* as a utilitarian justification of property. They enter to rebut the claim that because the proviso is violated no natural right to private property can arise by a Lockean process. The difficulty in working such an argument to show that the proviso is satisfied is in fixing the appropriate base line for comparison. Lockean appropriation makes people no worse off than they would be *how?*[17] This question of fixing the baseline needs more detailed investigation than we are able to give it here. It would be desirable to have an estimate of the general economic importance of original appropriation in order to see how much leeway there is for differing theories of appropriation and of the location of the baseline. Perhaps this importance can be measured by the percentage of all income that is based upon untransformed raw materials and given resources (rather than upon human actions), mainly rental income representing the unimproved value of land, and the price of raw material *in situ*, and by the percentage of current wealth which represents such income in the past.[18]

We should note that it is not only persons favoring *private* property who need a theory of how property rights legitimately originate. Those believing in collective property, for example those believing that a group of persons living in an area jointly own the territory, or its mineral resources, also must provide a theory of how such property rights arise; they must show why the persons living there have rights to determine what is done with the land and resources there that persons living elsewhere don't have (with regard to the same land and resources).

The Proviso

Whether or not Locke's particular theory of appropriation can be spelled out so as to handle various difficulties, I assume that any adequate theory of justice in acquisition will contain a proviso similar to the weaker of the ones we have

[17]Compare this with Robert Paul Wolff's "A Refutation of Rawls' Theorem on Justice," *Journal of Philosophy*, March 31, 1966, sect. 2. Wolff's criticism does not apply to Rawls's conception under which the baseline is fixed by the difference principle.

[18]I have not seen a precise estimate. David Friedman, *The Machinery of Freedom* (New York: Harper & Row, 1973), pp. xiv, xv, discusses this issue and suggests 5 percent of U.S. national income as an upper limit for the first two factors mentioned. However he does not attempt to estimate the percentage of current wealth which is based upon such income in the past. (The vague notion of "based upon" merely indicates a topic needing investigation.)

attributed to Locke. A process normally giving rise to a permanent bequeathable property right in a previously unowned thing will not do so if the position of others no longer at liberty to use the thing is thereby worsened. It is important to specify *this* particular mode of worsening the situation of others, for the proviso does not encompass other modes. It does not include the worsening due to more limited opportunities to appropriate (the first way above, corresponding to the more stringent condition), and it does not include how I "worsen" a seller's position if I appropriate materials to make some of what he is selling, and then enter into competition with him. Someone whose appropriation otherwise would violate the proviso still may appropriate provided he compensates the others so that their situation is not thereby worsened; unless he does compensate these others, his appropriation will violate the proviso of the principle of justice in acquisition and will be an illegitimate one.[19] A theory of appropriation incorporating this Lockean proviso will handle correctly the cases (objections to the theory lacking the proviso) where someone appropriates the total supply of something necessary for life.[20]

A theory which includes this proviso in its principle of justice in acquisition must also contain a more complex principle of justice in transfer. Some reflection of the proviso about appropriation constrains later actions. If my appropriating all of a certain substance violates the Lockean proviso, then so does my appropriating some and purchasing all the rest from others who obtained it without otherwise violating the Lockean proviso. If the proviso excludes someone's appropriating all the drinkable water in the world, it also excludes his purchasing it all. (More weakly, and messily, it may exclude his charging certain prices for some of his supply.) This proviso (almost?) never will come into effect; the more someone acquires of a scarce substance which others want, the higher the price of the rest will go, and the more difficult it will become for him to acquire it all. But still, we can imagine, at least, that

---

[19]Fourier held that since the process of civilization had deprived the members of society of certain liberties (to gather, pasture, engage in the chase), a socially guarenteed minimum provision for persons was justified as compensation for the loss (Alexander Gray, *The Socialist Tradition* (New York: Harper & Row, 1968), p. 188). But this puts the point too strongly. This compensation would be due those persons, if any, for whom the process of civilization was a net loss for whom the benefits of civilization did not counterbalance being deprived of these particular liberties.

[20]For example, Rashdall's case of someone who comes upon the only water in the desert several miles ahead of others who also will come to it and appropriates it all. Hastings Rashdall, "The Philosophical Theory of Property," in *Property, its Duties and Rights* (London: MacMillan, 1915).

We should note Ayn Rand's theory of property rights ("Man's Rights" in *The Virtue of Selfishness* (New York: New American Library, 1964), p. 94), wherein these follow from the right to life, since people need physical things to live. But a right to life is not a right to whatever one needs to live; other people may have rights over these other things. . . . At most, a right to life would be a right to have or strive for whatever one needs to live, provided that having it does not violate anyone else's rights. With regard to material things, the question is whether having it does violate any right of others. (Would appropriation of all unowned things do so? Would appropriating the water hole in Rashdall's example?) Since special considerations (such as the Lockean proviso) may enter with regard to material property, one *first* needs a theory of property rights before one can apply any supposed right to life (as amended above). Therefore the right to life cannot provide the foundation for a theory of property rights.

something like this occurs: someone makes simultaneous secret bids to the separate owners of a substance, each of whom sells assuming he can easily purchase more from the other owners; or some natural catastrophe destroys all of the supply of something except that in one person's possession. The total supply could not be permissibly appropriated by one person at the beginning. His later acquisition of it all does not show that the original appropriation violated the proviso (even by a reverse argument similar to the one above that tried to zip back from Z to A). Rather, it is the combination of the original appropriation *plus* all the later transfers and actions that violates the Lockean proviso.

Each owner's title to his holding includes the historical shadow of the Lockean proviso on appropriation. This excludes his transferring it into an agglomeration that does violate the Lockean proviso and excludes his using it in a way, in coordination with others or independently of them, so as to violate the proviso by making the situation of others worse than their baseline situation. Once it is known that someone's ownership runs afoul of the Lockean proviso, there are stringent limits on what he may do with (what it is difficult any longer unreservedly to call) "his property." Thus a person may not appropriate the only water hole in a desert and charge what he will. Nor may he charge what he will if he possesses one, and unfortunately it happens that all the water holes in the desert dry up, except for his. This unfortunate circumstance, admittedly no fault of his, brings into operation the Lockean proviso and limits his property rights.[21] Similarly, an owner's property right in the only island in an area does not allow him to order a castaway from a shipwreck off his island as a trespasser, for this would violate the Lockean proviso.

Notice that the theory does not say that owners do have these rights, but that the rights are overridden to avoid some catastrophe. (Overridden rights do not disappear; they leave a trace of a sort absent in the cases under discussion.)[22] There is no such external (and *ad hoc?*) overriding. Considerations internal to the theory of property itself, to its theory of acquisition and appropriation, provide the means for handling such cases. The results, however, may be coextensive with some condition about catastrophe, since the baseline for comparison is so low as compared to the productiveness of a society with private appropriation that the question of the Lockean proviso being violated arises only in the case of catastrophe (or a desert-island situation).

The fact that someone owns the total supply of something necessary for others to stay alive does *not* entail that his (or anyone's) appropriation of anything left some people (immediately or later) in a situation worse than the baseline one. A medical researcher who synthesizes a new substance that effectively treats a certain disease and who refuses to sell except on his terms does not worsen the situation of others by depriving them of whatever he has appropriated. The others easily can

[21]The situation would be different if his water hole didn't dry up, due to special precautions he took to prevent this. Compare our discussion of the case in the text with Hayek, *The Constitution of Liberty*, p. 136; and also with Ronald Hamowy, "Hayek's Concept of Freedom; A Critique," *New Individualist Review*, April 1961, pp. 28–31.

[22]I discuss overriding and its moral traces in "Moral Complications and Moral Structures," *Natural Law Forum*, 1968, pp. 1–50.

possess the same materials he appropriated; the researcher's appropriation or purchase of chemicals didn't make those chemicals scarce in a way so as to violate the Lockean proviso. Nor would someone else's purchasing the total supply of the synthesized substance from the medical researcher. The fact that the medical researcher uses easily available chemicals to synthesize the drug no more violates the Lockean proviso than does the fact that the only surgeon able to perform a particular operation eats easily obtainable food in order to stay alive and to have the energy to work. This shows that the Lockean proviso is not an "end-state principle"; it focuses on a particular way that appropriative actions affect others, and not on the structure of the situation that results.[23]

Intermediate between someone who takes all of the public supply and someone who makes the total supply out of easily obtainable substances is someone who appropriates the total supply of something in a way that does not deprive the others of it. For example, someone finds a new substance in an out-of-the-way place. He discovers that it effectively treats a certain disease and appropriates the total supply. He does not worsen the situation of others; if he did not stumble upon the substance no one else would have, and the others would remain without it. However, as time passes, the likelihood increases that others would have come across the substance; upon this fact might be based a limit to his property right in the substance so that others are not below their baseline position; for example, its bequest might be limited. The theme of someone worsening another's situation by depriving him of something he otherwise would possess may also illuminate the example of patents. An inventor's patent does not deprive others of an object which would not exist if not for the inventor. Yet patents would have this effect on others who independently invent the object. Therefore, these independent inventors, upon whom the burden of proving independent discovery may rest, should not be excluded from utilizing their own invention as they wish (including selling it to others). Furthermore, a known inventor drastically lessens the chances of actual independent invention. For persons who know of an invention usually will not try to reinvent it, and the notion of independent discovery here would be murky at best. Yet we may assume that in the absence of the original invention, sometime later someone else would have come up with it. This suggests placing a time limit on patents, as a rough rule of thumb to approximate how long it would have taken, in the absence of knowledge of the invention, for independent discovery.

I believe that the free operation of a market system will not actually run afoul of the Lockean proviso. (Recall that crucial to our story in Part I of how a protective agency becomes dominant and a *de facto* monopoly is the fact that it wields force in situations of conflict, and is not merely in competition, with other agencies. A similar tale cannot be told about other businesses.) If this is correct, the proviso

---

[23]Does the principle of compensation . . . introduce patterning considerations? Though it requires compensation for the disadvantages imposed by those seeking security from risks, it is not a patterned principle. For it seeks to remove only those disadvantages which prohibitions inflict on those who might present risks to others, not all disadvantages. It specifies an obligation on those who impose the prohibition, which stems from their own particular acts, to remove a particular complaint those prohibited may make against them.

will not play a very important role in the activities of protective agencies and will not provide a significant opportunity for future state action. Indeed, were it not for the effects of previous *illegitimate* state action, people would not think the possibility of the proviso's being violated as of more interest than any other logical possibility. (Here I make an empirical historical claim; as does someone who disagrees with this.) This completes our indication of the complication in the entitlement theory introduced by the Lockean proviso.

14

Neo-Libertarianism

James P. Sterba

Libertarians like to think of themselves as defenders of liberty. F. A. Hayek, for example, sees his work as restating an ideal of liberty for our times. "We are concerned," says Hayek, "with that condition of men in which coercion of some by others is reduced as much as possible in society."[1] Similarly, John Hospers believes that libertarianism is "a philosophy of personal liberty—the liberty of each person to live according to his own choices, provided that he does not attempt to coerce others and thus prevent them from living according to their choices."[2] And Robert Nozick claims that if a conception of justice goes beyond libertarian side-constraints, it cannot avoid the prospect of continually interfering with people's lives.

Taking liberty to be the absence of interference by other persons, libertarians generally agree that liberty only justifies a minimal or night-watchman state. According to Nozick,

> Our main conclusions about the state are that a minimal state, limited to the narrow functions of protecting against force, theft, fraud, enforcement of contracts, and so on, is justified; that any more extensive state will violate persons' rights not to be forced to do certain things, and is unjustified; and that the minimal state is inspiring as well as right.[3]

An earlier version of this paper appeared in the *American Philosophical Quarterly* (1978); 115–121.
[1] F. A. Hayek, *The Constitution of Liberty* (Chicago: University of Chicago Press, 1960), p. 11.
[2] John Hospers, *Libertarianism* (Los Angeles: Nash Publishers, 1971) p. 5.
[3] Robert Nozick, *Anarchy, State, and Utopia* (New York: Basic Books, 1977), p. IX.

Libertarians hold that while other social ideals, like equality and humanitarianism, if shown to be acceptable and of sufficient priority, may well justify a more extensive state, liberty never does. Or more precisely, they maintain that an ideal of liberty cannot be used to justify anything more extensive than a night-watchman state, as long as liberty is understood "negatively" as the absence of interference or coercion by other persons rather than "positively" as the presence of a particular activity or ability.

In what follows I shall argue that this commonly accepted libertarian view is mistaken. I shall show that moral commitment to an ideal of "negative" liberty does not lead to a night-watchman state but instead requires sufficient government to provide each person in society with the relatively high minimum of liberty that persons using Rawls' decision procedure would select. The political program actually justified by an ideal of negative liberty I shall call "neo-libertarianism."

The Argument for the Night-Watchman State

The libertarian argument for the night-watchman state begins with the acceptable premise that voluntary agreements represent an ultimate ideal for social interaction. This ideal, libertarians contend, finds its fullest expression in a market economy where buyers and sellers, employers and employees, voluntarily agree to exchange the goods they possess. Thus it is assumed that the requirements for voluntary agreements between persons with unequal resources are easily satisfied in a market economy. As long as alternative contractual arrangements make it possible for buyers and sellers, employers and employees, to take their business elsewhere, libertarians believe that agreements reached in market transactions are completely voluntary. On these grounds, libertarians claim that the only significant role left for the state is to prevent and rectify departures from a market economy resulting from fraud, theft, or the use of force. Any more extensive role for the state, they contend, would restrict people's liberty; that is to say, it would restrict liberty understood negatively as the absence of interference by other persons. Accordingly, libertarians conclude that only a night-watchman state can be justified in terms of an ideal of negative liberty.[4]

The libertarian argument for the night-watchman state also seeks to show that other social ideals cannot justify a more extensive state. Libertarians either maintain that other social ideals purporting to justify a more extensive state are

[4]In "Natural Property Rights," *Nous* (1976): 77-85, Allan Gibbard attacks the libertarian defense of a night-watchman state on the grounds that all fully-informed rational persons could only be expected to unanimously agree to "something resembling a welfare state." Assuming that persons so situated would agree to something resembling a welfare state—and whether they would agree at all is certainly problematic—libertarians could accept the premise and deny the conclusion. This is because libertarians are not committed to the view that the night-watchman state would meet the unanimous approval of every fully informed rational person. Rather, they are only committed to the view that the night-watchman state would best promote an ideal of negative liberty, either by respecting libertarian side constraints (Nozick) or by promoting liberty overall (Hayek and Hospers).

themselves without justification, or they claim that these social ideals have lower priority when compared with the ideal of negative liberty. But there is not always agreement as to which critical approach is appropriate. Thus with respect to an ideal of equality, Nozick and Hayek adopt different approaches: Nozick maintains that an ideal of equality has not been effectively justified, while Hayek maintains that the ideal has some validity but that negative liberty is the superior ideal. Allowing for such disagreements, both critical approaches could also be used by libertarians against various conceptions of positive liberty.

One conception of positive liberty, usually associated with Jean Jacques Rousseau and G. W. F. Hegel, but also found in the works of John Locke and John Stuart Mill, defines liberty in terms of the presence of a certain activity—the activity of doing what one ought. Locke, for example, uses this conception to define liberty in the state of nature. "The Natural Liberty of Man," Locke says, "is to have only the Law of Nature for his Rule." Since the "Law of Nature" for Locke is a moral law, it follows that having only the "Law of Nature" for one's rule or principle of action would always entail doing what one ought to do. On other occasions, Locke uses this conception of positive liberty to distinguish liberty from license. License is understood as the activity of doing what one ought not to do; liberty is understood as the activity of doing what one ought to do. Thus, for example, contemporary defenders of this conception of liberty would identify license with the selling of pornography or the promoting of prostitution or gambling. This conception of positive liberty is also the source of Rousseau's paradoxical claim that persons who refuse to obey the General Will should be "forced to be free." For the paradox of how persons can be free and forced at the same time is resolved if freedom means the activity of doing what one ought to do, since it is certainly possible to force people to do what they ought to do.

This conception of positive liberty—libertarians would have to admit—has some validity as a social ideal. An ideal requiring people to do what they ought to do cannot be all bad. Nevertheless, libertarians could argue that this ideal of positive liberty will not serve to justify a more extensive state. As Rousseau's paradoxical claim suggests, a state can guarantee its citizens complete liberty in this sense while still exercising whatever force is necessary to make them always do what they ought to do. Complete liberty in this sense is clearly compatible with the total enforcement of all aspects of morality. Consequently, this ideal of liberty could only suffice to justify a more extensive state if one could defend the view that people should always be prevented from doing what they ought not to do. But even Lord Devlin, a strong advocate of the enforcement of morality, would find this view too extreme. What is required, therefore, is a standard determining the extent to which morality should be enforced, a standard not provided for by this ideal of liberty.

More promising is the conception of positive liberty that defines liberty in terms of the presence of a certain ability—the ability to do whatever one might conceivably want. The advantage of this conception of positive liberty over the previous conception is that it cannot be used to claim that forcing a person to do what he ought to do thereby increases his liberty. If forcing a person to do what he ought to do increases anyone's liberty as determined by this ideal, it ordinarily increases the liberty of others who benefit from the person's doing what he ought; only in paternalistic practices would it be possible to increase the liberty of the person who is actually forced to do what he ought to do. Another advantage of this conception of liberty is that it does not make liberty depend solely on what a person actually happens to want. If liberty were specified solely in terms of the ability to do what one actually wants then it would be possible to increase a person's liberty by restricting his actual wants through social conditioning. Thus a government could increase the liberty of its citizens by socially conditioning them to always favor its policies. A person could also increase his own liberty by a process of self-denial that extinguished wants he was unable to satisfy. Liberty that could always be increased in this fashion, however, would be a somewhat questionable ideal. Since the value of having the ability to do whatever one actually wants is enhanced to the extent that one also has the ability to do whatever one might conceivably want, liberty defined in terms of this more general ability is clearly the more desirable ideal.

Yet it is obviously impossible for everyone in society to be guaranteed complete liberty as defined by this ideal: after all, people's actual wants as well as their conceivable wants can come into serious conflict. In this respect, however, this conception of positive liberty is no worse off than the conception of negative liberty defended by libertarians. Given people's actual and conceivable wants, it is also impossible for everyone in society to be completely free from the interference of other persons.

The main difficulty with this conception of positive liberty is that it identifies inability with lack of liberty, thereby construing liberties too broadly to satisfy the requirements of a social ideal. According to this conception, a person who is unable to vote due to legal restrictions, and a person who is unable to run a mile due to advanced age, would *both* be lacking in liberty. Yet it seems plausible to claim that for liberty to be a *social ideal*, it must be possible to assign moral responsibility for any lack of liberty. This means that for liberty to be a social ideal, an aged person's inability to run a mile cannot be regarded (except in rare circumstances) as a lack of liberty; consequently, only an inability like that of a person restricted by law from voting (an inability for which other persons are morally responsible by their interference) can ordinarily be regarded as a lack of liberty. Thus by defining liberty so broadly as to include all human inabilities, this conception of positive liberty ignores the requirement for assigning responsibility that is implicit in a social ideal.

Assuming that one rejects this conception of positive liberty, is it necessary to go further and adopt the libertarian view that liberty is a negative social ideal? Arguing against this view, Gerald MacCallum claims that every ideal of liberty has both its negative ("freedom from") and positive ("freedom to") aspects. Actually MacCallum contends that whenever the freedom of agents is in question, there is always a triadic relation implying the freedom of something (an agent or agents) from something, to do or become (or not do or not become) something.[5] Yet it is possible to accept MacCallum's thesis and still maintain that liberty functions primarily as a negative social ideal. One could argue that although we can always

[5]Gerald MacCallum, "Negative and Positive Freedom," *The Philosophical Review*. (1967): 312-334.

specify what it is to have complete liberty negatively in terms of a person's being totally free from the interference or coercion of other persons, if we tried to specify what it is to have complete liberty positively in terms of what a person is free to do or become (or not do or not become), we would have to provide a variety of different accounts for different persons and for different circumstances, an extremely difficult if not impossible task. One could, of course, say that what it is to have complete liberty positively is to be completely free to lead one's life. Yet if liberty so conceived is to be a social ideal, it cannot exclude every constraint or obstacle to the leading of one's life. Rather, it can only exclude those constraints or obstacles that result from the interference of other persons, that is, those resulting from the lack of negative liberty. This would seem to provide some justification for the libertarian view that liberty understood negatively is the more basic social ideal.

The Ideal of Negative Liberty

The libertarian argument for the night-watchman state is clearly strongest when it is directed against various conceptions of positive liberty and other social ideals such as equality and humanitarianism. The argument is weakest when it comes to assessing the implications of the libertarian's own social ideal of negative liberty. Libertarians are quite capable of enumerating a variety of ways in which governments deprive people of their liberty. Thus, it is said, governments restrict people's liberty by tariffs, taxes, wage and price regulations, credit restrictions, public monopolies, public work projects, and various welfare programs such as social security and health care. For the most part, these practices are thought to restrict people's liberty in undesirable ways. Commenting on social security programs, Hospers says,

> If I were given a choice, I would say, "No thanks" to social security: "I have found much better ways of saving for my old age than by subscribing to the government program"—or I might not want to save at all, or to stake everything on a business enterprise that requires my entire capital outlay *now*. But I am not given this choice: the government says, "You have to pay into this, whether you like it or not."[6]

Nozick even goes so far as to claim that taxation of earnings from labor is on a par with forced labor. Yet libertarians are not similarly sensitive to the loss of liberty that occurs in the marketplace. When an employer decides to lay someone off, for example, Hospers claims that the employer is simply deciding against continuing a voluntary exchange and is not restricting the person's liberty. Likewise, Hayek claims that as long as workers who are laid off can find alternative employment their liberty is not being restricted. But how can requiring a person to pay $500 into a social security program under threat of greater financial loss infringe upon the person's liberty when requiring a person to take a job paying $500 less under threat

[6]Hospers, *Libertarianism*, pp. 152-154.

of greater financial loss does not infringe upon the person's liberty? Surely it would seem that if one requirement restricts a person's liberty, the other will also.

To distinguish these cases, some libertarians claim that only intentional interference by others restricts a person's liberty. Requiring a person to pay $500 into a social security program under threat of greater financial loss, they contend, is intentional interference by others, and hence, restricts the person's liberty, while requiring a person to take a job paying $500 less under a similar threat is but the unintended result of individuals trying to better themselves in a market economy, and hence, does not restrict the person's liberty. But whether interference with a person's life is intentional or not is relevant only when determining the extent to which others are responsible for that interference. Although people are clearly more responsible for actions done intentionally they can still be responsible for actions does unintentionally, especially if they were morally negligent and should have foreseen the consequences of their actions. Since moral responsibility can extend to both intentional and unintentional interference with a person's life, there seems to be no reason for not considering both types of interference to be restrictions of a person's liberty. What is crucial to liberty as a social ideal is whether people are morally responsible for interfering with a person's life irrespective of whether that interference is intentional or not.

While granting that unintentional as well as intentional interference can restrict a person's liberty, W. A. Parent has recently argued that not every interference with a person's life for which others are morally responsible is a restriction of liberty.[7] In fact, Parent would not regard either of the two previous cases as a restriction of liberty. Each case would be said to violate a self-evident principle, to wit, that a person cannot be socially unfree to do what he can do or has already done. For a person can refuse to contribute to a required social security program, even when faced with a greater financial loss, and he can refuse to take a lower-paying job, even when faced with a comparable loss. Hence, Parent would conclude from applying his principle that in neither case is the person socially unfree, that is, in neither case is the interference with the person's life a restriction of liberty.

Parent's principle is certainly a reasonable requirement for an ideal of liberty. Parent simply misapplies it. When correctly applied the principle has the consequence that every interference with a person's life for which others are morally responsible is a restriction of liberty. What Parent fails to see is that in every such case of interference, there is always some action the person can no longer perform as a result of that interference. The person faced with greater financial loss if he refuses to pay $500 into a social security program cannot perform the action of refusing-to-pay-into-the-program-without-the-imminent-risk-of-a-greater-financial-loss. Interference by the state makes it impossible for the person to perform that action. Again, in the second case, the intentional interference with the person's life resulting from market transactions makes it impossible for him to perform the action of refusing-to-take-a-lower-paying-job-without-incurring-the-

[7]W. A. Parent, "Some Recent Work on the Concept of Liberty," *American Philosophical Quarterly* (1974): 149–167.

imminent-risk-of-greater-financial-loss. In short, in both cases, there is an action that the person cannot perform because of the interference of other persons. And it is that action that the person is socially unfree to do. Thus, in both cases, Parent's principle is satisfied. In general, therefore, when we speak of a person's liberty being restricted by the laws of the state, this implies not that it is impossible for the person to violate those laws, but rather that it is impossible for the person to perform the action of violating-the-laws-of-the-state-without-incurring-some-risk-of-punishment-or-penalty.

So far it has been argued that any intentional or unintentional interference with a person's life for which other persons are morally responsible is a restriction of liberty. Disagreement can arise, however, over what constitutes an interference with a person's life. If a sick person is simply left alone and dies for lack of treatment, for example, has his liberty been restricted? Or is a person's liberty restricted if he is left alone to starve to death? Put more generally, can acts of omission as well as acts of commission interfere with a person's life? The importance of this question derives from the fact that libertarians believe that interference requires an act of commission from which they think it follows that it is impossible to justify the practices of a welfare state in terms of an ideal of negative liberty.

No doubt in standard cases the interference that restricts a person's liberty results from an act of commission. A prisoner's liberty, for example, is restricted by what his jailers do rather than by what they refrain from doing. A prisoner could, of course, retain his liberty if his jailers gave him the keys and turned their backs, but the omitted acts are certainly not causally sufficient to restrict the prisoner's liberty. If these omitted acts restrict the prisoner's liberty at all they do so only in virtue of the coercive actions already performed by the jailers.

But suppose a person were starving to death and the only causally relevant actions for which others were morally responsible were actions of failing to give him the food he needs. Would those acts of omission interfere with the person's life? C. B. Macpherson believes they would. For Macpherson, any humanly alterable condition that prevents a person from doing something either directly or indirectly interferes with the person's life, and hence restricts his liberty.[8] No doubt construing interference in this fashion would make it possible to defend the practices of a welfare state in terms of an ideal of negative liberty, but it would not win many converts among libertarians. Libertarians would think that Macpherson's interpretation simply begs the question of whether acts of omission interfere with a person's life.

Yet it is possible to grant libertarians that interference with a person's life requires an act of commission and still maintain that liberty is restricted when people in need are simply left alone. In the first place, most people would be able to take from others the goods and resources they need if they were not prohibited from doing so by those who possess the goods and resources. Such prohibitions would obviously be acts of commission that interfere with people's lives, and hence, restrict their liberty. Secondly, with respect to those persons who are in such dire need that they cannot even take from others the goods and resources they need, restrictions of liberty will also arise if there are other persons who are interested in transferring

[8] C. B. Macpherson, *Democratic Theory* (Oxford: Oxford University Press, 1973), pp. 95-119.

goods and resources to them but are prohibited from doing so by some of those who possess the goods and resources. Consequently, in virtually every case in which people in need are left alone to care for themselves their liberty and/or the liberty of others is actually restricted. For this reason, even if one accepts the libertarian view that interference with a person's life requires an act of commission, it still may be possible to justify the practices of a welfare state in terms of an ideal of negative liberty.

From what has been argued, it is apparent that restrictions of liberty are more pervasive than libertarians are usually willing to admit. In fact, attempting a more general account, it seems plausible to claim that

> Any intentional or unintentional act of commission for which others are morally responsible interferes with a person's life, and thereby, restricts his liberty, if that act prevents him from doing something he could otherwise do.

And in accordance with Parent's principle that a person cannot be socially unfree to do what he can do or has already done, we could add that

> If a person's action prevents another from doing some action he could otherwise do, then the person's action renders it impossible for the other person to perform that action.

Of course, some libertarians may object to this account on the grounds that to interfere with a person's life so as to restrict his liberty, one must violate his rights. Thus it may be claimed that in the social security example where a person is required to pay $500 under threat of a greater financial loss, the person's liberty is being restricted because his rights to his justly acquired possessions are being violated, whereas in the employment example where a person is required to take a job paying $500 less under threat of a greater financial loss, the person's liberty is not being restricted since his rights are not being violated, presumably because he has no right to a higher paying job. But to define liberty in this fashion, would make liberty a derivative social ideal. Whether a person's liberty is being restricted would thus depend on what a person's rights are at any given moment. This would have the odd consequence that if we were to justly imprison someone for committing a crime, we would not be restricting his liberty because he would have forfeited his right to live his life as he pleases. Likewise, it could turn out that in a society in which people voluntarily contracted into extensive paternalistic practices, there may be no more restriction of liberty, understood as the nonviolation of people's rights, than in the most individualistic society, even though it would seem that the reason people have for contracting into paternalistic practices from Christmas clubs to monastic orders is in fact to restrict their liberty for some good purpose. Thus while it must be granted that people's rights should determine how much liberty they should have at any given time, if liberty is to serve as an ultimate social ideal for libertarians, then it must be specified in a manner similar to the account just proposed.

According to that account, restrictions of liberty can be quite severe (like forcing a person to give over all of his possessions at gunpoint) or they can be very slight and even trivial (like accidentally stepping on a person's toe). The relative significance of a restriction of liberty depends upon the relative significance of the action(s) prevented by that restriction. Significant restrictions of liberty can be imposed either by the government (like a steeply progressive income tax) or by private individuals and groups (like dehumanizing work conditions in a market economy). Significant restrictions of liberty are called coercive when they prevent a person from doing something he could otherwise do, either by applying considerable physical force or by threatening some highly undesirable consequence. Although libertarians are quick to point out that significant restrictions of liberty by the government are greater under a more extensive state than under a night-watchman state, they are slow to see that significant restrictions of liberty by private individuals and groups can also be greater under a night-watchman state than under a more extensive state. Given the practical impossibility of avoiding all restrictions of liberty, the crucial question for the advocate of negative liberty is: In what ways should liberty be restricted? What is needed, therefore, is an acceptable procedure for deciding upon principles for restricting liberty in society. The libertarian's hope is that from such a procedure it is possible to derive principles that justify a night-watchman state.

A Rawlsian Decision Procedure

In keeping with the libertarian's concern for negative liberty, we might consider the possibility of determining principles for restricting liberty by having a meeting of all the members of a society. Such a meeting, assuming it were practically possible, might result in a greater appreciation of all the relevant viewpoints, if, that is, each member were given a chance to argue in favor of his or her particular interests. However, it is unrealistic to think that the members at this meeting would be able to reach a unanimous agreement with respect to principles for restricting liberty. The chances of that occurring would be very slight unless the members had some procedure for compromising their particular interests.

Suppose, then, that the members of this society were to adopt a procedure analogous to the one developed by John Rawls in *A Theory of Justice*.[9] Suppose, that is to say, that the members of this society in deciding upon principles for restricting liberty were to discount the knowledge of which particular interests happen to be their own. Although they would actually know what their own particular interests were, they would not take that knowledge into account when selecting principles for restricting liberty. In selecting such principles, they would reason from their knowledge of all the particular interests in their society but not from their knowledge of which particular interests happen to be their own.[10] In employing this decision procedure, the members of this society (like judges who discount prejudicial information in order to reach fair decisions) would be able to give a fair hearing to

[9] John Rawls, *A Theory of Justice* (Cambridge, Mass.: Harvard University Press, 1971).

[10] In discounting the knowledge of which particular interests happen to be their own, it is assumed that persons would also be discounting the knowledge of with what probability they would have various particular interests in their society.

everyone's particular interests. If we further assume that the members were well informed of all the particular interests in their society and were fully capable of rationally deliberating with respect to that information, then their deliberations would culminate in a unanimous decision. This is because each of them would be deliberating in a rationally correct manner with respect to the same information and would be using a decision procedure leading to a uniform evaluation of the alternatives; consequently, each would favor the same principles for restricting liberty in society. Given that the principles that would be selected by this procedure would result from a unanimous agreement in which everyone's particular interests received a fair hearing, there seems to be no reasonable grounds for libertarians to object to the principles that would be derived.

But *what* principles would be derived from this procedure? Some philosophers have argued that persons employing analogous decision procedures (in which they assume ignorance of their own particular interests) would reason as if they had an equal chance of having each person's particular interests, and hence, would select principles for restricting liberty that maximized average utility in society.[11] Yet clearly, since persons employing the proposed decision procedure would not be using their knowledge of which particular interests happen to be their own, they would be quite concerned about the pattern according to which utilities would be distributed in their society. Employing this decision procedure, they would reason as though their particular interests might be those of persons with the lowest utilities in their society. Hence, it would only be reasonable for them to consider adopting principles that maximized average utility in society if the pattern of distribution were such that each of them could expect to realize at least approximately the average utility of the society. In a society that maximized average utility by providing very high utilities to some and very low utilities to others, however, such an expectation would not be justified. Consequently, persons employing this decision procedure would not favor the adoption of principles that maximized average utility, since such principles could be satisfied in a society with considerable inequality.

The previous argument suggests that persons employing the proposed decision procedure would be primarily concerned with securing an acceptable minimum of liberty for each person in their society. In fact, Rawls has argued that securing the highest possible minimum would be the only concern of persons employing such a decision procedure.[12] But a policy of always favoring the least advantaged is an extreme view that persons employing this decision procedure would have reason to avoid.[13] And they would also want to secure a higher minimum of liberty than could be guaranteed by adopting principles that maximized average utility in society. Persons employing this decision procedure could meet these requirements by specifying an acceptable minimum of liberty in terms of a person's basic needs.

[11] R. M. Hare, "Rawls' Theory of Justice," *Philosophical Quarterly* (1973): 144-155, 241-255; Richard Brandt, "Utilitarianism and the Rules of War," *Philosophy and Public Affairs* (1972): 145-165.

[12] Rawls, *Theory of Justice*, pp. 150-166.

[13] See James P. Sterba, "Distributive Justice," *American Journal of Jurisprudence* (1977): 55-79.

Although the criterion of need is not appropriate for distributing all social goods because of the difficulty of determining both what a person's nonbasic needs are and how they should be arranged according to priority, the criterion can be effectively used to determine an acceptable minimum of liberty. A person's basic needs are those that must be satisfied in order not to seriously endanger the person's health and sanity. Thus, the needs a person has for food, shelter, companionship, medical care, protection and self-development are, at least in part, needs of this sort. Naturally, societies will vary in their ability to satisfy a person's basic needs but the needs themselves will not be similarly subject to variation, unless there is corresponding variation in what constitutes health and sanity in different societies.

Obviously, people have other needs that are nonbasic. Some of these needs are functional or instrumental needs. For example, a barber needs a comb, scissors, and maybe a barber chair to cut hair; a carpenter needs lumber, a hammer, and maybe an electric saw in order to ply his trade; and a husband may need meat, potatoes, and certain other ingredients in order to prepare his wife's favorite stew. As in the last example, a person can have functional or instrumental needs for the same sorts of goods that he requires to satisfy his basic needs. There can also be serious disagreement as to what a person's functional or instrumental needs are. For example, de Jouvenel thought that a professor's functional needs extended beyond his office and classroom and included the need to be able to entertain his colleagues and students in a comfortable manner.[14] Other people would want to restrict a professor's functional needs to his office and classroom. And it is not apparent how to resolve such disputes. Yet even if it were possible to reach agreement as to what people's functional and instrumental needs are, it is clear that not all such functional and instrumental needs ought to be satisfied. For example, a safecracker may need two sticks of dynamite and a fuse to blow up a safe, and a would-be murderer may need some arsenic to poison his intended victim, but satisfying such functional or instrumental needs would not be morally justified. For these reasons, only when the criterion of need is restricted to basic needs does it appear to be an acceptable standard for determining the minimum of primary social goods a person should receive.

Actually, specifying a minimum of this sort seems to be the goal of the poverty index used in the United States since 1964.[15] This poverty index is based on the U.S. Department of Agriculture's Economy Food Plan (for an adequate diet) and on evidence showing that low income families spend about one-third of their income on food. The index is then adjusted yearly to take into account changing prices. Thus, while a minimum defined in terms of a person's basic needs would generally (depending on what incentives are required to motivate people to contribute to society) be lower than that required by the strategy of always favoring the least advantaged, it would not be unreasonably low when one considers that over 25 million people in the United States fall below the poverty level.[16]

It is possible, of course, to specify a minimum in terms of a standard of

---

[14]Bertrand de Jouvenel, *The Ethics of Redistribution* (Cambridge, 1952), pp. 54–55.
[15]See *Old Age Insurance*, submitted to the Joint Economic Committee of the Congress of the United States in December 1967, p. 186; and *Statistical Abstracts of the United States for 1977*, p. 426.
[16]*Statistical Abstracts*, p. 454.

living that is conventional and varies over time and between societies. Following this approach, Benn and Peters have suggested that an acceptable minimum could be specified in terms of the income received by the most numerous group in a society.[17] Specified in this manner, an acceptable minimum could only be reached in some societies by satisfying a considerable number of nonbasic needs. For example, in the United States today the greatest number of family units fall within the $15,000-$19,999 income bracket (in 1976 dollars).[18] Consequently, to specify a minimum in terms of this income group would certainly provide for the satisfaction of many nonbasic needs. Moreover, suppose that the most numerous group of family units in a society with the wealth of the United States fell within a $500-$999 income bracket (in 1976 dollars). Certainly it would not thereby follow that a guarantee of $1000 per family unit would constitute an acceptable minimum for such a society. Or suppose that the income of the most numerous group of family units in such a society fell within the $95,000-$100,000 income bracket (in 1976 dollars). Certainly a minimum of $100,000 per family unit would not thereby be required. What this suggests is that an acceptable minimum is neither a direct function of the number of family units that share a particular income nor a direct function of the wealth of a particular society.

Nevertheless, it still seems that an acceptable minimum should vary over time and between societies at least to some degree. For example, it could be argued that a television set is almost a necessity in the typical North American household today, which was not true 30 years ago, nor is it true today in most other countries of the world. Happily, a basic needs approach to defining an acceptable minimum can appropriately account for such variation. For there is variation in the basic needs approach to defining an acceptable minimum, but the variation does not enter into the definition of the basic needs themselves, which are, for the most part, understood to be invariant over time and between societies. Instead, variation enters into the cost of satisfying those same needs at different times and in different societies.[19] For in the same society at different times, and in different societies at the same time, the normal costs of satisfying a person's basic needs can and do vary considerably. This is because the most readily available means for satisfying a person's basic needs in more affluent societies are usually processed so as to satisfy certain nonbasic needs at the same time that they satisfy a person's basic needs. This processing is carried out to make the means more attractive to persons in higher income brackets who can easily afford the extra cost. As a result, the most readily available means for satisfying a person's basic needs are much more costly in more affluent societies than they are in less affluent societies. This occurs most obviously with respect to the most readily available means for satisfying a person's basic needs for food, shelter, and transportation, but it also occurs with respect to the most readily available means for satisfying a person's basic needs for companionship, self-esteem, and self-development. For a person cannot normally satisfy even these latter needs in more affluent societies without participating in at least some

[17]S. I. Benn and R. S. Peters, *The Principles of Political Thought* (New York, 1959), p. 167.
[18]*Statistical Abstracts*, p. 440.
[19]See Bernard Gendron, *Technology and the Human Condition* (New York: St. Martin's Press, 1977), pp. 222-227.

relatively costly educational and societal development practices. Thus, there can be considerable variation in the normal costs of satisfying a person's basic needs as a society becomes more affluent over time, and at any one time, in societies at different levels of affluence. Consequently, a basic needs approach to defining an acceptable minimum would guarantee a person the liberty necessary to meet the normal costs of satisfying his basic needs in the society in which he lives. A minimum of liberty determined in this way would enable a person to acquire the goods and resources necessary for satisfying his own basic needs. Other liberties would enable a person to transfer goods and resources, not necessarily his own, to provide for the basic needs of others. Persons using this decision procedure would want liberties of both types to ensure equal consideration for everyone's basic needs.

Of course, the exact minimum of liberty that persons using this decision procedure would require necessarily depends upon the particular economic and social resources available in a society. Yet whatever the acceptable minimum of liberty for a particular society, how social goods are to be distributed above the minimum would simply be a matter of private appropriation and voluntary agreement and exchange. Provided each person is guaranteed the acceptable minimum of liberty, persons using this decision procedure would have little reason to object to the results of private appropriation and voluntary agreement and exchange.[20] For example, people could voluntarily agree to set up for themselves various forms of government, from direct democracies to dictatorships, as long as the right to the acceptable minimum of liberty were respected. Nor would each person be required to keep the minimum of liberty he is guaranteed. A person could give up part of it or all of it or risk losing it for the chance of gaining a greater share of liberties or other social goods.[21] Thus the most general principle of neo-libertarianism is the following:

Needs and Agreement Principle

The results of private appropriation and voluntary agreement and exchange are morally justified provided each person is guaranteed the liberty necessary to meet the normal costs of satisfying his basic needs in the society in which he lives.

In neo-libertarianism, the right to an acceptable minimum of liberty functions in the same way as the Lockean proviso does in Nozick's libertarianism.[22] According to Nozick's view, the results of voluntary agreement and private appropriation are morally justified so long as the Lockean proviso against catastrophe is not violated. Similarly, in neo-libertarianism, the results of voluntary agreement and private appropriation are morally justified so long as the right to an

---

[20]Of course, persons using this decision procedure would have to determine acceptable means of private appropriation. There would also be limits to private appropriation if the decision procedure were modified to take into account the interests of future generations. See James P. Sterba, "Distributive Justice," *American Journal of Jurisprudence* (1977).

[21]The person cannot, however, give up his or her children's right to that minimum.

[22]Nozick, *Anarchy, State, and Utopia*, Chapter 7.

acceptable minimum of liberty is guaranteed. Only with respect to the minimum of liberty it requires does neo-libertarianism differ significantly from Nozick's libertarianism.

It may be objected, however, that to require a high minimum of liberty is a significant difference since most libertarians would definitely oppose such a minimum on the grounds that it would conflict with a person's right to acquire property. But while guaranteeing such a minimum of liberty would certainly place some restriction on a person's right to acquire property over and above what is necessary to satisfy his basic needs, why should a person's right to acquire property take precedence over guaranteeing that minimum?

Surely we cannot expect that people will universally consent to a lower minimum of liberty so as to have a greater opportunity to acquire property. After all, a minimum that provides each person with the liberty necessary to satisfy his or her basic needs would be quite attractive to many people.

It may be claimed, of course, that property rights can legitimately arise either by some Lockean process of creatively mixing one's labor with previously unowned goods or by the voluntary transfer of goods that have been subjected to such a Lockean process. But whether a person can come to have property rights through these processes of acquisition and transfer will depend on whether others can rightfully interfere with such processes, and if others can rightfully interfere, on whether they have forfeited their rights to do so.

For example, let us assume that I can acquire property rights to a piece of unowned land by creatively mixing my labor with the land and that the piece of land is more than I really need to satisfy my basic needs. Could others then rightfully appropriate that part of it that I did not require for my basic needs if no other means of satisfying their basic needs were available? Surely others could not be morally required to do nothing to avoid seriously endangering their health and sanity just because I have already creatively mixed my labor with all the available resources for satisfying their basic needs. Therefore, persons in such dire need or their agents would seem to be within their rights to appropriate the surplus goods I possess unless they have forfeited their rights to an adequate minimum of liberty, for example, either by squandering their possessions or by gambling away their rights to an adequate minimum of liberty for the chance of acquiring greater possessions and thereby greater liberty.

No doubt it will frequently be possible to prevent persons in dire need or their agents from interfering with processes of appropriation and transfer, but this does not show that it would be right to do so. Since a moral solution to the conflict between persons who possess surplus goods and persons in dire need would have to be one each party could accept as reasonable, such a solution could not demand that persons in dire need renounce the only available means they have at their command for satisfying their basic needs. Although providing an adequate minimum of liberty is certainly not a productive exchange between persons possessing surplus goods and persons in dire need since each party would presumably be better off if the other did not exist; nevertheless, providing such a minimum is certainly the only reasonable solution if both parties are presumed to have the right to exist.

Furthermore, a person's right to an adequate minimum of liberty would not be unconditional, but would apply to the surplus goods of others only when there is no other means at the person's command for satisfying his basic needs.

Yet libertarians sometimes argue that persons in need would be even better off in a society that did not guarantee as high a minimum as is required by the Needs and Agreement Principle. In a society without a guaranteed high minimum, it is claimed, persons would be more productive because they would be able to keep more of what they produced; and, with this greater productivity, it is claimed, persons in need would benefit even more from private charity than they would from having as high a minimum as that required by the Needs and Agreement Principle. But it is certainly doubtful that this would occur, because it would only make sense to secure the minimum of the Needs and Agreement Principle in a manner that would have the least tendency to reduce productivity in a society. For the greater the productivity in a society the greater the possibilities would be for private charity to supplement that minimum. It is also difficult to even comprehend how persons in need could ever be better off in a society without a guaranteed high minimum, assuming, as seems likely, that they would experience a considerable loss of self-respect once they had to depend on private charity rather than on a guaranteed high minimum for the satisfaction of their basic needs. It would seem, therefore, that persons in need would only be better off without the high minimum requirement of the Needs and Agreement Principle if persons who are productive in a society would so dislike having to contribute to such a minimum that they would choose to produce less, thus sustaining a significant loss to themselves, in order to reduce the contribution they would have to make toward providing that minimum. Yet there seems to be no reason to expect that this sort of behavior would be generally characteristic of intelligent and creative persons in society. In any case, if the previous argument is correct, then it follows that persons in need would still be justified in claiming a right to the minimum required by the Needs and Agreement Principle irrespective of what might result from their relying on private charity.

This requirement of a relatively high minimum of liberty for each person in society results from employing a particular decision procedure to determine the ways that liberty should be restricted in society. That some procedure is needed is obvious—people are constantly restricting each other's liberty in society. Neo-libertarianism combines the libertarian's moral commitment to negative liberty with a procedure that selects principles for restricting liberty on the basis of a unanimous agreement in which everyone's particular interests receive a fair hearing.[23] In this way, neo-libertarianism justifies the Needs and Agreement Principle and the more extensive state necessary to implement that principle. Given the evident moral basis for adopting this particular decision procedure, libertarians would have to abandon their moral commitment to the ideal of negative liberty to avoid endorsing the political program of neo-libertarianism. One would think that price is more than any libertarian would want to pay.

[23]Hence, there is a place for an appeal to unanimous agreement in a critique of libertarianism. However, it functions as part of a procedure for deciding between alternative ways of restricting liberty only after an ideal of negative liberty has been shown to require such a procedure. An appeal to unanimous agreement should not be, as it is for Gibbard (see footnote 4), a starting point for an argument against libertarianism.

V
SOCIALIST JUSTICE: DEFENSES AND A CRITIQUE

15

The Socialist Ideal

Karl Marx and Friedrich Engels

A spectre is haunting Europe—the spectre of Communism. All the Powers of old Europe have entered into a holy alliance to exorcise this spectre: Pope and Czar, Metternich and Guizot, French Radicals and German police-spies.

Where is the party in opposition that has not been decried as Communistic by its opponents in power? Where the Opposition that has not hurled back the branding reproach of Communism, against the more advanced opposition parties, as well as against its reactionary adversaries?

Two things result from this fact.

I. Communism is already acknowledged by all European Powers to be itself a Power.

II. It is high time that Communists should openly, in the face of the whole world, publish thier views, their aims, their tendencies, and meet this nursery tale of the Spectre of Communism with a Manifesto of the party itself . . .

The Communist Program

The Communists do not form a separate party opposed to other working-class parties.

They have no interests separate and apart from those of the proletariat as a whole.

From the *Communist Manifesto*, first published in English by Friedrich Engels in 1888 and the *Critique of the Gotha Program*, edited by C. P. Dutt (1966), pp. 5-11. Reprinted by permission of International Publishers.

They do not set up any sectarian principles of their own, by which to shape and mould the proletarian movement.

The Communists are distinguished from the other working-class parties by this only: (1) In the national struggles of the proletarians of the different countries, they point out and bring to the front the common interests of the entire proletariat, independently of all nationality. (2) In the various stages of development which the struggle of the working class against the bourgeoisie has to pass through they always and everywhere represent the interests of the movement as a whole.

The Communists, therefore, are on the one hand, practically, the most advanced and resolute section of the working-class parties of every country, that section which pushes forward all others; on the other hand, theoretically, they have over the great mass of the proletariat the advantage of clearly understanding the line of march, the conditions, and the ultimate general results of the proletarian movement.

The immediate aim of the Communists is the same as that of all the other proletarian parties: formation of the proletariat into a class, overthrow of the bourgeois supremacy, conquest of political power by the proletariat.

The theoretical conclusions of the Communists are in no way based on ideas or principles that have been invented, or discovered, by this or that would-be universal reformer.

They merely express, in general terms, actual relations springing from an existing class struggle, from a historical movement going on under our very eyes. The abolition of existing property relations is not at all a distinctive feature of Communism.

All property relations in the past have continually been subject to historical change consequent upon the change in historical conditions.

The French Revolution, for example, abolished feudal property in favour of bourgeois property.

The distinguishing feature of Communism is not the abolition of property generally, but the abolition of bourgeois property. But modern bourgeois private property is the final and most complete expression of the system of producing and appropriating products, that is based on class antagonisms, on the exploitation of the many by the few.

In this sense, the theory of the Communists may be summed up in the single sentence: Abolition of private property.

We Communists have been reproached with the desire of abolishing the right of personally acquiring property as the fruit of a man's own labour, which property is alleged to be the groundwork of all personal freedom, activity and independence.

Hard-won, self-acquired, self-earned property! Do you mean the property of the petty artisan and of the small peasant, a form of property that preceded the bourgeois form? There is no need to abolish that; the development of industry has to a great extent already destroyed it, and is still destroying it daily.

Or do you mean modern bourgeois private property?

But does wage-labour create any property for the labourer? Not a bit. It creates capital, *i.e.*, that kind of property which exploits wage-labour, and which cannot increase except upon condition of begetting a new supply of wage-labour for fresh exploitation. Property, in its present form, is based on the antagonism of capital and wage-labour. Let us examine both sides of this antagonism.

To be a capitalist, is to have not only a purely personal, but a social *status* in production. Capital is a collective product, and only by the united action of many members, nay, in the last resort, only by the united action of all members of society, can it be set in motion.

Capital is, therefore, not a personal, it is a social power.

When, therefore, capital is converted into common property, into the property of all members of society, personal property is not thereby transformed into social property. It is only the social character of the property that is changed. It loses its class-character.

Let us now take wage-labour.

The average price of wage-labour is the minimum wage, *i.e.*, that quantum of the means of subsistence, which is absolutely requisite to keep the labourer in bare existence as a labourer. What, therefore, the wage-labourer appropriates by means of his labour, merely suffices to prolong and reproduce a bare existence. We by no means intend to abolish this personal appropriation of the products of labour, an appropriation that is made for the maintenance and reproduction of human life, and that leaves no surplus wherewith to command the labour of others. All that we want to do away with, is the miserable character of this appropriation, under which the labourer lives merely to increase capital, and is allowed to live only in so far as the interest of the ruling class requires it.

In bourgeois society, living labour is but a means to increase accumulated labour. In Communist society, accumulated labour is but a means to widen, to enrich, to promote the existence of the labourer.

In bourgeois society, therefore, the past dominates the present; in Communist society, the present dominates the past. In bourgeois society capital is independent and has individuality, while the living person is dependent and has no individuality.

And the abolition of this state of things is called by the bourgeois, abolition of individuality and freedom! And rightly so. The abolition of bourgeois individuality, bourgeois independence, and bourgeois freedom is undoubtedly aimed at.

By freedom is meant, under the present bourgeois conditions of production, free trade, free selling and buying.

But if selling and buying disappears, free selling and buying disappears also. This talk about free selling and buying, and all the other "brave words" of our bourgeoisie about freedom in general, have a meaning, if any, only in contrast with restricted selling and buying, with the fettered traders of the Middle Ages, but have no meaning when opposed to the Communistic abolition of buying and selling, of the bourgeois conditions of production, and of the bourgeoisie itself.

You are horrified at our intending to do away with private property. But in your existing society, private property is already done away with for nine-tenths of the population; its existence for the few is solely due to its non-existence in the hands of those nine-tenths. You reproach us, therefore, with intending to do away with a form of property, the necessary condition for whose existence is the non-existence of any property for the immense majority of society.

In one word, you reproach us with intending to do away with your property. Precisely so; that is just what we intend.

From the moment when labour can no longer be converted into capital, money, or rent, into a social power capable of being monopolised, *i.e.*, from the moment when individual property can no longer be transformed into bourgeois property, into capital, from that moment, you say, individuality vanishes.

You must, therefore, confess that by "individual" you mean no other person than the bourgeois, than the middle-class owner of property. This person must, indeed, be swept out of the way, and made impossible.

Communism deprives no man of the power to appropriate the products of society; all that it does is to deprive him of the power to subjugate the labour of others by means of such appropriation.

It has been objected that upon the abolition of private property all work will cease, and universal laziness will overtake us.

According to this, bourgeois society ought long ago to have gone to the dogs through sheer idleness; for those of its members who work, acquire nothing, and those who acquire anything, do not work. The whole of this objection is but another expression of the tautology: that there can no longer be any wage-labour when there is no longer any capital.

All objections urged against the Communistic mode of producing and appropriating material products, have, in the same way, been urged against the Communistic modes of producing and appropriating intellectual products. Just as, to the bourgeois, the disappearance of class property is the disappearance of production itself, so the disappearance of class culture is to him identical with the disappearance of all culture.

That culture, the loss of which he laments, is, for the enormous majority, a mere training to act as a machine.

But don't wrangle with us so long as you apply, to our intended abolition of bourgeois property, the standard of your bourgeois notions of freedom, culture, law, [and so on]. Your very ideas are but the outgrowth of the conditions of your bourgeois production and bourgeois property, just as your jurisprudence is but the will of your class made into a law for all, a will, whose essential character and direction are determined by the economical conditions of existence of your class.

The selfish misconception that induces you to transform into eternal laws of nature and reason, the social forms springing from your present mode of production and form of property—historical relations that rise and disappear in the progress of production—this misconception you share with every ruling class that has preceded you. What you see clearly in the case of ancient property, what you admit in the case of feudal property, you are of course forbidden to admit in the case of your own bourgeois form of property.

Abolition of the family! Even the most radical flare up at this infamous proposal of the Communists.

On what foundation is the present family, the bourgeois family, based? On capital, on private gain. In its completely developed form this family exists only among the bourgeoisie. But this state of things finds its complement in the practical absence of the family among the proletarians, and in public prostitution.

The bourgeois family will vanish as a matter of course when its complement vanishes, and both will vanish with the vanishing of capital.

Do you charge us with wanting to stop the exploitation of children by their parents? To this crime we plead guilty.

But, you will say, we destroy the most hallowed of relations, when we replace home education by social.

And your education! Is not that also social, and determined by the social conditions under which you educate, by the intervention, direct or indirect, of society, by means of schools, [and so on]? The Communists have not invented the intervention of society in education; they do but seek to alter the character of that intervention, and to rescue education from the influence of the ruling class.

The bourgeois clap-trap about the family and education, about the hallowed co-relation of parent and child, becomes all the more disgusting, the more, by the action of Modern Industry, all family ties among the proletarians are torn asunder, and their children transformed into simple articles of commerce and instruments of labour.

But you Communists would introduce community of women, screams the whole bourgeoisie in chorus.

The bourgeois sees in his wife a mere instrument of production. He hears that the instruments of production are to be exploited in common, and, naturally, can come to no other conclusion than that the lot of being common to all will likewise fall to the women.

He has not even a suspicion that the real point aimed at is to do away with the status of women as mere instruments of production.

For the rest, nothing is more ridiculous than the virtuous indignation of our bourgeois at the community of women which, they pretend, is to be openly and officially established by the Communists. The Communists have no need to introduce community of women; it has existed almost from time immemorial.

Our bourgeois, not content with having the wives and daughters of their proletarians at their disposal, not to speak of common prostitutes, take the greatest pleasure in seducing each other's wives.

Bourgeois marriage is in reality a system of wives in common and thus, at the most, what the Communists might possibly be reproached with, is that they desire to introduce, in substitution for a hypocritically concealed, an openly legalised community of women. For the rest, it is self-evident that the abolition of the present system of production must bring with it the abolition of the community of women springing from that system, i.e., of prostitution both public and private.

The Communists are further reproached with desiring to abolish countries and nationality.

The working men have no country. We cannot take from them what they have not got. Since the proletariat must first of all acquire political supremacy, must rise to be the leading class of the nation, must constitute itself *the* nation, it is, so far, itself national, though not in the bourgeois sense of the word.

National differences and antagonisms between peoples are daily more and more vanishing, owing to the development of the bourgeoisie, to freedom of commerce, to the world-market, to uniformity in the mode of production and in the conditions of life corresponding thereto.

The supremacy of the proletariat will cause them to vanish still faster. United action, of the leading civilised countries at least, is one of the first conditions for the emancipation of the proletariat.

In proportion as the exploitation of one individual by another is put an end to, the exploitation of one nation by another will also be put an end to. In proportion as the antagonism between classes within the nation vanishes, the hostility of one nation to another will come to an end.

The charges against Communism made from a religious, a philosophical, and, generally, from an ideological standpoint, are not deserving of serious examination.

Does it require deep intuition to comprehend that man's ideas, views and conceptions, in one word, man's consciousness, changes with every change in the conditions of his material existence, in his social relations and in his social life?

What else does the history of ideas prove, than that intellectual production changes its character in proportion as material production is changed? The ruling ideas of each age have ever been the ideas of its ruling class.

When people speak of ideas that revolutionise society, they do but express the fact, that within the old society, the elements of a new one have been created, and that the dissolution of the old ideas keeps even pace with the dissolution of the old conditions of existence.

When the ancient world was in its last throes, the ancient religions were overcome by Christianity. When Christian ideas succumbed in the 18th century to rationalist ideas, feudal society fought its death battle with the then revolutionary bourgeoisie. The ideas of religious liberty and freedom of conscience merely gave expression to the sway of free competition within the domain of knowledge.

"Undoubtedly," it will be said, "religious, moral, philosophical and juridical ideas have been modified in the course of historical development. But religion, morality, philosophy, political science, and law, constantly survived this change."

"There are, besides, eternal truths, such as Freedom, Justice, etc., that are common to all states of society. But Communism abolishes eternal truths, it abolishes all religion, and all morality, instead of constituting them on a new basis; it therefore acts in contradiction to all past historical experience."

What does this accusation reduce itself to? The history of all past society has consisted in the development of class antagonisms, antagonisms that assumed different forms at different epochs.

But whatever form they may have taken, one fact is common to all past ages, *viz.*, the exploitation of one part of society by the other. No wonder, then, that the social consciousness of past ages, despite all the multiplicity and variety it displays, moves within certain common forms, or general ideas, which cannot completely vanish except with the total disappearance of class antagonisms.

The Communist revolution is the most radical rupture with traditional property relations; no wonder that its development involves the most radical rupture with traditional ideas.

But let us have done with the bourgeois objections to Communism.

We have seen above, that the first step in the revolution by the working class, is to raise the proletariat to the position of ruling class, to win the battle of democracy.

The proletariat will use its political supremacy to wrest, by degrees, all capital from the bourgeoisie, to centralise all instruments of production in the hands of the State, *i.e.*, of the proletariat organised as the ruling class; and to increase the total of productive forces as rapidly as possible.

Of course, in the beginning, this cannot be effected except by means of despotic inroads on the rights of property, and on the conditions of bourgeois production; by means of measures, therefore, which appear economically insufficient and untenable, but which, in the course of the movement, outstrip themselves, necessitate further inroads upon the old social order, and are unavoidable as a means of entirely revolutionising the mode of production.

These measures will of course be different in different countries.

Nevertheless in the most advanced countries, the following will be pretty generally applicable.

1. Abolition of property in land and application of all rents of land to public purposes.
2. A heavy progressive or graduated income tax.
3. Abolition of all right of inheritance.
4. Confiscation of the property of all emigrants and rebels.
5. Centralisation of credit in the hands of the State, by means of a national bank with State capital and an exclusive monopoly.
6. Centralisation of the means of communication and transport in the hands of the State.
7. Extension of factories and instruments of production owned by the State; the bringing into cultivation of waste-lands, and the improvement of the soil generally in accordance with a common plan.
8. Equal liability of all to labour. Establishment of industrial armies, especially for agriculture.
9. Combination of agriculture with manufacturing industries; gradual abolition of the distinction between town and country, by a more equable distribution of the population over the country.
10. Free education for all children in public schools. Abolition of children's factory labour in its present form. Combination of education with industrial production [and so on].

When, in the course of development, class distinctions have disappeared, and all production has been concentrated in the hands of a vast association of the whole nation, the public power will lose its political character. Political power, properly so called, is merely the organised power of one class for oppressing another. If the proletariat during its contest with the bourgeoisie is compelled, by the force of circumstances, to organise itself as a class, if, by means of a revolution, it makes itself the ruling class, and, as such, sweeps away by force the old conditions of production, then it will, along with these conditions, have swept away the conditions for the existence of class antagonisms and of classes generally, and will thereby have abolished its own supremacy as a class.

In place of the old bourgeois society, with its classes and class antagonisms, we shall have an association, in which the free development of each is the condition for the free development of all. . . .

Critique of Social Democracy

In present-day society, the instruments of labour are the monopoly of the capitalist class; the resulting dependence of the working
class is the cause of misery and servitude in all its forms.

This sentence, borrowed from the Statutes of the International, is incorrect in this "improved" edition.

In present-day society the instruments of labour are the monopoly of the landowners (the monopoly of property in land is even the basis of the monopoly of capital) *and* the capitalists. In the passage in question, the Statutes of the International do not mention by name either the one or the other class of monopolists. They speak of the *"monopoly of the means of labour, that is the sources of life."* The addition, *"sources of life"* makes it sufficiently clear that land is included in the instruments of labour.

The correction was introduced because Lassalle, for reasons now generally known, attacked *only* the capitalist class and not the landowners. In England, the capitalist is usually not even the owner of the land on which his factory stands.

The emancipation of labour demands the promotion of the
instruments of labour to the common property of society, and the
co-operative regulation of the total labour with equitable
distribution of the proceeds of labour.

"Promotion of the instruments of labour to the common property" ought obviously to read, their "conversion into the common property," but this only in passing.

What are the "proceeds of labour"? The product of labour or its value? And in the latter case, is it the total value of the product or only that part of the value which labour has newly added to the value of the means of production consumed?

The "proceeds of labour" is a loose notion which Lassalle has put in the place of definite economic conceptions.

What is "equitable distribution"?

Do not the bourgeois assert that the present-day distribution is "equitable"? And is it not, in fact, the only "equitable" distribution on the basis of the present-day mode of production? Are economic relations regulated by legal conceptions or do not, on the contrary, legal relations arise from economic ones? Have not also the socialist sectarians the most varied notions about "equitable" distribution?

To understand what idea is meant in this connection by the phrase "equitable distribution," we must take the first paragraph and this one together. The latter implies a society wherein "the instruments of labour are common property, and the total labour is co-operatively regulated," and from the first paragraph we learn that "the proceeds of labour belong undiminished with equal right to all members of society."

"To all members of society"? To those who do not work as well? What remains then of the "undiminished proceeds of labour"? Only to those members of society who work? What remains then of the "equal right" of all members of society?

But "all members of society" and "equal right" are obviously mere phrases. The kernel consists in this, that in this communist society every worker must receive the "undiminished" Lassallean "proceeds of labour."

Let us take first of all the words "proceeds of labour" in the sense of the product of labour, then the co-operative proceeds of labour are the *total social product.*

From this is then to be deducted:

First, cover for replacement of the means of production used up.

Secondly, additional portion for expansion of production.

Thirdly, reserve or insurance fund to provide against mis-adventures, disturbances through natural events, etc.

These deductions from the "undiminished proceeds of labour" are an economic necessity and their magnitude is to be determined by available means and forces, and partly by calculation of probabilities, but they are in no way calculable by equity.

There remains the other part of the total product, destined to serve as means of consumption.

Before this is divided among the individuals, there has to be deducted from it:

First, the general costs of administration not belonging to production.

This part will, from the outset, be very considerably restricted in comparison with present-day society and it diminishes in proportion as the new society develops.

Secondly, that which is destined for the communal satisfaction of needs, such as schools, health services, etc.

From the outset this part is considerably increased in comparison with present-day society and it increases in proportion as the new society develops.

Thirdly, funds for those unable to work, etc., in short, what is included under so-called official poor relief today.

Only now do we come to the "distribution" which the programme, under Lassallean influence, alone has in view in its narrow fashion, namely that part of the means of consumption which is divided among the individual producers of the co-operative society.

The "undiminished proceeds of labour" have already quietly become converted into the "diminished" proceeds, although what the producer is deprived of in his capacity as a private individual benefits him directly or indirectly in his capacity as a member of society.

Just as the phrase "undiminished proceeds of labour" has disappeared, so now does the phrase "proceeds of labour" disappear altogether.

Within the co-operative society based on common ownership of the means of production, the producers do not exchange their products; just as little does the labour employed on the products appear here *as the value* of these products, as a material quality possessed by them, since now, in contrast to capitalist society, individual labour no longer exists in an indirect fashion but directly as a component part of the total labour. The phrase "proceeds of labour," objectionable even today on account of its ambiguity, thus loses all meaning.

What we have to deal with here is a communist society, not as it has *developed* on its own foundations, but, on the contrary, as it *emerges* from capitalist society; which is thus in every respect, economically, morally and intellectually, still stamped with the birthmarks of the old society from whose womb it emerges. Accordingly the individual producer receives back from society—after the deductions have been made—exactly what he gives to it. What he has given to it is his individual amount of labour. For example, the social working day consists of the sum of the individual labour hours; the individual labour time of the individual producer is the part of the social labour day contributed by him, his share in it. He receives a certificate from society that he has furnished such and such an amount of labour (after deducting his labour for the common fund), and with this certificate he draws from the social stock of means of consumption as much as the same amount of labour costs. The same amount of labour which he has given to society in one form, he receives back in another.

Here obviously the same principle prevails as that which regulates the exchange of commodities, as far as this is exchange of equal values. Content and form are changed, because under the altered circumstances no one can give anything except his labour, and because, on the other hand, nothing can pass into the ownership of individuals except individual means of consumption. But, as far as the distribution of the latter among the individual producers is concerned, the same principle prevails as in the exchange of commodity-equivalents, so much labour in one form is exchanged for an equal amount of labour in another form.

Hence, *equal right* here is still in principle—*bourgeois right*, although principle and practice are no longer in conflict, while the exchange of equivalents in commodity exchange only exists on the *average* and not in the individual case.

In spite of this advance, this *equal right* is still stigmatised by a bourgeois limitation. The right of the producers is *proportional* to the labour they supply; the equality consists in the fact that measurement is made with an *equal standard*, labour.

But one man is superior to another physically or mentally and so supplies more labour in the same time, or can labour for a longer time; and labour, to serve as a measure, must be defined by its duration or intensity, otherwise it ceases to be a standard of measurement. This *equal* right is an unequal right for unequal labour. It recognises no class differences, because everyone is only a worker like everyone else; but it tacitly recognises unequal individual endowment and thus productive capacity as natural privileges. *It is therefore a right of inequality in its content, like every right.* Right by its very nature can only consist in the application of an equal standard; but unequal individuals (and they would not be different individuals if they were not unequal) are only measurable by an equal standard in so far as they are brought under an equal point of view, are taken from one *definite* side only, *e.g.*, in the present case are regarded *only as workers*, and nothing more seen in them, everything else being ignored. Further, one worker is married, another not; one has more children than another and so on and so forth. Thus with an equal output, and hence an equal share in the social consumption fund, one will in fact receive more than another, one will be richer than another, and so on. To avoid all these defects, right, instead of being equal, would have to be unequal.

But these defects are inevitable in the first phase of communist society as it is when it has just emerged after prolonged birth pangs from capitalist society. Right can never be higher than the economic structure of society and the cultural development thereby determined.

In a higher phase of communist society, after the enslaving subordination of individuals under division of labour, and therewith also the antithesis between mental and physical labour, has vanished; after labour, from a mere means of life, has itself become the prime necessity of life; after the productive forces have also increased with the all-round development of the individual, and all the springs of co-operative wealth flow more abundantly—only then can the narrow horizon of bourgeois right be fully left behind and society inscribe on its banners: from each according to his ability, to each according to his needs!

I have dealt more at length with the "undiminished proceeds of labour" on the one hand, and with "equal right" and "equitable distribution" on the other, in order to show what a crime it is to attempt, on the one hand, to force on our party again, as dogmas, ideas which in a certain period had some meaning but have now become obsolete rubbishy phrases, while on the other, perverting the realistic outlook, which has cost so much effort to instill into the party, but which has now taken root in it, by means of ideological nonsense about "right" and other trash common among the democrats and French Socialists.

Quite apart from the analysis so far given, it was in general incorrect to make a fuss about so-called *"distribution"* and put the principal stress on it.

The distribution of the means of consumption at any time is only a consequence of the distribution of the conditions of production themselves. The latter distribution, however, is a feature of the mode of production itself. The capitalist mode of production, for example, rests on the fact that the material conditions of production are in the hands of non-workers in the form of property in capital and land, while the masses are only owners of the personal condition of production, *viz.*, labour power. Once the elements of production are so distributed, then the present-day distribution of the means of consumption results automatically. If the material conditions of production are the co-operative property of the workers themselves, then this likewise results in a different distribution of the means of consumption from the present one. Vulgar socialism (and from it in turn a section of democracy) has taken over from the bourgeois economists the consideration and treatment of distribution as independent of the mode of production and hence the presentation of socialism as turning principally on distribution. After the real position has long been made clear, why go back again?

16
Justice Under Socialism
Edward Nell and Onora O'Neill

> *"From each according to his ability, to each according to his need."*

The stirring slogan that ends *The Critique of the Gotha Program* is generally taken as a capsule summary of the socialist approach to distributing the burdens and benefits of life. It can be seen as the statement of a noble ideal and yet be found wanting on three separate scores. First, there is no guarantee that, even if all contribute according to their abilities, all needs can be met; the principle gives us no guidance for distributing goods when some needs must go unmet. Second, if all contribute according to their abilities, there may be a material surplus after all needs are met; again, the principle gives us no guidance for distributing such a surplus. Third, the principle incorporates no suggestion as to why each man would contribute according to his ability; no incentive structure is evident.

These apparent shortcomings can be compared with those of other principles a society might follow in distributing burdens and benefits. Let us call

1. "From each according to his ability, to each according to his need," the *Socialist Principle of Justice*. Its Capitalist counterpart would be
2. From each according to his choice, given his assets, to each according to his contribution. We shall call this the *Laissez-Faire Principle*.

These two principles will require a good deal of interpretation, but at the outset we can say that in the Socialist Principle of Justice "abilities" and "needs" refer to persons, whereas the "choices" and "contributions" in the Laissez-Faire Principle refer also to the management of impersonal property, the given assets. It goes without saying that some of the "choices," particularly those of the propertyless, are

From "Justice under Socialism," *Dissent* (1972), pp 483–491. Reprinted by permission of the authors and Dissent Publishing Corporation.

normally made under considerable duress. As "choice" is the ideologically favored term, we shall retain it.

In a society where the Socialist Principle of Justice regulates distribution, the requirement is that everyone use such talents as have been developed in him (though this need not entail any allocation of workers to jobs), and the payment of workers is contingent not upon their contributions but upon their needs. In a laissez-faire society, where individuals may be endowed with more or less capital or with bare labor power, they choose in the light of these assets how and how much to work (they may be dropouts or moonlighters), and/or how to invest their capital, and they are paid in proportion.

None of the three objections raised against the Socialist Principle of Justice holds for the Laissez-Faire Principle. Whatever the level of contribution individuals choose, their aggregate product can be distributed in proportion to the contribution—whether of capital or of labor—each individual chooses to make. The Laissez-Faire Principle is applicable under situations both of scarcity and of abundance, and it incorporates a theory of incentives: people choose their level of contribution in order to get a given level of material reward.

Principles 1 and 2 can be crossfertilized, yielding two further principles:

3. From each according to his ability, to each according to his contribution.
4. From each according to his choice, to each according to his need.

Principle 3 could be called an *Incentive Socialist Principle* of distribution. Like the Socialist Principle of Justice, it pictures a society in which all are required to work in proportion to the talents that have been developed in them. Since unearned income is not available and rewards are hinged to contribution rather than need, all work is easily enforced in an economy based on the Incentive Socialist Principle. This principle, however, covers a considerable range of systems. It holds for a Stalinist economy with an authoritarian job allocation. It also holds for a more liberal, market socialist economy in which there is a more or less free labor market, though without an option to drop out or live on unearned income, or the freedom to choose the level and type of qualification one is prepared to acquire. The Incentive Socialist Principle rewards workers according to their contribution: it is a principle of distribution in which an incentive system—reliance on material rewards—is explicit. Marx believed this principle would have to be followed in the early stages of socialism, in a society "still stamped with the birthmarks of the old society."

Under the Incentive Socialist Principle, each worker receives back the value of the amount of work he contributes to society in one form or another. According to Marx, this is a form of bourgeois right that "tacitly recognizes unequal individual endowments, and thus natural privileges in respect of productive capacity." So this principle holds for a still deficient society where the needs of particular workers, which depend on many things other than their productive capacity, may not be met. Although it may be less desirable than the Socialist Principle of Justice, the Incentive Socialist Principle clearly meets certain criteria the Socialist Principle of Justice cannot meet. It provides a principle of allocation that can be applied equally well to the various situations of scarcity, sufficiency, and abundance. Its material incentive structure explains how under market socialism, given a capital structure and a skill structure, workers will choose jobs and work hard at them—and also why under a Stalinist economy workers will work hard at jobs to which they have been allocated.

Under the Incentive Socialist Principle, workers—whether assigned to menial work or to specific jobs—respond to incentives of the same sort as do workers under the Laissez-Faire Principle. The difference is that, while the Laissez-Faire Principle leaves the measurement of the contribution of a worker to be determined by the level of wage he is offered, the Incentive Socialist Principle relies on a bureaucratically determined weighting that takes into account such factors as the difficulty, duration, qualification level, and risk involved in a given job.

There is another difference between societies living under the Laissez-Faire Principle and those following the Incentive Socialist Principle. Under the Laissez-Faire Principle, there is no central coordination of decisions, for assets are managed according to the choices of their owners. This gives rise to the well-known problems of instability and unemployment. Under the Incentive Socialist Principle, assets are managed by the central government; hence one would expect instability to be eliminated and full employment guaranteed. However, we do not regard this difference as a matter of principle on the same level with others we are discussing. Moreover, in practice some recognizable capitalist societies have managed to control fluctuations without undermining the Laissez-Faire Principle as the principle of distribution.

Let us call Principle 4 the *Utopian Principle of Justice*. It postulates a society without any requirement of contribution or material incentives, but with guaranteed minimal consumption. This principle suffers from the same defect as the Socialist Principle of Justice: it does not determine distributions of benefits under conditions either of scarcity or of abundance, and it suggests no incentive structure to explain why enough should be contributed to its economy to make it possible to satisfy needs. Whether labor is contributed according to choice or according to ability, it is conceivable that the aggregate social product should be such that either some needs cannot be met or that, when all needs are met, a surplus remains that cannot be divided on the basis of needs.

On the surface, this Utopian Principle of Justice exudes the aroma of laissez-faire: though needs will not go unmet in utopia, contributions will be made for no more basic reason than individual whim. They are tied neither to the reliable effects of the incentive of material reward for oneself, nor to those of the noble ideal of filling the needs of others, nor to a conception of duty or self-sacrifice. Instead, contributions will come forth, if they do, according to the free and unconstrained choices of individual economic agents, on the basis of their given preferences. Preferences, however, are not "given"; they develop and change, are learned and unlearned, and follow fashions and fads. Whim, fancy, pleasure, desire, wish are all words suggesting this aspect of consumer choice. By tying the demand for products to needs and the supply of work to choice, the Utopian Principle of Justice ensures stability in the former but does not legislate against fluctuations and unpredictable variability in the latter.

So the Socialist Principle of Justice and the Utopian Principle of Justice suffer from a common defect. There is no reason to suppose these systems will operate at precisely the level at which aggregate output is sufficient to meet all needs without surplus. And since people do not need an income in money terms but rather an actual and quite precisely defined list of food, clothing, housing, etc. (bearing in mind the various alternatives that might be substituted), the aggregate measured in value terms could be right, yet the *composition* might still be unable to meet all the people's needs. People might choose or have the ability to do the right amount of work, but on the wrong projects. One could even imagine the economy growing from a situation of scarcity to one of abundance without ever passing through any point at which its aggregate output could be distributed to meet precisely the needs of its population.

So far, we have been considering not the justification or desirability of alternative principles of distribution, but their practicality. It appears that, in this respect, principles hinging reward on contribution rather than on need have a great advantage. They can both provide a general principle of distribution and indicate the pattern of incentives to which workers will respond.

It might be held that these advantages are restricted to the Incentive Socialist Principle in its various versions, since under the Laissez-Faire Principle there is some income—property income—which is not being paid in virtue of any contribution. This problem can be dealt with either, as we indicated above, by interpreting the notion of contribution to cover the contribution of one's assets to the capital market, or by restricting the scope of the Laissez-Faire Principle to cover workers only, or by interpreting the notion of property income so as to regard wages as a return to property, i.e., property in one's labor power. One can say that under capitalism part of the aggregate product is set aside for the owners of capital (and another part, as under market socialism, for government expenditure) and the remainder is distributed according to the Laissez-Faire Principle. Or one may say that property income is paid in virtue of past contributions, whose reward was not consumed at the time it was earned but was stored. Apologists tend to favor interpretations that make the worker a sort of capitalist or the capitalist a sort of slow-consuming worker. Whichever line is taken, it is clear that the Laissez-Faire Principle—however undesirable we may find it—is a principle of distribution that can be of general use in two senses. Appropriately interpreted, it covers the distribution of earned and of unearned income, and it applies in situations both of scarcity and of abundance.

So we seem to have reached the paradoxical conclusion that the principle of distribution requiring that workers' needs be met is of no use in situations of need, since it does not assign priorities among needs, and that the principle demanding that each contribute according to his ability is unable to explain what incentives will lead him to do so. In this view, the Socialist Principle of Justice would have to be regarded as possibly noble but certainly unworkable.

The Socialist Principle Defended

But this view should not be accepted. Marx formulated the Socialist Principle of Justice on the basis of a conception of human abilities and needs that will yield some guidance to its interpretation. We shall now try to see whether the difficulties discussed above can be alleviated when we consider this principle in the light of Marxian theory.

Marx clearly thought that the Socialist Principle of Justice was peculiarly relevant to situations of abundance. In the last section we argued that, on the contrary, it was an adequate principle of distribution only when aggregate output exactly covered total needs. The source of this discrepancy lies in differing analyses of human needs.

By fulfillment of needs we understood at least a subsistence income. Needs are not met when a person lacks sufficient food, clothing, shelter, medical care, or socially necessary training/education. But beyond this biological and social minimum we can point to another set of needs, which men do not have qua men but acquire qua producers. Workers need not merely a biological and social minimum, but whatever other goods—be they holidays or contacts with others whose work bears on theirs or guaranteed leisure, which they need to perform their jobs as well as possible. So a principle of distribution according to needs will not be of use only to a subsistence-level economy. Very considerable goods over and above those necessary for biological subsistence can be distributed according to a principle of need.

But despite this extension of the concept of need the Socialist Principle of Justice still seems to face the three problems listed [earlier]:

1. What guarantees are there that even under abundance the *composition of the output*, with all contributing according to their abilities, will suffice to fill all needs? (There may still be scarcities of goods needed to fill either biological or job-related needs.)
2. What principle can serve to distribute goods that are surplus both to biological and to job-related needs?
3. What system of incentives explains why each will contribute to the full measure of his abilities, though he is not materially rewarded for increments of effort? Whether or not there is authoritative job allocation, job performance cannot be guaranteed.

Marx's solution to these problems does not seem too explicit. But much is suggested by the passage at the end of the *Critique of the Gotha Program* where he describes the higher phase of communist society as one in which "labor is no longer merely a means of life but has become life's principal need."

To most people it sounds almost comic to claim that labor could become life's principal need: it suggests a society of compulsive workers. Labor in the common view is intrinsically undesirable, but undertaken as a means to some further, typically material, end. For Marx this popular view would have been confirmation of his own view of the degree to which most labor under capitalism is alienating. He thought that under capitalism laborers experienced a threefold alienation: alienation from the *product* of their labor, which is for them merely a means to material reward; alienation from the *process* of labor, which is experienced as forced labor rather than as desirable activity; and alienation from *others*, since activities undertaken with others are undertaken as a means to achieving further ends, which are normally scarce and allocated competitively. Laborers cooperate in production but, under capitalism, compete for job and income, and the competition overrides the cooperation. Hence Marx claims (in the *Economic and Philosophical Manuscripts*) that "life itself appears only as a means to life." Though the horror of that situation is apparent in the very words, many people accept that labor should be only a means to life—whose real ends lie elsewhere; whether in religion, consumption, personal relations, or leisure.

Marx, on the other hand, held that labor could be more than a means; it could also be an end of life, for labor in itself—*the activity*—can, like other activities, be something for whose sake one does other things. We would be loath to think that activity itself should appear only as a means to life—on the contrary, life's worth for most people lies in the activities undertaken. Those we call labor do not differ intrinsically from the rest, only in relation to the system of production. In Marx's view a system was possible in which all activities undertaken would be nonalienating. Nobody would have to compete to engage in an activity he found unpleasant for the sake of a material reward. Instead, workers would cooperate in creative and fulfilling activities that provide occasions for the exercise of talents, for taking responsibilities, and that result in useful or beautiful products. In such a situation one can see why labor would be regarded as life's greatest need, rather than as its scourge. Nonalienated labor is humanly fulfilling activity.

In the course of switching from the conception of alienating labor to that of nonalienating labor, it might seem that we have moved into a realm for which principles of distribution may be irrelevant. What can the Socialist Principle of Justice tell us about the distribution of burdens and benefits in "the higher phase of Communist society"?

In such a society each is to contribute according to his abilities. In the light of the discussion of nonalienated labor, it is clear that there is no problem of incentives. Each man works at what he wants to work at. He works because that is his need. (This is not a situation in which "moral incentives" have replaced material ones, for both moral and material incentives are based on alienating labor. The situation Marx envisages is one for which incentives of *all* sorts are irrelevant.)

Though this disposes of the problem of incentives under the Socialist Principle of Justice, it is much less clear whether this principle can work for a reasonable range of situations. Can it cope with both the situation of abundance and that of scarcity?

In the case of abundance, a surplus of goods over and above those needed is provided. But if all activities are need-fulfilling, then no work is done that does not fulfill some need. In a sense there is no surplus to be distributed, for nothing needless is being done. Nevertheless, there may be a surplus of material goods that are the by-product of need-fulfilling activity. In a society where everybody fulfills himself by painting pictures, there may be a vast surplus of pictures. If so, the Socialist Principle of Justice gives no indication of the right method for their distribution; they are not the goal for which the task was undertaken. Since they do not fulfill an objective need, the method for their distribution is not important. In this the higher phase of communist society is, as one might expect, the very antithesis of consumerism; rather than fabricate reasons for desiring and so acquiring what is not needed, it disregards anything that is not needed in decisions of distribution.

There, nevertheless, is a problem of distribution the Socialist Principle of Justice does not attempt to solve. Some of the products of need-fulfilling activity may be things other people either desire or detest. When need-fulfilling activity yields works of art or noisy block parties, its distribution cannot be disregarded. Not all planning problems can be solved by the Socialist Principle of Justice. We shall not discuss the merits of various principles that could serve to handle these cases, but shall only try to delimit the scope of the Socialist Principle of Justice.

This brings us to the problem of scarcity. Can the Socialist Principle of Justice explain why, when all contribute to the extent of their abilities, all needs can be met? Isn't it conceivable that everyone should find fulfillment in painting, but nobody find fulfillment in producing either biological necessities or the canvases, brushes, and paints everybody wants to use? Might not incentive payments be needed, even in this higher phase of communist society, to guarantee the production of subsistence goods and job-related necessities? In short, will not any viable system involve some alienating labor?

Marx at any rate guarantees that communism need not involve much alienating labor. He insists that the Socialist Principle of Justice is applicable only in a context of abundance. For only when man's needs can be met is it relevant to insist that they ought to be met. The Socialist Principle of Justice comes into its own only with the development of the forces of production. But, of course, higher productivity does not by itself guarantee the right composition of output. Subsistence goods and job-related services and products might not be provided as the population fulfills itself in painting, poetry, and sculpture. Man cannot live by works of art alone.

This socialist version of the story of Midas should not alarm us too much. The possibility of starvation amidst abundant art works seemed plausible only because we abstracted it from other features of an abundant socialist society. Such a society is a planned society, and part of its planning concerns the ability structure of the population. Such a society would include people able to perform all tasks necessary to maintain a high level of material well-being.

Nevertheless, there may be certain essential tasks in such a society whose performance is not need-fulfilling for anybody. Their allocation presents another planning problem for which the Socialist Principle of Justice, by hypothesis, is not a solution. But the degree of coercion need not be very great. In a highly productive society the amount of labor expended on nonfulfilling tasks is a diminishing proportion of total labor time. Hence, given equitable allocation of this burden (and it is here that the planning decisions are really made), nobody would be prevented from engaging principally in need-fulfilling activities. In the limiting case of abundance, where automation of the production of material needs is complete, nobody would have to do any task he did not find intrinsically worthwhile. To the extent that this abundance is not reached, the Socialist Principle of Justice cannot be fully implemented.

However, the degree of coercion experienced by those who are allocated to necessary but nonfulfilling chores may be reducible if the planning procedure is of a certain sort. To the extent that people participate in planning and that they realize the necessity of the nonfulfilling chores in order for everyone to be able to do also what he finds need-fulfilling, they may find the performance of these chores less burdensome. As they want to achieve the ends, so—once they are informed—they cannot rationally resent the means, provided they perceive the distribution of chores as just.

The point can be taken a step further. Under the Socialist Principle of Justice, households do not put forth productive effort to be rewarded with an aliquot portion of time and means for self-fulfillment. It is precisely this market mentality from which we wish to escape. The miserable toil of society should be

> performed gratis for the benefit of society . . . performed not as a definite duty, not for the purpose of obtaining a right to certain products, not according to previously established and legally fixed quotas, but voluntary labor . . . performed because it has become a habit to work for the common good, and because of a conscious realization (that has become a habit) of the necessity of working for the common good. [V. I. Lenin, "From the Destruction of the Old Social System to the Creation of the New," April 11, 1920. From *Collected Works*, English trans., 40 vols. (London: Lawrence & Wishart, 1965), vol. 30, p. 517.]

Creative work should be done for its own sake, not for any reward. Drudgery should be done for the common good, not in order to be rewarded with opportunity and means for creative work. Of course, the better and more efficient the performance of drudgery, the more will be the opportunities for creative work. To realize this, however, is to understand the necessity of working for the common good, not to be animated by private material incentives. For the possibilities of creative work are opened by the simultaneous and parallel development of large numbers of people. To take the arts, poets need a public, authors readers, performers audiences, and all need (though few want) critics. One cannot sensibly wish, under the Socialist Principle of Justice, to be rewarded *privately* with opportunities and means for nonalienated work.

There is a question regarding the distribution of educational opportunities. Before men can contribute according to their abilities, their abilities must be developed. But in whom should society develop which abilities? If we regard education as consumption, then according to the Socialist Principle of Justice, each should receive it according to his need.

It is clear that all men require some early training to make them viable social beings; further, all men require certain general skills necessary for performing work. But we could hardly claim that some men need to be doctors or economists or lawyers, or need to receive any other specialized or expensive training. If, on the other hand, we regard education as production of those skills necessary for maintaining society and providing the possibility of fulfillment, then the Socialist Principle of Justice can determine a lower bound to the production of certain skills: so-and-so many farmers/doctors/mechanics must be produced to satisfy future subsistence and job-related needs. But the Socialist Principle of Justice cannot determine who shall get which of these educational opportunities. One traditional answer might be that each person should specialize at whatever he is relatively best suited to do. Yet this only makes sense in terms of tasks done as onerous means to desirable ends. Specialization on the basis of comparative advantage minimizes the effort in achieving given ends; but if work is itself fulfilling, it is not an "effort" that must be minimized.

In conditions of abundance, it is unlikely that anyone will be denied training they want and can absorb, though they may have to acquire skills they do not particularly want, since some onerous tasks may still have to be done. For even in conditions of abundance, it may be necessary to compel some or all to undertake certain unwanted training in the interests of the whole. But it is not necessary to supplement the Socialist Principle of Justice with an incentive scheme, whether material or moral. The principle already contains the Kantian maxim: develop your talents to the utmost, for only in this way can a person contribute to the limits of his ability. And if a society wills the end of self-fulfillment, it must will sufficient means. If the members of society take part in planning to maintain and expand the opportunities for everyone's nonalienated activity, they must understand the necessity of allocating the onerous tasks, and so the training for them.

Perhaps we can make our point clearer by looking briefly at Marx's schematic conception of the stages of modern history—feudalism, capitalism, socialism, communism—where each stage is characterized by a higher productivity of labor than the preceding stage. In feudalism, the principle of distribution would be:

5. From each according to his status, to each according to his status—the Feudal Principle of Justice.

There is no connection between work and reward. There are no market incentives in the "ideal" feudal system. Peasants grow the stuff for their own subsistence and perform traditional labor services for their lord on domain land. He in turn provides protection and government in traditional fashion. Yet, though labor is not performed as a means to a distant or abstract end, as when it is done for money, it still is done for survival, not for its own sake, and those who do it are powerless to control their conditions of work or their own destinies. Man lives on the edge of famine and is subject to the vagaries of the weather and the dominion of tradition. Only a massive increase in productive powers frees him. But to engender this increase men must come to connect work directly with reward. This provides the incentive to labor, both to take those jobs most needed (moving from the farm to the factory) and to work sufficiently hard once on the job.

But more than work is needed; the surplus of output over that needed to maintain the work force (including managers) and replace and repair the means of production (machines, raw materials) must be put to productive use; it must be reinvested, not consumed. In capitalism, station at birth determines whether one works or owns capital; workers are rewarded for their contribution of work, capitalists for theirs of reinvestment. There is a stick as well as a carrot. Those workers who do not work, starve; those capitalists who fail to reinvest, fail to grow and will eventually be crushed by their larger rivals. Socialism rationalizes this by eliminating the two-class dichotomy and by making reinvestment a function of the institutions of the state, so that the capital structure of the society is the collective property of the citizenry, all of whom must work for reward. In this system the connection between work and reward reaches its fullest development, and labor in one sense is most fully alienated. The transition to communism then breaks this link altogether.

The link between work and rewards serves a historical purpose; namely, to encourage the development of the productive forces. But as the productive forces continue to develop, the demand for additional rewards will tend to decline, while the difficulty of stimulating still further growth in productivity may increase. This, at least, seems to be implied by the principles of conventional economics—diminishing marginal utility and diminishing marginal productivity. Even if one rejects most of the conventional wisdom of economics, a good case can be made for the diminishing efficacy of material incentives as prosperity increases. For as labor productivity rises, private consumption needs will be met, and the most urgent needs remaining will be those requiring *collective* consumption—and, indeed, some of these needs will be generated by the process of growth and technical progress. These last needs, if left unmet, may hinder further attempts to raise the productive power of labor. So the system of material incentives could in principle come to a point where the weakened encouragements to extra productivity offered as private reward for contribution might be offset by the accumulated hindrances generated by the failures to meet collective needs and by the wastes involved in competition. At this point, it becomes appropriate to break the link between work and reward. Breaking the link, however, is not enough. Both the Socialist Principle of Justice and the Utopian Principle of Justice break the link between work and reward. But the Utopian Principle of Justice leaves the distinction between them. Work is a means, the products of work are the ends. Given a high productivity of labor, workers would in principle choose their occupations and work-leisure patterns, yet still producing enough to satisfy everyone's needs. This would be a society devoted to minimizing effort, a sort of high-technology Polynesia. Since it neither makes consumption dependent upon work nor regards work as other than a regrettable means to consumption, it fails to explain why sufficient work to supply basic needs should ever be done. The alienation of labor cannot be overcome by eliminating labor rather than alienation.

Breaking the link between work and reward, while leaving the distinction itself intact, may also lead to the loss of the productive powers of labor. For without reward, and when the object is to work as little as possible, why expend the effort to acquire highly complex skills? What is the motive to education, self-improvement, self-development? A high-technology Polynesia contains an inner contradiction.

By contrast, the Socialist Principle of Justice not only does not make reward depend upon work but denies that there is a distinction between the two. Because man needs fulfilling activity—work that he chooses and wants—men who get it contribute according to their ability.

Yet there still may remain routine and menial, unfulfilling jobs. But who wills the end wills the means. The society must plan to have such jobs done. No doubt many will be mechanized or automated, but the remaining ones will form a burden that must be allocated.

The Socialist Principle of Justice cannot solve this problem of allocation. But everyone has some interest in getting uncoveted but essential work done. Hence it should not be difficult to find an acceptable supplementary principle of distribution for allocating these chores. For instance, the Principle of Comparative Advantage might be introduced to assign each the drudgery at which he is relatively best. There can be no quarrel with this so long as such alienating work is only a small fraction of a man's total activity, conferring no special status. It is only when alienating work takes up the bulk of one's waking hours, and determines status, that specialization inevitably entails some form of class structure.

The Socialist Principle of Justice cannot solve all allocation problems. But once one understands that it is based on a denial of a distinction between work, need, and reward, it is clear that it can solve an enormous range of such problems. In a highly productive society the only allocation problems the Socialist Principle of Justice cannot solve are the distribution of unmechanized and uncoveted chores and of the material by-products of creative endeavor.

17

Socialism and Equality

Steven Lukes

> . . . there is now, with the existence of a large amount
> of sociological research on inequality of opportunity and
> inequality of result, and with the resurgence of interest
> among moral philosophers in inequality, as manifested in
> John Rawls's work, the possibility of serious examination
> of social ideals and social reality in this area.
>
> —James S. Coleman[1]

In assessing the contemporary viability of the socialist idea, three questions demand to be faced: first, why is "greater equality in the conditions of life", desirable?[2] Second, how unequal are such conditions in contemporary industrial societies, capitalist and state socialist, and what explains these inequalities? And third, are these inequalities ineradicable, or eradicable only at an unacceptable cost? Clearly, I cannot begin to answer these momentous questions here. What I shall try to do is to offer some suggestions as to how they might be answered. Concerning the first (philosophical) question, I shall seek to suggest a modified Kantian ethical basis for the social, political, and economic equalities socialists have traditionally sought to establish. As for the second (sociological) question, I shall briefly sketch some of the evidence about actual inequalities and the range of explanations for them. And with regard to the third question I shall briefly consider a number of arguments for the inevitability of inequality. Having done these things, it will be clear to even the most sympathetic reader that everything remains to be done.

From "Socialism and Equality," *Dissent* (1975), pp. 154–168. Reprinted by permission of Dissent Publishing Corporation and A D Peters & Co. Ltd.

[1]James S. Coleman, "Equality of Opportunity and Equality of Results," *Harvard Educational Review*, 43 (February 1973), p. 137.

[2]Though equality is an objective central to socialism, socialists have not, in general, been very explicit about its content or the values on which it rests. I have (perhaps surprisingly) found the ideas of certain English egalitarians and socialists (Arnold, Morris, Tawney, Cole, Orwell) especially helpful.

The Social Ideals of Equality

The Ideal of Equality has been made to seem absurd in either of two opposing ways. It has been interpreted as based either on the principle of absolute and unconditional equality—"treat everyone equally in every respect"—or else on the empty formal principle, "treat people equally unless there are relevant or sufficient reasons for treating them unequally." In fact, few serious thinkers, let alone socialists, have advocated the former[3] and all the interesting forms of egalitarianism have put content into the latter in two ways: negatively, by ruling out certain sorts of reasons as justifications for treating people unequally; and positively, by advancing, or presupposing, a set of reasons for treating them equally. Historically, the fight for equality has taken the form of attacking specific inequalities and their alleged justifications: inequalities of privilege and power—legal and political, then social and economic—have been attacked as unjustifiable, because arbitrary, capricious, or irrational. For example, it has been suggested that inequalities are unjustifiable unless they can be shown to satisfy one or more of the following criteria: (1) merit or deserts; (2) need; (3) social benefit (and on such a basis it would be hard to justify the present extreme inequality of inherited wealth in Britain).[4] But, quite apart from the difficulty of interpreting these criteria, especially the last, such an approach always presupposes a view of what is justifiable, that is, what are relevant and sufficient sorts of reasons for unequal treatment, and over this individuals, classes, and cultures conflict. What, then, of the positive way?

One influential argument for treating people equally—and in particular for according them equal income and wealth—is the utilitarian argument for attaining the maximum aggregate satisfaction, on the assumption of diminishing marginal utility: as Dalton put it, an "unequal distribution of a given amount of purchasing power among a given number of people is . . . likely to be a wasteful distribution from the point of view of economic welfare."[5] In their recent important study of inequality, Christopher Jencks and his associates state their position as follows:

> We begin with the premise that every individual's happiness is of equal value. From this it is a short step to Bentham's dictum that society should be organized so as to provide the greatest good for the greatest number. In addition, we assume that the law of

[3]Babeuf came perhaps the nearest to doing so, proclaiming, "Let there be no other difference between people than that of age or sex. Since all have the same needs and the same faculties, let them henceforth have the same education and the same diet. They are content with the same sun and the same air for all; why should not the same portion and the same quality of nourishment suffice for each of them?" *Manifeste des égaux* [1796] in M. Leroy, ed., *Les Précurseurs français du socialisme de Condorcet à Proudhon* (Paris: Editions du temps présent, 1948), pp. 67–68 (trans. S. Lukes).

[4]See A. B. Atkinson, *Unequal Shares: Wealth in Britain* (London: Allen Lane and Penguin, 1972), pp. 80 ff.

[5]H. Dalton, *Some Aspects of Inequality of Incomes in Modern Communities* (London: Routledge, 1925), cited in *ibid.*, p. 84.

diminishing returns applies to most of the good things in life. In economic terms this means that people with low incomes value extra income more than people with high incomes. It follows that if we want to maximize the satisfaction of the population, the best way to divide any given amount of money is to make everyone's income the same. Income disparities (except those based on variations in "need") will always reduce overall satisfaction, because individuals with low incomes will lose more than individuals with high incomes gain.[6]

But this assumption is questionable. Why assume that a given amount of purchasing power yields equal utility for everyone (assuming one could make the interpersonal comparison), and why assume that it diminishes as income or wealth increases?

In any case, egalitarians and socialists have not rested their case on this precarious basis alone: there is an alternative tradition of thought on the subject, of which Rousseau is the classical figure and Rawls the major contemporary exponent, which offers an alternative interpretation of equality and which appeals to deeper values than the utilitarian. This interpretation may be called the principle of equality of consideration or respect. In this view, all human beings have certain basic features that entitle them to be considered or respected as equals, and this is seen as implying practical policies for implementing substantial political, social, and economic equality.[7]

What, then, are the basic features of human beings that command equal consideration or respect? For Christians the answer is that they are all children of God, for Kant that they are rational wills and thus members of the Kingdom of Ends, for classical liberals that they share "common rights to which they are called by nature,"[8] for many socialists and anarchists that they share a "common humanity." These are all transcendental answers, whether religious or secular. Others speak of man's "inherent dignity," "intrinsic or infinite value," or "human worth."

But in all these cases, no *independent* reasons are given for respecting people equally—or at least none that would convince a skeptic disposed to do so unequally, according to, say, birth or merit. But it is arguable that there are a number of empirical features that could provide such reasons, to which, throughout their history, egalitarian doctrines have, implicitly or explicitly, appealed. On the one hand, there are basic human needs—minimally, the means to life and health—without which they could not function in a recognizably human manner. On the other hand, there are certain basic capacities (of which more below), characteristic of human beings, whose realization is essential to their enjoyment of freedom. It may be objected that, since people have these needs and capacities to different degrees, they are therefore worthy of unequal respect. But to this it may be replied that it is

---

[6]Christopher Jencks *et al.*, *Inequality: A Reassessment of the Effects of Family and Schooling in America* (London: Allen Lane, Penguin, 1974), pp. 9–10.

[7]The argument that follows, spelling out the principle of equal respect, is taken from the present author's *Individualism* (Oxford: Blackwell, 1973), Part III.

[8]Condorcet, *Sketch for the Progress of the Human Mind* [1793], transl. June Barraclough (London: Weidenfeld & Nicolson, 1955), p. 184.

the existence of the needs and capacities, not the degree to which the former are met and the latter realized or realizable, that elicits the respect, and that respecting persons precisely consists in doing all that is necessary and possible to satisfy their basic needs and to maintain and enhance their basic capacities (and to discriminate between them in this regard is to fail to show them equal respect).

The principle of equal respect for needs tells against all humanly alterable economic and social arrangements that discriminate between individuals' access to the means of sustenance and health (and it is not irrelevant in contemporary Britain, where there are still marked class differences in the risks of death and infant mortality). But "need" is a concept to which appeal cannot be made beyond this basic (if rising) minimum level: beyond that point, it becomes a question of individuals' entitlement to the means of realizing certain basic capacities. Three such capacities appear to be of particular significance.

There is, first, the capacity of human beings to form intentions and purposes, to become aware of alternatives and choose between them, and to acquire control over their own behavior by becoming conscious of the forces determining it, both internally, as with unconscious desires and motives, and externally, as with the pressures exerted by the norms they follow or the roles they fill. In other words, human beings have the capacity to act with relative autonomy and to be or become relatively self-determining, to become conscious of the forces determining or affecting them, and either consciously to submit to them or become independent of them. Obviously, not all exercise this capacity to an equal degree, but all, except the mentally defective or deranged, possess it.

Second, human beings have the capacity to think thoughts, perform actions, develop involvements, and engage in relationships to which they attach value but which require a certain area of noninterference in order to have that value. Enjoyments and delights of all kinds, intellectual and artistic activities, love and friendship are examples: all these require a space free and secure from external invasion or surveillance in order to flourish. There is, of course, considerable room for differences about which of these activities and relationships are of most value, and about what kind of value they have, and indeed about which of them people should be left alone to engage in. But what seems indisputable is that there is a range of such activities and relationships, in some of which all persons have the capacity to engage and to which they attach value.

Third, human beings have the capacity for self-development. By this I mean that everyone has the capacity to develop in himself some characteristic human excellence or excellences—whether intellectual, aesthetic or moral, theoretical or practical, personal or public, and so on. Obviously, not everyone will be able to develop any given excellence to the same degree—and perhaps, pace Marx, not all will be able to develop them in a many-sided, all-round fashion. But all human beings share the capacity to realize potentialities that are worthy of admiration. What counts as worthy of admiration will be subject to moral disagreement and cultural variation, but it is arguable that there is a delimited range of human excellences that are intrinsically admirable, though the forms they take differ from society to society, and that all human beings are capable of achieving some of them to some degree.

I have argued that these three characteristics of persons are at least part of the ground on which we accord them respect. What, then, does that respect consist of? The unsurprising answer is that, whatever else it involves, respecting them involves treating them as (actually or potentially) autonomous, as requiring a free and secure space for the pursuit of valued activities and relationships, and as capable of self-development. That answer has, given certain further assumptions, far-reaching social, economic, and political implications, and points toward a society with substantially reduced inequalities, both of material and symbolic rewards and of political power.

What, we may ask, constitutes a denial of such respect? We fail to respect someone by denying his autonomy, not only when we control or dominate his will, but also when we unreasonably restrict the range of alternatives between which he can choose. Such control and restriction is as likely to be social and economic as political, and as typical of the work situation and the family and of opportunities for education and employment as of the relation between the state and the citizen. In this sense, Tawney saw a central aim of "measures correcting inequalities or neutralizing their effects" as increasing "the range of alternatives open to ordinary men, and the capacity of the latter to follow their own preferences in choosing between them."[9]

But we also cease to respect someone when we fail to treat him as an agent and a chooser, as a self from which actions and choices emanate, when we see him and consequently treat him, not as a person, but as merely the bearer of a title or the occupant of a role, or as merely a means to securing a certain end, or, worst of all, as merely an object. We deny his status as an autonomous person to the extent that we allow our attitudes to him to be dictated solely by some contingent and socially defined attribute of him, such as his "merit" or success or occupational role or place in the social order—or what Tawney called "the tedious vulgarities of income and social position."[10] This denial of autonomy was what William Godwin had in mind when he urged universal and equal political participation on the grounds that "each man will thus be inspired with a consciousness of his own importance, and the slavish feelings that shrink up the soul in the presence of an imagined superior will be unknown."[11] It is what William Morris meant when he wrote of socialism as a "condition of equality" in which a man "would no longer take his position as the dweller in such and such a place, or the filler of such and such an office, or (as now) the owner of such and such property, but as being such and such a man."[12] It is what Tawney intended when he wrote of an egalitarian society as one in which "money and position count for less, and the quality of human personalities for more,"[13] and what George Orwell was thinking of when he wrote of "breathing the air of equality" in revolutionary Spain, with "no boss-class, no menial-class, no beggars, no

[9]R. H. Tawney, *Equality*, 4th edition, 1952 (London: Allen & Unwin, 1931), p. 260.
[10]*Ibid.*, p. 153.
[11]William Godwin, *Enquiry Concerning Political Justice and its influence on Morals and Happiness* [1793], 3rd edition, vol. 1 (London, 1798), pp. 214–15.
[12]William Morris, *Letters on Socialism* [1888] (privately printed, London, 1894), Letter I, p. 5.
[13]*Op. cit.*, p. 254.

prostitutes, no lawyers, no priests, no boot-licking, no cap-touching."[14] Respecting persons in this way, as Bernard Williams has well put it, implies that they be "abstracted from certain conspicuous structures of inequality" in which they are found and seen, "not merely under professional, social, or technical titles, but with consideration of their own views and purposes," as "conscious beings who necessarily have intentions and purposes and see what they are doing in a certain light."[15]

But more is involved in respecting autonomy than looking behind the surface of socially defined titles or labels and seeing the world (and the labels) from the agent's point of view. Social existence in part determines consciousness; and the most insidious and decisive way of denying the autonomy of persons is to diminish or restrict their opportunity to increase their consciousness of their situation and activities. It is for this reason that respecting autonomy points toward a "single-status society" and away from the ideal of a stable hierarchy, since

> what keeps stable hierarchies together is the idea of necessity, that it is somehow foreordained or inevitable that there should be these orders; and this idea of necessity must be eventually undermined by the growth of people's reflective consciousness about their role, still more when it is combined with the thought that what they and others have always thought about their roles in the social system was the product of the social system itself.[16]

Second, one manifestly fails to respect someone if one invades his private space and interferes, without good reason, with his valued activities and relationships (and above all with his inner self). Examples of where it can be justifiable so to interfere are in cases, say, of imprisonment or conscription during wartime—where it may be claimed that there is "good reason" for interference and thus no denial of respect insofar as they are necessary infringements of a person's freedom, either to preserve the freedom of others, or his own and others' in the long run, or as the only way of realizing other cherished values. But, in the absence of these justifications, such an invasion or interference is clearly a denial of human respect. It is easy to think of extreme forms of such a denial, as in the prison camps described by Solzhenitsyn or in the total institutions described by Erving Goffman. But less extreme forms result from inequalities of power and privilege in all contemporary societies. Liberals characteristically attack such invasions of liberty, especially in nonliberal societies, when they take the form of political authoritarianism, bureaucratic tyranny, social pressures to conformity, religious and racial discrimination. But interference with valued activities and relationships occurs in other ways to which liberals are less sensitive—through class discrimination,

[14]George Orwell, *Homage to Catalonia* (London: Secker & Warburg, 1938, and Penguin, 1962) p. 66.

[15]Bernard Williams, "The Idea of Equality" in P. Laslett and W. G. Runciman, eds., *Philosophy, Politics and Society: Second Series* (Oxford: Blackwell, 1962), pp. 117, 118.

[16]Ibid., pp. 119-20.

remediable economic deprivation and insecurity, and what Hayek has called the "hard discipline of the market,"[17] where nominally equal economic and social rights are unequally operative because of unequal but equalizable conditions and opportunities.

Finally, one also importantly fails to respect someone if one limits or restricts his opportunities to realize his capacities of self-development. It is the systematic and cumulative denial of such opportunities to the less favored citizens of stratified societies, both capitalist and state socialist, that constitutes perhaps the strongest argument against the structured inequalities they exhibit. That argument really has two parts.

The first part is simply an argument against discrimination, against the failure to "bring the means of a good life within the reach of all."[18] Thus the principal argument against a discriminatory educational system is not that it creates social inequality (which, as Jencks shows, it scarcely does, serving, "primarily to legitimize inequality, not to create it,"[19]) but rather that it blocks the self-development of the less favored and thereby fails to respect them. Again, where it is possible to make certain types of work more challenging and require a greater development of skill or talent or responsibility, it is a denial of human respect to confine workers within menial, one-sided, and tedious tasks. Furthermore, workers—and citizens of political society as a whole—are denied respect to the degree to which they are denied possibilities of real participation in the formulation and taking of major decisions affecting them, for they are thereby denied the opportunity to develop the human excellence of active self-government celebrated by Rousseau and John Stuart Mill and central to the various forms of classical democratic theory.

The second part of this argument against structured inequalities is that they provide an unfavorable climate for the self-development of ordinary people. The assumption that this is so was well expressed by Matthew Arnold, who claimed that for

> the common bulk of mankind . . . to live in a society of equals tends in general to make a man's spirits expand, and his faculties work easily and actively; while, to live in a society of superiors, although it may occasionally be a very good discipline, yet in general tends to tame the spirits and to make the play of the faculties less secure and active.[20]

Tawney made the same assumption, arguing that "individual differences, which are a source of social energy, are more likely to ripen and find expression if

---

[17]Friedrich A. Hayek, *Individualism, True and False* (Dublin: Hodges, Figgis & Co., and Oxford: Blackwell, 1946), p. 24.

[18]Tawney, *op. cit.*, p. 87.

[19]*Op. cit.*, p. 135.

[20]Matthew Arnold, "Democracy" [1861] in Lionel Trilling, ed., *The Portable Matthew Arnold* (New York: Viking Press, 1949), pp. 442–43.

social inequalities are, as far as practicable, diminished."[21] Individuals, Tawney argued

> differ profoundly . . . in capacity and character but they are equally entitled as human beings to consideration and respect, and . . . the well-being of a society is likely to be increased if it so plans its organization that, whether their powers are great or small, all its members may be equally enabled to make the best of such powers as they possess.[22]

His case was that establishing "the largest possible measure of equality of environment, and circumstance, and opportunity," was a precondition for ensuring "that these diversities of gifts may come to fruition."[23]

I have argued, then, that certain basic human needs and capacities provide at least part of the ground for equality of respect, and give some content to that notion of "respect," and I have further suggested that a society practicing equal respect would be one in which there were no barriers to reciprocal relations between relatively autonomous persons, who see each other and themselves as such, who are equally free from political control, social pressure, and economic deprivation and insecurity to engage in valued pursuits, and who have equal access to the means of self-development. Such a society would not be marked by inequalities of power and privilege (which is not to say that a society without such inequalities would necessarily practice equal respect).

However, I should conclude this section by noting an important tension, between the notion of equality of respect, as discussed here, and that of "equality of opportunity," as normally understood. In the context of public debate, especially about education, this latter principle is *not* generally taken to refer to equality of opportunity to develop individual powers or gifts, but rather equality of opportunity to achieve scarce social rewards. Thus understood, it comes into conflict with equal respect, since it focuses attention upon forms of differentiation and grading, which carry status and prestige. It endorses and serves to perpetuate those very structures of inequality, characterized by competition and emulation, of which equality of respect makes light—and, practiced seriously, it would abolish. The distinction was well drawn by Tawney when he contrasted "the claim for an open road to individual advancement" with the desire "to narrow the space between valley and peak."[24] The former aspiration has, of course, a central place in the history of socialism: it represents the meritocratic policy of widening the social base of recruitment to privileged positions, which has always been the central plank of social democracy. C. A. R. Crosland wrote:

> The essential thing is that every citizen should have an equal chance—that is his basic democratic right; but provided the start is

[21]*Op. cit.*, p. 49.
[22]*Ibid.*, pp. 35–36.
[23]*Ibid.*, p. 47.
[24]*Ibid.*, p. 108.

fair, let there be the maximum scope for individual self-advancement. There would then be nothing improper in either a high continuous status ladder . . . or even a distinct class stratification . . . since opportunities for attaining the highest status or the topmost stratum would be genuinely equal. Indeed the continuous traffic up and down would inevitably make society more mobile and dynamic, and so less class-bound.[25]

By contrast, the egalitarian socialist focuses on equalizing the rewards and privileges attached to different positions, not on widening the competition for them. In fact, of course, these two strands are often intertwined in socialist theory and practice. But, although there are well-known arguments (an example of which we shall consider) to the effect that unequal rewards, together with equal opportunity to reap them, have essential economic and social functions, they are in tension with the social, political, and economic implications of the principle of equal respect, which, as we have seen, points toward greater equality in the conditions of life, that is, of wealth, income, status, and power.

The Realities of Inequality

Contemporary industrial societies manifest structured inequalities of such conditions, and of much else besides, such as access to education, social services and other public benefits, economic security, promotion prospects, etc. Some patterns of inequality appear to be common to all such societies, both capitalist and state socialist, others to the one system or the other, yet others to particular countries. But three myths, prevalent in recent times, are belied by the evidence. The first is that of "convergence," according to "the logic of industrialism." This is misleading insofar as it suggests a continuing trend in the development of industrial societies toward greater overall economic equality, toward an ever-increasing consistency of stratification systems around the occupational order (e.g., toward the congruence of middle incomes and middle-class lifestyle and status), and toward a uniform pattern of social mobility.[26] The second is that "affluence" in capitalist societies has eroded inequalities of income, wealth, and security of life and that the power of private capital has been tamed, from within by the "managerial revolution" and the divorce between ownership and control, and from without by the growth of the state and/or a pluralistic diffusion of power among competing interest groups. The third myth is the official communist (especially Soviet) interpretaion of state socialist societies, which, while acknowledging the existence of nonantagonistic classes (working class and peasantry) and the stratum of the intelligentsia—and the existence of inequalities of income, consumption goods, education, etc., between rural and urban population and between occupational strata—maintains that these inequalities are

[25]C. A. R. Crosland, *The Future of Socialism* (London: Cape, 1956), pp. 150–51.

[26]See J. H. Goldthorpe, "Social Stratification in Industrial Society," reprinted in R. Bendix and S. M. Lipset, eds., *Class, Status and Power: Social Stratification in Comparative Perspective*, 2nd edition, (London: Routledge, 1967).

in the process of continuing decline (the so-called process of *sblizhenie*, or "drawing together"), denies that there is a hierarchy of status, and is silent about the hierarchy of power.

Of the patterns of inequality common to industrial societies, it appears broadly true to say that, in contrast with traditional or nonindustrial societies, "the occupational order comes increasingly to be the primary source of symbolic as well as material advantages,"[27] thus

> The occupational structure in modern industrial society not only constitutes an important foundation for the main dimensions of social stratification, but also serves as the connecting link between different institutions and spheres of social life, and therein lies its great significance. The hierarchy of prestige strata and the hierarchy of economic classes have their roots in the occupational structure; so does the hierarchy of political power and authority, for political authority in modern society is largely exercised as a full-time occupation. . . .[28]

As for income, there appears to be a remarkable similarity in capitalist and communist societies in the structure of earnings—more precisely, in the distribution of pretax money wages or salaries of fully employed male adult workers in all industries but farming.[29] There is a broad relationship between the hierarchy of skills and knowledge demanded by occupations on the one hand, and the hierarchy of material rewards on the other (though there is a narrower range of differentials under command than market economies), and, related to this, there are certain more specific trends: high rewards accruing to those in management and the technically highly qualified and skilled, and a relative decline in the rewards of clerical work. As for status inequality (allowing for the "softness" of the data and their paucity for socialist systems, except Poland), various studies suggest a common structure of occupational prestige. For example, according to Sarapata, the correlation between the occupational prestige hierarchies of Poland and the U.S. is 0.882, Poland and England 0.862 and Poland and West Germany 0.879.[30] As for inequalities of power, apart from the obvious differences, parallels can be seen in the differential distribution of power and authority (whether in the form of legal ownership or directive control) within "imperatively coordinated associations," such as the industrial enterprise; conversely, a tendency toward political pluralism, albeit of a highly restricted and managed type, has been observed in communist systems.[31]

Of the inequalities characteristic of capitalism, the most obvious is that of wealth. It has been justly said that "capitalism produces extremely rich people with a

[27]Frank Parkin, *Class, Inequality and Political Order* (London: MacGibbon & Kee, 1971), p. 39.
[28]P. M. Blau and O. D. Duncan, *The American Occupational Structure* (New York: John Wiley, 1967), p. 7.
[29]See H. F. Lydall, *The Structure of Earnings* (London: Oxford University Press, 1968).
[30]Cited in David Lane, *The End of Inequality? Stratification under State Socialism* (London: Penguin, 1971), p. 81.
[31]See, e.g., H. Gordon Skilling and Franklyn Griffiths, eds., *Interest Groups in Soviet Politics* (Princeton: Princeton University Press, 1971).

great deal of capital, and this is the most striking difference between the two systems."[32] Moreover, such capital "means so much more than the income it provides: security, diminished pressure to save and (in very large quantities) political power."[33] The most recent study of the subject, in Britain,[34] estimates that the top 5 percent of wealthholders own between one-half and three-quarters of the total personal wealth. There has, it is true, been a long-term trend toward a greater spread of such wealth, but this has mainly been from the top 1 percent to the next 2-5 percent (i.e., to relatives and others), as a defense against taxation.[35] It has been estimated that, equally divided, the yield from private property would substantially change the overall income distribution, providing a married couple with something over £9.00 a week.[36] Similar (though less extreme) concentrations of property ownership are found in other capitalist countries. Its impact is considerable because it "leads to unequal incomes, and concentrates control over the economy in a few hands."[37] This is

> accentuated by the fact that the very rich tend to hold their wealth in the form of company shares and real property yielding a higher return than the assets typically owned by small savers. The concentration of share ownership is even greater than that in the distribution of wealth as a whole, which is important since shares convey not only income but also rights of control, and even allowing for the increasing power of corporation managers these still remain of considerable significance.[38]

As for income inequality, after a temporary narrowing in the 1940s, it has remained relatively fixed and in some cases somewhat widened—both before direct taxation and (as far as one can estimate) after it. Overall taxation appears to be almost neutral in relation to income and in certain cases (the U.S., West Germany) directly regressive, while redistribution through the welfare state, although it obviously aids the poor more than the rich in relative terms, is paid for by wage-earners themselves, and is mainly "horizontal" rather than "vertical"—i.e., it takes the form of a "life-cycle" transfer *within* social classes; moreover, these welfare facilities often tend to favor more privileged groups.[39] In general, the social democratic "welfare approach" brings about little disturbance of the stratification system[40]—and some have claimed that there is increasing inequality at its base, with the growth of an

[32]P. J. D. Wiles and S. Markowski, "Income Distribution under Communism and Capitalism: Some Facts about Poland, the U.K., the U.S.A. and the U.S.S.R." *Soviet Studies*, 22 (1971), p. 344.

[33]*Ibid.*, p. 353.

[34]Atkinson, *op. cit.*

[35]See John Westergaard and Henrietta Resler, *Class in Contemporary Britain* (London: Heinemann, 1976).

[36]Atkinson, *op. cit.*, pp. 37–38.

[37]*Ibid.*, p. 251.

[38]*Ibid.*, p. 77.

[39]See Westergaard and Resler, *op. cit.*, and Parkin, *op. cit.*, pp. 125–26.

[40]Parkin, *op. cit.*, p. 127.

underclass of unemployed and unemployables.[41] In capitalist societies that stratification system exhibits a cleavage between the manual and nonmanual categories of occupation—not merely with respect to income (here, indeed, there is substantial overlap), but with respect to a whole range of privileges and advantages: white-collar workers have strikingly better sick pay and pension schemes, holidays and other fringe benefits, life-cycle promotion and career opportunities, long-term economic stability (including for many guaranteed salary increases), working environment, freedom of movement and from supervision, etc. Nonmanual workers "even when they diverge are more like one another than they are like manual workers" and "the big divide still comes between manual workers on the one hand and nonmanual grades on the other."[42] As for status inequality, such evidence as exists appears to point away from the thesis of an accommodative *embourgeoisement* of affluent workers and increasingly toward different forms of polarization between what Kerr terms "the managers" and the "managed.[43]

Inequalities of political power in capitalist societies are of course manifest in the inequalities already considered, since these represent the power of the dominant class to command a disproportionate share of rewards and privileges *vis-à-vis* the subordinate class. A full consideration of this topic would also involve an examination of all the means available to the former to preserve its rewards and privileges; not only within governmental institutions, but within the administrative service, the educational system, industry, the law, mass communications, etc.; not only through coercive power but also through "the mobilization of bias," operating anonymously through the structure of institutions (especially private property and the market), the rituals of social and political life, and ideological assumptions.[44]

The inequalities typical of state socialist societies display a different pattern. Property, in the sense of legal ownership, is, of course, largely absent: as Lane writes, "the really significant difference in the system of social stratification compared to Western industrial societies is the absence of a private propertied class possessing great concentrations of wealth."[45] On the other hand, following Djilas, one can argue that the white-collar intelligentsia, and the *apparatchiki* above all, exercise rights of control over the use and products of collective property and expropriate surplus value from the subordinate class. On the other hand, there is no direct inheritance of such rights, as with private property, although there is evidence of *de facto* inheritance of educational privileges. The analogy between "legal" and "sociological" ownership cannot be taken too far, but clearly there is a considerable hierarchy of monetary privilege and power based upon such authority

[41] See Goldthorpe, *art. cit.*, p. 653.

[42] D. Wedderburn and C. Craig, "Relative Deprivation in Work," paper presented at the British Association for the Advancement of Science (Exeter, 1969), cited in Parkin, *op. cit.*, p. 26.

[43] C. Kerr *et al.*, *Industrialism and Industrial Man* (Cambridge, Mass.: Harvard University Press, 1960).

[44] See Westergaard and Resler, *op. cit.*, and the present author's *Power: A Radical View* (London: Macmillan, 1974), and "Political Ritual and Social Integration," *Sociology* (forthcoming).

[45] Lane, *op. cit.*, p. 69.

roles and above all upon party membership. With respect to income inequality, this has gone through a number of phases in all socialist regimes. The general pattern is this: a highly egalitarian stage of "socialist reconstruction," followed by a substantial widening of differentials (most pronounced in the U.S.S.R. with Stalin's attacks on "equality mongering") in order to increase material incentives, followed by a subsequent move toward greater equality.[46]

The current picture is one of a substantially narrower range of money incomes in socialist than in capitalist societies; thus, for example, the ratio of the lowest wage to the average in the U.S.S.R. is 60:112.6, and even the most extreme estimate of the total range is substantially less than what is widely accepted as true of the U.S.[47] Moreover, apart from Yugoslavia, there is no structural unemployment. The stratification system has a different pattern from that in capitalist systems: social strata are distinguished by money incomes, consumption patterns, styles of life, education, use of the social services, housing, "cultural level," but there appears to be no major "break" or "big divide," as under capitalism, between the manual and the nonmanual strata. As Parkin suggests, in many state socialist societies highly skilled or craft manual workers enjoy a higher position in the scale of material and status rewards, and promotion prospects, than do lower white-collar employees.[48] Thus, for example, in both Poland and Yugoslavia skilled manual positions have higher occupational prestige than do lower routine white-collar positions. Parkin suggests that the overall reward hierarchy is as follows: "(1) White-collar intelligentsia (i.e., professional, managerial and administrative positions), (2) Skilled manual positions, (3) Lower or unqualified white-collar positions, (4) Unskilled manual positions," and that the major break lies between the skilled and the unskilled.[49] Thus "the most obvious break in the reward hierarchy occurs along the line separating the qualified professional, managerial and technical positions from the rest of the occupational order."[50] Thus the status hierarchy does not appear to reflect and reinforce a dichotomous class structure on the Western capitalist model (though Machonin provides conflicting evidence on this point from Czechoslovakia).[51] Clearly, however, the most significant contrast between the systems lies in the hierarchy of political power. Here, despite the pluralistic tendencies identified by certain Western observers, the explicitly hierarchical, monistic, and all-pervasive structure of party control, increasingly manned by the white-collar intelligentsia, is altogether distinctive.

[46]See Parkin, op. cit., p. 144 and his article, "Class Stratification in Socialist Societies," British Journal of Sociology, December 1969.

[47]Lane, op. cit., pp. 72–74.

[48]Parkin, op. cit., p. 146.

[49]Parkin, op. cit., p. 147, cf. Lane, op. cit., p. 78.

[50]Parkin, op. cit., p. 149.

[51]P. Machonin, "Social Stratification in Contemporary Czechoslovakia," American Journal of Sociology, 75 (1970), pp. 725–41. For an English summary of Machonin and his associates' full-scale study of this subject, see Ernest Gellner, "The Pluralist Anti-levelers of Prague," European Journal of Sociology, 12 (1971), pp. 312–25, and Dissent, Summer 1972.

Finally, brief mention should be made of inequalities characteristic of particular societies within these two broad systems. Thus, with respect to income inequality, the U.K. is more equal than the U.S.,[52] and Norway is substantially more equal still, while the U.S.S.R. has carried income equalization very far within the socialist bloc, especially through the redistributive effects of collective consumption.[53] whereas Yugoslavia has seen a marked widening of the span of incomes and life-chances, with the introduction of "market socialism," as to a lesser extent did Czechoslovakia in the later 1960s. Other peculiarities relate to racial, religious, and linguistic factors (the U.S., Northern Ireland, Canada), where inconsistencies between income and status hierarchies are to be seen, and long-range historical factors, as, for example, in Britain, where the stratification takes a distinctive form and the concentration of wealth is especially high.[54]

The explanation of inequality can be approached in either of two ways. On the one hand, one may seek to explain why individuals attain different positions, rewards and privileges; on the other hand, one may seek to account for the allocation of rewards and privileges to different social positions. The first approach implies a focus upon inequality of opportunity among persons; the second upon inequality of reward among occupational positions. In the foregoing, I have implicitly concentrated on the second question and I have also implicitly suggested a range of explanations for inequality at different levels. Some such explanations will be historically and geographically specific. Examples are, say, the particular circumstances explaining the exceptionally high status of Poland's intelligentsia,[55] or the cultural factors in ethnically or religiously divided communities or the long-range historical factors referred to above. Other factors explaining the differences between income distributions in different countries, and in the same country over time, are the activities of the central government and local authorities in allocating taxes and distributing benefits, the control of entry into occupations by professional associations and unions, national rates of economic growth, level of unemployment, etc. Other explanations will be at the level of the economic system, and will focus primarily on the institution of private property, and all that protects and legitimates it, under capitalism; and on political intervention, allocating rewards and privileges, in accordance with the ruling elite's policy objectives, under state socialism. However, at the next level, the constraints operating on both systems come into view: the division of labor under advanced industrialism, it has been argued, creates a certain role structure inevitably accompanied by differentials of material reward, status, and power, which are in turn perpetuated by the nuclear family.[56] Some writers have sought explanations of inequality at a higher level still: according to them social inequalities arise from the functional prerequisites or basic features of all human societies, or, more universally still, from the genetic, biological, or psychological differentiation of human nature itself.

[52]Wiles and Markowski, art. cit., p. 344.

[53]Ibid.

[54]See Atkinson, op. cit., p. 77, and Lydall, op. cit.

[55]See Michalina Vaughan, "Poland," in Margaret Scotford Archer and Salvador Giner (eds.), Contemporary Europe: Class, Status and Power (London: Weidenfeld & Nicolson, 1971).

[56]Lane, op. cit., pp. 129–37.

The Realizability of Equality

This leads us naturally to the question of the alleged inevitability of inequality. There are a number of such arguments (of which I shall cite some typical contemporary examples), ranging from the "hard" to the "soft." The hardest are those that appeal to biological and psychological data, which, it is argued, set sharp limits to the possibility of implementing egalitarian social ideals: "biology," writes Eysenck, "sets an absolute barrier to egalitarianism."[57] Then there are sociological arguments that maintain inequalities are functional to, or inherent in, all possible social systems—or less strongly, in all industrial societies. Finally, there are arguments of a different order, which seek to show that the cost of implementing equality in contemporary societies are unacceptably high, because they conflict with other values.

The hard-line approach to the realizability of equality is currently taken by various participants in the contemporary debate about genetics, environment, and intelligence. Professors Jensen, Herrnstein, and Eysenck assert that "intelligence" is mainly determined by heredity—specifically that about 80 percent of the variance in IQ scores is genetically determined. Eysenck urges "recognition of man's biological nature, and the genetically determined inequality inevitably associated with his derivation."[58] Social class is "determined quite strongly by IQ," and educational attainment depends "closely" on IQ: "talent, merit, ability" and "largely innate factors."[59] Eysenck maintains that "regression to the mean" through social mobility and the redistribution of genes prevents social classes from calcifying into hereditary castes, and he concludes that a "society which would come as near to our egalitarian desires as is biologically attainable would give the greatest scope possible to this social mobility."[60] Herrnstein,[61] by contrast, ignores "regression to the mean" and stresses the process of "assortative mating" between partners of similar IQ levels, and he foresees a future in which, as the environment becomes more favorable to the development of intelligence, social mobility increases, and technological advance sets a higher premium on intelligence, social classes will become ever more castelike, stratifying society into a hereditary meritocracy. Finally, Jensen, observing that some racial groups, especially American whites and blacks, differ markedly in their distribution of IQ scores (the mean IQ differing from 10 to 15 points), concludes that, since no known environmental factors can explain such differences, their explanation must be largely genetic. In his latest book, he affirms the hypothesis that "something between one-half and three-fourths of the average IQ difference between American Negroes and whites is attributable to genetic factors, and the remainder to environmental factors and their interaction with the genetic differences."[62] He attaches much importance to this conclusion, since he believes that IQ is a major determinant of success in our society.

[57]H. J. Eysenck, *The Inequality of Man* (London: Temple Smith, 1973), p. 224.
[58]*Ibid.*, p. 270.
[59]*Ibid.*, pp. 159, 224.
[60]*Ibid.*, p. 224.
[61]R. Herrnstein, *IQ in the Meritocracy* (London: Allen Lane, and Penguin, 1973).
[62]Arthur R. Jensen, *Educability and Group Differences* (London: Methuen, 1973), p. 363.

These claims obviously cannot be adequately considered here, but a few remarks are worth making. First the estimate of 80 percent genetic determination of IQ is controversial. Others suggest a substantially lower figure. According to Jencks it is something like 45 percent: Jencks and his colleagues estimate that "genotype explains about 45 percent of the variance in IQ scores, that environment explains about 35 percent, and that the correlation between genotype and environment explains the remaining 20 percent."[63] Moreover the evidence with respect to genetic determination is far less univocal than these writers imply; "different methods of estimating the heritability of test scores yield drastically different results" and "studies of different populations yield somewhat different results."[64] Again, children's test scores are not immune to considerable improvement by effecting changes in their environment. Eysenck suggests that "Clearly [sic] the whole course of development of a child's intellectual capabilities is largely laid down genetically,"[65] yet this is strikingly contradicted by a number of twin and adoption studies.[66] Second, psychologists notoriously differ about what IQ tests measure: some, such as Jensen, Herrnstein, and Eysenck, believe it measures some basic property of the intellect; others believe that intelligence is multidimensional, that it cannot be measured by a single number, and (according to many authorities) that that number in any case measures educationally and culturally specific aptitudes with limited wider applicability. Third, and related to this last point, it has been established (at least for the U.S.) that (1) social class is not, pace Eysenck, "determined strongly" by IQ; (2) educational attainment depends less on IQ than on family background; and (3) IQ is not a major determinant of economic and social success.[67] Fourth, the difference in average IQ-test performance between blacks and whites is consistent with all three of the following hypotheses: that it is explained by genes, by environment, and by both.[68] Moreover it appears indisputable that present data and techniques cannot resolve this issue. It certainly has not been established that one can extrapolate from genetic determinants of differences within a population to explain mean differences between populations. And it is worth observing that, in any case, genetic differences within races are far greater than those between them, accounting for 60–70 percent of all human genetic variation. In general, it appears entirely reasonable to conclude with Jencks that it is "wrong to argue that genetic inequality dictates a hierarchical society."[69] This is so even if Jensen should turn out to be nearer the truth than Jencks, and heredity does substantially constrain the maximum achievable by different individuals in the best of all possible environments. For, as we have argued, the principle of equal respect requires, in Tawney's words, that society's organization be planned so that "whether their powers are great or small, all its members may be equally enabled to make the best of such

[63]Jencks, op. cit., p. 315.
[64]Ibid., p. 71.
[65]Op. cit., p. 111.
[66]See Jencks, op. cit., Appendix A.
[67]See Jencks, op. cit.
[68]Ibid., Chapter 3, Part II.
[69]Ibid., p. 72.

powers as they possess." Since this requires the equalization of rewards and privileges, biological differences would correlate with social positions but not with unequal rewards and privileges attaching to those positions.

Sociological arguments for the inevitability of inequality are of two broad types. One is that inequalities are functionally necessary for any society, the other that they are inherent in the very nature of social life. A much-discussed example of the former is the so-called functionalist theory of stratification; an interesting instance of the latter is furnished by Ralf Dahrendorf.

Davis and Moore's "functionalist theory of stratification" seeks to demonstrate "the universal necessity which calls forth stratification in any social system.[70] It advances the following propositions:

1. Certain positions in any society are functionally more important than others.
2. Adequate performance in these positions requires appropriate talents and training.
3. Some such talents are scarce in any population.
4. It is necessary (a) to induce those with the requisite talents to undergo the sacrifice of acquiring the appropriate training; (b) to attract them to the functionally important positions; and (c) to motivate them to perform in these positions adequately.
5. To achieve these objectives, differential incentives must be attached to the posts in question—and these may be classified into those things which contribute to (i) "sustenance and comfort"; (ii) "humor and diversion"; and (iii) "self-respect and ego expansion."[71]
6. These differential incentives (unequal rewards) constitute social inequality, which, in securing that the most talented individuals occupy and adequately perform in the functionally important positions, fulfills a necessary function in any society: "Social inequality is thus an unconsciously evolved device by which societies insure that the most important positions are conscientiously filled by the most qualified persons."[72]

Controversy over this theory has raged for well over two decades,[73] and it is fair to say that the balance of the argument has largely lain with the theory's critics. There is the evident difficulty of identifying the "functionally important" positions, as distinct from those that a given society values as important (bankers or miners? elementary or university teachers?) and the dubious assumption that training for these positions is sacrificial (especially since there would, presumably,

---

[70]K. Davis and W. E. Moore, "Some Principles of Stratification" in Bendix and Lipset, *Class Status and Power* (see n. 26), p. 47.

[71]*Ibid.*, p. 48.

[72]*Ibid.*, p. 48.

[73]See G. A. Huaco, "The Functionalist Theory of Stratification: Two Decades of Controversy," *Inquiry*, 9 (Fall 1966), pp. 215–40.

be no material loss in an egalitarian society). Also, it ignores the point that a stratified society itself restricts the availability of talent, and the further point that an advanced industrial society is in principle able substantially to increase the availability of talent and training. A further weakness of the theory is its assumption that unequal rewards (defined in a most culture-specific way) are the only possible means of mobilizing qualified individuals into adequately performing important jobs. It leaves out of account the intrinsic benefits of different positions, in relation to the expectations, aptitudes, and aspirations of different individuals (potential surgeons being anyway attracted by practicing surgery and potential carpenters by carpentry); and it fails in general to consider functional alternatives to a system of unequal rewards—such as intrinsic job satisfaction, the desire for knowledge, skills, and authority, an ethos of social or public service and a diminution of acquisitiveness and status-seeking, the use of negotiation, persuasion or direct planning, changes in the organization of work and decision-making, and so on. Finally, to the extent to which the thesis does remain valid, at least for contemporary industrial societies— that is, insofar as unequal rewards are needed so that certain jobs are adequately filled—this in no way implies a societywide system of structured social inequality, linking wealth, income, status, and power (indeed, it would probably imply the reverse); nor is it plausible to suggest that the range and scope of actual inequalities, such as those surveyed in the previous section of this essay, can be explained in this beneficently functional manner. It is, incidentally, noteworthy that liberal reformers in East European countries have used arguments analogous to Davis's and Moore's to justify the widening of income differentials (as did Stalin in the 1930s). But the Davis-Moore theory does not specify any particular range of inequality as functionally necessary—or rather, it all too easily serves to justify any such range which its proponents may seek to defend or establish.

Dahrendorf's theory seeks to demonstrate that "inequalities among men follow from the very concept of societies as moral communities . . . the idea of a society in which all distinctions of rank between men are abolished transcends what is sociologically possible and has its place in the sphere of poetic imagination alone."[74] The thesis is essentially this: that "(1) every society is a moral community, and therefore recognises norms which regulate the conduct of its members; and (2) there have to be sanctions connected with these norms which guarantee their obligatory character by acting as rewards for conformism and penalties for deviance,"[75] from which Dahrendorf concludes that "the sanctioning of human behaviour in terms of social norms necessarily creates a system of inequality of rank and that social stratification is therefore an immediate result of the control of social behaviour by positive and negative sanctions."[76] But the conclusion does not follow from the premises. It does not follow from the mere existence of social norms and the fact that their enforcement discriminates against those who do not or cannot (because of their social position) conform to them that a societywide system of

[74]Ralf Dahrendorf, "On the Origin of Social Inequality," in P. Laslett and W. G. Runciman, eds., *Philosophy, Politics and Society: Second Series* (Oxford: Blackwell, 1962), p. 107.
[75]*Ibid.*, p. 103.
[76]*Ibid.*, p. 103.

inequality and "rank order of social status" are "bound to emerge."[77] Dahrendorf slides unaccountably from the undoubted truth that within groups norms are enforced that discriminate against certain persons and positions (he cites the example of gossiping neighbors making the professional woman an outsider) to the unsupported claim that, within society as a whole, a system of inequality between groups and positions is inevitable. To support that claim he would need to show the necessity of societywide norms whose enforcement necessarily discriminates between persons and social positions, and this he fails to do. Nothing he says rules out the empirical possibility of a society containing a plurality of norms, each conferring and withholding status and prestige (so that gossiping neighbors look down on professional women, and vice versa), without themselves being ranked within a single system of inequality or stratification.

Finally, I turn to the argument that inequality is eradicable only at an unacceptable cost. This argument has been voiced in many forms, by those both friendly and hostile to socialism. A forceful contemporary formulation is that of Frank Parkin, who argues that

> A political system which guarantees constitutional rights for groups to organise in defence of their interests is almost bound to favour the privileged at the expense of the disprivileged. The former will always have greater organising capacities and facilities than the latter, such that the competition for rewards between different classes is never an equal contest. This is not merely because the dominant class can more easily be mobilized in defence of its interests, but also because it has access to the all-important means of social control, both coercive and normative. Given this fundamental class inequality in the social and economic order, a pluralist or democratic political structure works to the advantage of the dominant class.[78]

What this argument perhaps suggests, Parkin writes, is that

> socialist egalitarianism is not readily compatible with a pluralist political order of the classic western type. Egalitarianism seems to require a political system in which the state is able continually to hold in check those social and occupational groups which, by virtue of their skills or education or personal attributes, might otherwise attempt to stake claims to a disproportionate share of society's rewards. The most effective way of holding such groups in check is by denying them the right to organise politically or in other ways to undermine social equality.[79]

But historical experience of this approach has been pretty uniform: gross abuses of constitutional rights, terrorism and coercion, and, even when these latter are

[77]*Ibid.*, p. 102.
[78]Parkin, *op. cit.*, pp. 181–82.
[79]*Ibid.*, p. 183.

relaxed, the continuance of party control over all areas of social life, including literature and the arts. As Parkin observes,

> The fact that the humanistic ideals central to the socialist tradition have found little, if any, expression in the European socialist states highlights an unresolved dilemma; namely, whether it is possible to establish the political conditions for egalitarianism while also guaranteeing civil rights to all citizens within a system of "socialist legality."[80]

Conclusions

Fortunately, this is not the place to enter into the whole question of the "socialist transition." I merely wish to conclude this essay with three brief observations. The first is that the massive inequalities of power and privilege outlined in the second part are, for many socialists, intolerable mainly because they violate something like the principle of equal respect delineated in the first part—a principle that derives from liberal premises, but takes them seriously. The second is that the arguments for the unrealizability of equality considered in the third part all fail to show that these inequalities are ineradicable, whether on psychological or sociological grounds. And the third is that the argument that the costs of implementing equality are too high is the most crucial facing any socialist today. And it is perhaps the inclination to see the accumulated weight of historical evidence for the apparent need to pay such costs—from the rise of Stalin to the fall of Allende—as a challenge rather than as a source of despair that is, in the end, the distinguishing mark of an egalitarian socialist.

[80]*Ibid.*, p. 184.

18
Socialism and Liberty
John Hospers

"Socialism," says Webster, "is any of various economic and political theories advocating collective or governmental ownership and administration of the means of production and distribution of goods." In socialism's purest form, as in the Soviet Union, the government owns not only the means of production but the real estate—the individual is a perpetual renter. In a less extreme form, as in Great Britain and Sweden, the individual may own real estate, and only some of the industries and other means of production are owned by the government, but every individual in the nation is subjected to a central economic plan, to which each must conform; and in addition, heavy taxes are levied to pay for the benefits of unemployment, medical care, etc., provided in the central economic plan.

With increasing degrees of socialism, the control of the government over the lives of individuals tends to become complete. The state (that is, the bureaucrats who administer the functions of government) decides who is to be educated—in government schools of course—and who is not; how many doctors there shall be, how many teachers, and so on, and who these shall be; how many theaters, how many parks and playgrounds, etc. If a foreigner asks a Russian, "Have you decided on a profession?" the Russian citizen will typically answer, "The state has not yet decided where it can best use me." In America such a reply would be greeted with, "The state? What's the state got to do with it? Why don't *you* decide?" Since it decides what profession you will pursue, it also decides where you shall go to pursue it—if there is a shortage in town X, you will be sent to town X, and you will have nothing to say about it; one cannot after all control the work without controlling the worker. You live in a house owned by the government; your medical care is arranged by the

From *Libertarianism* (1971), pp. 245–280. Reprinted by permission of the author.

government, and if it is inadequate you can turn nowhere else; you cannot buy food without a card issued by government (which can be withdrawn the moment you disagree with the government or for any reason become "an enemy of the people"). The government has power of life and death over you, in virtually every aspect of your life.

Suppose, for example, that a planning bureau regulates the entire economy, as in Soviet Russia. The state then becomes the sole employer. "If the worker fails to please the powers that be in the State, or if he arouses their active animosity, there is no one else to whom he can turn. A far greater tyranny may be exercised over him under socialism than . . . was ever possible under capitalism. For if a worker failed to please a particular employer under capitalism . . . he was free to go to another. . . . But under socialism, if a worker falls out of favor with the powers that constitute the State he can be forced to starve; there is no one else to whom he can turn."[1] Trotsky himself once said, "The old maxim, 'He that does not work shall not eat,' has been replaced by the maxim, 'He that does not obey shall not eat.'"

Every part of our lives, every decision we make, is dependent on and affects someone's "economic activities." If you decide to go to the movies, the planner must agree. He must determine how many movie theaters there will be, how many ushers, how many movies. Your decision to go on a picnic depends on prior decisions of (for example) the Department of Parks. If you decide to read a book, it will affect either the economic activities of the Department of Publishing and Distribution of Literature or the economic activities of the Department of Libraries. All of these decisions by you must be planned by the government. It is no accident that in Russia the question of how to organize the people's leisure is a problem of planning—of the leisure being planned for them, not by them. The State will handle every major decision from the cradle to the grave. The type of planning and control involved is often not obvious to superficial inspection. If the planner does not want people to read books, all he has to do is make the price of a book very high. If books were $100 a piece, not many people could buy them. In a free market the fact that the books are not selling would force the publisher to lower his price. But not so in a planned economy.

But can there not be "democratic socialism," socialism without dictatorship? Such a state is likely to be an unstable one, and lead back to free enterprise without centralized planning or to centralized planning imposed by dictatorship. There will always be disagreement on what plans should be adopted, and here the advocate of "democratic socialism" is faced with a difficult choice: either he must forget about planning (give up socialism) or forget about reaching agreement on a common plan (give up parliamentary government). Unless he hopes for the miracle of a majority agreement on a particular plan for the organization of all society, the democratic statesman who sets out to plan economic life will soon be confronted with the alternative of either assuming dictatorial powers or abandoning his plans; for how else but by force will he impose his plans on others who want no part of

[1]Henry Hazlitt, *Time Will Run Back*, p. 95. (Originally published by Appleton-Century-Crofts, 1952, under the title *The Great Idea*. Published in Great Britain as *Time Will Run Back*, and also reprinted under this title by Arlington House, New Rochelle, N. Y. Page references are to the British edition.)

them? Planning will lead to dictatorship because dictatorship is the most efficient instrument of coercion, and coercion will have to be employed if central planning on a large scale is going to work.

Many socialists are aware of this and do not shrink from the dictatorship which their view leads to. Harold Laski, the most eminent contemporary advocate of socialism,[2] writes,

> I believe that the attainment of power by the Labor Party in the normal election fashion must result in a radical transformation of parliamentary government. Such an administration could not, if it sought to be effective, accept the present form of its procedure. It would have to take vast powers, and legislate under them by ordinance and decree; it would have to suspend the classic formulae of normal opposition. . . . A labor government may take office and embark on its policy; but it may be met with resistance, either tacit or overt, which strikes at the root of its purposes; under such conditions the suspension of the Constitution is inevitable.

And according to Sidney and Beatrice Webb, well-known British socialist writers,[3]

> In any corporate action a loyal unity of thought is so important that, if anything is to be achieved, public discussion must be suspended between the promulgation of the decision and the accomplishment of the task. Whilst the work is in progress, any public expression of doubt, or even fear that the plan will not be successful, is an act of disloyalty and even of treachery because of its possible effects on the will and on the efforts of the rest of the staff.

What has happened now to freedom of the speech and of the press? The entire socialist society would be an army, for a military-type organization would be the only one which could possibly carry out what the socialists are advocating. The individual will be relieved of the responsibility of making his own decisions; they will be made for him. The delegation of authority to a central commission must be employed because matters could not be settled by general rules which a majority of the people could act on. What should be the price of milk in New York? What should be the train rates from Los Angeles to Chicago? What type of car shall we produce next year? All these decisions must be made by government officials, rather than being left to the operation of the free market. It wouldn't be practicable to vote on all of them. And so they must be left to the decisions of a central planning bureau, which forces them upon each individual by means of the enormous coercive powers of the state.

In a free-enterprise society, people who disagree with the government,

[2]Harold Laski, *Democracy in Crisis*, p. 87 (Chapel Hill: University of North Carolina Press, 1933.)
[3]Sidney and Beatrice Webb, *Soviet Communism: A New Capitalism?*, p. 1038. (New York: Scribners, 1936.)

even those who disagree with the whole system, can still find employment. They can in fact usually earn their living by attacking the existing state of affairs. In a socialist society, people who disagree with the government can easily be disposed of. In both systems there will always be people who disagree; but with socialism the political leader has the power to shut up the opposition. In Russia what happens is that an economic demand is "created" for a worker in the salt-mines of Siberia. Only in a free-enterprise economy can the individual be in a position where his income is *independent* of the government. In a centrally planned economy, the worker must ultimately lose his freedom to choose his own line of work. For, if no one wants to go to a certain area for a certain type of job and the government determines the wages, the government must force him to go there. It must control the worker along with the work.

When we discuss "freedom to choose one's job" we mean freedom in its primary sense, as absence of coercion, not as the power to do something. Someone who wants to be a college professor and isn't, is not necessarily unfree. If nobody is willing to buy his services because he is ignorant, he may call himself "not free to become a professor" but the fact is simply that others choose not to avail themselves of his services. He may not get the job he wants, but he is still free because he is uncoerced.

But in a socialist system all such choices *would* be coerced, because of the power of unlimited government. Perhaps the most foolish thing that Marx ever said was that under socialism the state would eventually wither away. For ". . . it is above all under socialism, where the state owns all the means of production, does all the planning and assigns and controls all the jobs, that the state is and must be closest to omnipotence. . . . It is precisely under a socialist state that the least liberty can exist. Under complete socialism, in fact, liberty for the individual is simply impossible."[4]

In a free-enterprise economy, of course, all this is different. There, if someone plans to start a business, and his plan is unwise or short-sighted, he goes bankrupt. No one forces him to start the business, and no one will stop him. Nor can he coerce employees into working for him: he cannot command their services by edict, but only by paying them at least as much as the going wage for the type of work in question. The worker voluntarily chooses to work for him, and consumers voluntarily choose to buy his product (if they don't, he goes broke). The manufacturer of the product cannot coerce the consumer. In a free economy, the consumer determines the economic fate of the manufacturer (and with him, his employees). This provides the manufacturer, of course, with a natural motive for providing the best possible product at the lowest possible price, so that his product will outvote that of his competitors in the economic plebiscite of the consumers.

It should be clear by now how closely freedom of speech is based upon economic freedom. Many intellectuals in America, including, it would seem, the majority of college professors, are deeply concerned about freedom of speech—and quite rightly so, of course—but they couldn't care less about economic freedom. Indeed, many of them are socialists, and some of those who aren't or haven't

[4]Hazlitt, *Time Will Run Back*, p. 96.

thought about the matter very much retain in their minds a collection of tired clichés about the greedy capitalist who exploits his workers and ought to be controlled, and that "redistribution of wealth" is required for humanitarian reasons. But the fact is that without economic freedom, the continuation of freedom of speech is extremely precarious. One example will suffice:

> Imagine a socialist society that has a sincere desire to preserve the freedom of the press. The first problem would be that there would be no private capital—no private fortunes that could be used to subsidize an anti-socialist, pro-capitalist press. So the socialist state would have do it. But now the men and women undertaking this task would have to be released from the socialist labor pool and would have to be assured that they would never be discriminated against in employment opportunities if they were to wish to change occupations later. Then these pro-capitalist members of the socialist society would have to go to other functionaries of the state to secure the buildings, the presses, the paper, the skilled and the unskilled workmen, and all the other components of a working newspaper. Then they would face the problem of finding distribution outlets, either creating their own—a frightening task—or using the same ones used by the official socialist propaganda organs. Finally, where would they find readers? How many men and women would risk showing up at their government-controlled jobs carrying copies of the *Daily Capitalist?*[5]

If a government has control over your economic life, it has control over your very means of survival. The government can cut you off from food by refusing to employ you, or by taking away your ration card, and it can deprive you of a physician's care by taking away your state-controlled medical benefits. One can be safe only if one's livelihood is *independent of* government by having the government divorced from economic affairs. But give a government control over a man's economic actions, and it controls his very means of survival.

Since the government subsidizes research in the socialist state—no private sources being available—people will perforce undertake only such projects as the government bureaucrats are willing to have them pursue. And candidates for research grants, knowing where their hoped-for money is coming from, will fall over each other trying to get their projects approved by the bureaucrats who hold the purse-strings and accepting any kind of party line that will permit them to do so. And the psychologists who must depend on government to get any of their projects through, will gladly do what the government asks of them in return: they will devise methods of thought-control, and the technicians will devise methods of wiretapping and other more subtle invasions of privacy. To the extent that the economy of a nation is centrally controlled, as with Soviet Russia and its satellites, the educated elite of these countries, who depend for their future on favors from the

[5]Benjamin R. Rogge, "The Case for the Free Market," *The Freeman*, September 1963.

government, will be forced to fawn on every local bureaucrat who has it in his power to dispense these favors, and give them whatever devices the government requests in return for the favors, including finally the noose that will hang the researchers themselves. Can anyone doubt that the other freedoms are dependent on the preservation of economic freedom? When economic freedom goes, the other freedoms will soon follow, to be replaced by centralized control over the economy, over workers, over speech, and finally over thought.

Planning

"But," it is objected, "socialism is at least a *planned* economy, and don't we need planning? Isn't something planned better than something unplanned?"

The question is who is to do whatever planning there is to be. Are we to have one plan imposed on all of us from the outside, or is each of us to be free to make and execute *his own* plans? The difference between a free-enterprise economy and a centrally planned one is that in a free-enterprise economy every individual is free to construct and implement his own plans to the best of his ability, and as far as his initiative will carry him; whereas in a centrally planned economy the planner *eliminates everyone's plan except his own*. A socialist scheme can be made to work only by imposing one central plan on everyone in the nation, whether they like it or not. It is amazing how many people delight to indulge in armchair planning, fitting everybody into the plan like pawns on their own private chessboard. They never think of themselves as victims of other people's plans; no, as they imagine it everyone is to be subjected to *their* plan. But of course, different people will have different plans. And if one central plan does become adopted, what are the chances that it will be *your* plan, or your neighbor's plan? The chances are millions to one that instead of being able to impose your plan on other people, you will become the victim of someone else's plan, the pawn on someone else's chessboard.[6]

And by what right does some other person or group force me to conform against my will to *his* plan? If A has a right to impose his plan on B, C, and D, then doesn't B have a right to impose his very different plan on A, C, and D—and so on? Does any human being have a right to plan other people's lives against the will of those whose lives are being planned?

"But," it will be said, "aren't you doing the same as they are? Aren't you setting forth your plan, your political ideal or utopia, to which you would like everyone else to conform?" The answer is no, and we should be quite clear why. The political philosophy of libertarianism is one which leaves everyone free to implement his own plans, to do his own thing, compatible with the equal right of everyone else to do the same.

In a free-enterprise society, a group of people who wanted to get together

[6]See Ludwig von Mises, *Socialism* (New Haven, Conn.: Yale University Press, 1951). This monumental work is probably the best and most thorough treatment of the consequences of socialism to be found anywhere.

and form a communist colony somewhere would have a perfect right to do so. They would have to buy the land, of course—if they took it by force they would be violating the rights of the people who owned it. But with some expenditure of time and labor they could do it, as they often have in the past in the United States, and they could then go into the hills and do their thing with perfect legality and without encroaching on anyone else's rights. They can form a commune in which the policy is share-and-share-alike, if this is how they prefer to live; this would be *voluntary* collectivism, in which each person freely enters upon the scheme and leaves it again if he elects to do so. It is a far cry from the *enforced* collectivism to which everyone is subjected in the Soviet Union and other countries.

Contrast this situation with one in a socialist country where a group of people want to form a free-enterprise enclave. This is the very thing they would not be permitted to do. At once the government officials would descend upon them, forcing them to contribute to the National Health Plan and every other government scheme even if they preferred not to and desired no benefits from it.

The truth is of course that *every* plan that involves the forced submission of other people means a considerable loss of liberty. Under capitalism, however, there is no such loss of liberty. If a man plans to start a clothing store in a town and is not foresighted enough to realize that there are already more clothing stores in the community than the traffic will bear, he will lose his investment, and the consequences of his bad planning will be on his own head. On the other hand, if a Central Planning Board makes an unwise decision, the ill consequences are borne by every taxpayer; they must pay for the incompetence of another person. And under those conditions, such incompetence is far more likely to occur.

Consider a specific example, the publishing business. Authors and would-be authors are constantly complaining that publishers don't accept manuscripts which are not going to make money. On the whole this is true enough: the publisher can, and occasionally does, publish a book that is pretty sure to lose money, either for the sake of prestige or because he considers it of unusual worth; but he can do this only with the surplus from other books which do make money. He cannot make this a constant policy without going bankrupt himself, after which he is of course unable to publish any books at all, good *or* bad.

Now at this point our objector will say, "That's just the trouble; there should be a Central Planning Commission which decides which books should be published. These men should be devoted to quality, and should publish only the best books, whether they will make money or not." Very well—and who pays for the books that don't make money? It has to come from somewhere—and it comes, of course, from the taxpayer—who is forced to subsidize the book, whether he approves it or not. His liberty is interfered with every time he is forced to pay in taxes for a project of which he disapproves.

And is there any guarantee that books of higher quality will now be published? On the contrary. A central committee will make the decisions, and they are not likely to be any more far-sighted than the private publisher. Besides, they are employees of the government, and the end result will usually be that only those books get published which are in accord with the opinions of those persons who are in political power. Dissenters will not be able to get their books published at all—whereas under capitalism, a book that is turned down by one publisher has a chance of being accepted by one of a hundred *other* publishers. Where there are competitors in the market, the author has at least a chance; but when the government owns all the printing presses, there is no appeal from the Planning Board's decision. If your book disagrees with the views of the government or if you are disliked by some bureaucrat in power, it is most unlikely that what you write will ever see the light of day. The government will squelch your ideas, and perhaps you along with it.

Of course, planning may not go as far as this. The government may not own all the printing presses, but one might say, it should still own all the means of production. But are advocates of this policy aware of its implications? Even if we do not consider human rights or liberty, the practical task of economic planning is so bewilderingly complex as to be impossible. A socialist state could not do it were there not free economies whose prices on the open market could be used as guidelines for what price to charge for what product.

No better illustration of these points could be given than is contained in Henry Hazlitt's novel, *Time Will Run Back.* . . . In the passage quoted here, the main character, Peter, is about to become dictator of Wonworld (centered at Moscow), since his father Stalenin has just had a stroke. Nothing is known about capitalism, since all records of it have been destroyed and nothing except Marxist literature is permitted in Wonworld. Step by step Peter rediscovers capitalism entirely on his own, as the only feasible economic system for Wonworld. But at the early stage of the book in which this quotation occurs, Peter has not yet discovered capitalism, but is only speculating about the ills of the socialist regime which he is about to inherit. He is discussing the issues with his second in command, Adams.

> "But of course people ought to consider it a privilege to work for the State, because when they work for the State they are working for themselves; they are working for each other. . . ."
>
> Peter stopped. He found that he was mechanically repeating the arguments of Bolshekov.
>
> "I agree that people ought to feel this way," said Adams, "but our experience shows that they just don't. The hard fact is that some people simply have to do more unpleasant chores than others, and the only way we can get the unpleasant chores done is by compulsion. Not everybody can be a manager, or an actor or an artist or a violin player. Somebody has to dig the coal, collect the garbage, repair the sewers. Nobody will deliberately *choose* these smelly jobs. People will have to be assigned to them, forced to do them."
>
> "Well, perhaps we could compensate them in some way, Adams—say by letting them work shorter hours than the others."
>
> "We thought of that long ago, chief. It didn't work. It unluckily turned out that it was only the pleasant jobs, like acting or violin playing, that could be reduced to short hours. But we simply can't afford to have people work only a few hours on the

nasty jobs. These are precisely the jobs that have to be done. We couldn't afford to cut our coal production in half by cutting the hours in half, for example; and we just haven't got the spare manpower to rotate. Besides, we found that on most such jobs a considerable loss of time and production was involved in merely changing shifts."

"All right," agreed Peter; "so under our socialist system we can't have freedom in choice of work or occupation. But couldn't we provide some freedom of initiative—at least for those who direct production? Our propaganda is always urging more initiative on the part of commissars or individual plant managers. Why don't we get it?"

"Because a commissar or plant manager, chief, is invariably shot if his initiative goes wrong. The very fact that he was using his own initiative means that he was not following orders. How can you reconcile individual initiative with planning from the centre? When we draw up our Five Year Plans, we allocate the production of hundreds of different commodities and services in accordance with what we assume to be the needs of the people. Now if every plant manager decided for himself what things his plant should produce or how much it should produce of them, our production would turn out to be completely unbalanced and chaotic."

"Very well," Peter said; "so we can't permit the individual plant manager to decide what to produce or how much to produce of it. But this is certainly a big disadvantage. For if someone on the Central Planning Board doesn't think of some new need to be satisfied, or some new way of satisfying an old need, then nobody thinks of it and nobody dares to supply it. And . . . how can we encourage individual plant managers to devise more efficient ways of producing the things they are ordered to produce? If these plant managers can't be encouraged to invent new or better consumption goods, at least they can be encouraged to invent new methods or machines to produce more economically the consumption goods they are ordered to produce, or to produce a higher quality of those consumption goods."

"You're just back to the same problem," Adams said. "If I'm a plant manager, and I invent a new machine, I'll have to ask the Central Planning Board to get somebody to build it, or to allocate the materials to me so that I can build it. In either case I'll upset the preordained central plan. I'll have a hard job convincing the Central Planning Board that my invention or experiment won't fail. If my invention does fail, and it turns out that I have wasted scarce labour and materials, I will be removed and probably shot. The member of the Central Planning Board who approved my project will be lucky if he isn't shot himself. Therefore, unless the success of my invention or experiment seems absolutely certain in advance, I will be well advised to do what everybody else does. Then if I fail, I can prove that I failed strictly according to the rules. . . . Suppose I devise a more economical method of making the product assigned to my factory. I will probably need different proportion of labour and materials, or different kinds of labour and materials, than I would with the old method. And in that case I will again be upsetting the central plan."

Peter sighed. "That doesn't seem to leave much room under our system for initiative, improvement and progress."

Adams shrugged his shoulders.

"Very well then, Adams. So under our socialist system we can't have freedom of choice of work or occupation; we can't have freedom of initiative. But can't we at least give people more freedom in the choice of what they consume?"

"How are you going to do that?" Adams asked. "We issue ration tickets for everything we produce, and we try to distribute them evenly—at least within each of the Four Functional Groups. We can't let people have ration tickets for more than we produce. They complain about that already."

"No, Adams; but some people like cigarettes and others don't; some like beer and others don't; some prefer spinach to potatoes, and some like it the other way round. Why not permit everyone his choice?"

"Well, maybe we could work out something better than the present rationing system, chief, but the fundamental problem remains. People can consume only what is produced. We must draw up our production plans in advance, on the basis of the known needs and assumed wants of consumers. And then . . . well, I repeat: people can consume only what is produced. So how can they have freedom of choice?"

"I think there are two answers to that," said Peter, after blowing a few more smoke rings. "We could still give consumers considerable freedom of choice *individually*, even if they did not have much when considered *collectively*. In other words, out of the stock of goods already produced, we could devise some method under which one person could get more spinach if he preferred, and the other more potatoes, instead of each having to take the exact proportion in which the total supplies of spinach and potatoes were raised."

"Well—maybe, chief. But I still insist that the fundamental problem would remain unsolved. Considered collectively, how can consumers have any freedom of choice? They have to take what there is."

"But can't we find out in advance what it is they really want, and then make that? In other words, can't we guide production to anticipate the wants of consumers, instead of merely obliging consumers to take what we have produced?"

"We are always trying, chief; but it isn't so simple. Suppose, for example, that in relation to the wants of consumers we turn out too many peanuts as compared with pins? Then we will run out of pins sooner than we run out of peanuts. In other words, people will use up their ration tickets for pins before they use them up for peanuts. They will then start taking peanuts because they can't get any more pins—"

"Oh, come!"

"Well, change the illustration— They will start taking more spinach, for example, because they can't get any more potatoes. But because they are entitled by their ration tickets to the entire supply of *both*, and because their need for goods exceeds the entire supply of goods, they will end by consuming the entire supply of spinach as well as of potatoes."

"But if people consume all of one product before they turn to another," asked Peter, "don't we know that we are producing too little of the first or too much of the second?"

"Usually we do, chief. But we can't know from that just how *much more* of the first we should have produced and *how much* less of the second."

"Can't we tell from the preceding *rate* at which the two products have been consumed?"

"No. Because if people begin to think that soap is going to run short before salt, they will all scramble for soap. Therefore soap will run short in the state commissaries sooner than otherwise. The relative rate at which soap is taken by consumers while it lasts will be faster than if people thought that both soap and salt were going to last them throughout the consuming year."

"But can't we keep making readjustments in the relative amounts produced, Adams, based on this experience, until we get consumption of soap and salt and everything else to come out even?"

"That's what we are always trying to do, chief. But I still haven't got to some of the real problems. The trouble is that very few things are consumed evenly throughout the year even if we should get the relative production of each thing exactly right. People can't burn coal evenly throughout the year, but only in winter. And if they have the storage room, they ask for the entire supply they are entitled to as soon as the ration ticket permits it. Yet the fact that three-quarters of the whole supply of coal is asked for in the first week of the consuming year doesn't necessarily mean that the coal supply is short or is going to run short. Again, ice is consumed mainly during the summer, and all sorts of other things are wanted only seasonally. The only reason people turn in their coupons for new clothes evenly each month throughout the year is that we stagger the validity dates on the clothes coupons in the first place so only one-twelfth become due each month. . . . And still again, some things, like vegetables and fruit, are consumed entirely within a few months of the year for the simple reason that that's when they come on the market, and they won't keep. In short, trying to figure relative shortages and surplusses by relative rates of consumption throughout the year is a tough problem. In most cases we who direct the economy have to solve it by pure guesswork."

"Couldn't we figure it out by mathematics?" asked Peter.

Adams grinned and shrugged his shoulders. "How are you going to find the mathematical formula for somebody's wayward desires? How are you going to find the equation for when I want a cocktail—or whether I want a Marxattan or a Stalini? . . . And I haven't even mentioned one problem. Suppose there is some product, or some potential product, which is not produced but which, if it were invented or discovered or produced, people would want in great quantities? How are you going to find by mathematics that people would want such a product *if* it existed? Or even that such a product is missing?"

Peter sighed. "It's all pretty discouraging. We seem to be reduced to the conclusion that under our socialist system we can't have freedom of choice of work or occupation and we can't permit freedom of choice for consumers. Is that right?"

"People are free to use or not to use their ration tickets," answered Adams.

"In other words," said Peter, "they are free to consume what we tell them they can consume. They are free to consume what we, the rulers, have decided to produce."

"Right, chief."

There was a long pause. . . .

"What did Engels mean when he said that socialism was 'a leap from the kingdom of necessity to the kingdom of freedom?'"

. . . "He meant, I take it," answered Adams, "that under capitalism the individual was not free but enslaved, because one class was dominated and exploited by another; . . . the worker had to obey the orders of his employer or starve. And socialism means freedom from all this."

"I don't quite see it," Peter said. "Under any system of production whatever, there has to be social organization. There have to be those who direct the work and those who are directed; those who give orders and those who follow them; those who boss and those who are bossed. There has to be, in other words, a managerial hierarchy. If it is merely a question of building a single house, there has to be someone to decide that the house has to be put up, and what kind and where. There has to be an architect to design it, a builder to interpret the plans and to decide what workers to use and what to tell them to do—"

"But under socialism, chief, unlike capitalism, there is no exploitation of the workers for the profit of the employer."

"Under socialism," retorted Peter, "the State is the sole employer. If the worker fails to please the powers that be in the State, or if he arouses their active animosity, there is no one else to whom he can turn. A far greater tyranny may be exercised over him under socialism than I imagine was even possible under capitalism. For if a worker failed to please a particular employer under capitalism, I imagine he was free to go to another. And the fear of losing his exploited workers to some other employer must have mitigated the exploitation practiced by each employer. . . .

But under socialism, if a worker falls out of favour with the powers that constitute the State, he can be forced to starve; there is no one else to whom he can turn."

"What I think Engels meant, chief, is that under capitalism the workers were exploited by the capitalist class, and crises and depressions seemed to come like visitations apart from anybody's wishes; while under socialism, society takes its destiny into its own hands and is in that sense free."

"I see," said Peter sarcastically. "And in practice, who constitutes 'society'? Who *is* 'society'?"

"Society is everyone."

"Oh, come now! *Everyone* can't make the decisions. No two persons' decisions would ever agree."

"Well, by society I mean the State."

"And by the State—?"

Adams grinned, "I mean us."

"Exactly. The hierarchy momentarily headed by me," said Peter. He had a sick feeling as he thought once more of his appalling responsibility. "What it comes down to is this, Adams. Society consists, and consists necessarily, of a small body of rulers and a large body of ruled. And this body of rulers itself consists of a hierarchy, finally topped by one man with the power to resolve disputes and make final decisions. So when we say that 'society' does this or that, we mean that the State does this or that. And when we say State, we mean the ruling hierarchy. We mean the Protectors; we mean the Party; we mean the Central Committee; we mean the Politburo; we mean merely the Dictator himself— or," Peter grinned, "the Dictator's Deputy."

"But under socialism," protested Adams, "the State reflects not the will of the exploiters against the proletariat, but, the will of the proletariat themselves. The State is just the mechanism by which the people express their will. It is a dictatorship of the proletariat—"

"Or a dictatorship *over* the proletariat? Let's face the real facts. Under our socialist system a few people—say the Central Planning Board—make the economic plan, and the rest of the people are ordered to carry out the plan. All initiative must come from the centre, and none can come from the periphery."

"It *has* to be that way, chief. There would be no point in having a master overall plan, deciding just what goods should be produced, and just how much of each, and by just whom, if anybody anywhere were free to decide to make or do something else. That would be chaos."

"But isn't there any productive system that would allow more liberty, Adams? Isn't there any system that would allow more centres of initiative? What actually happened under capitalism? Were workers free to change from one job to another that they liked better? Was the individual capitalist free to decide to make what he pleased, and in the way he pleased? Was the

consumer free to consume what he preferred, and to reject what
he didn't like?"

"I don't know what happened under capitalism, chief.
Nobody knows. And we destroyed the capitalist literature so
completely that I don't see how we are going to find out. But
surely we are not going to turn back to that discredited and vicious
system—which the world got rid of at the cost of so much blood
and sacrifice—to take lessons in how to improve socialism!"

"All right," agreed Peter, "let's forget about capitalism.
But I still don't understand what Engels meant when he called
socialism 'the kingdom of freedom.' I still don't know what Marx
meant when he said that under socialism the State would 'wither
away.' For it seems to me that it is above all under socialism, where
the State owns all the means of production, does all the planning
and assigns and controls all the jobs, that the State is and must be
closest to omnipotence. . . ."

He gazed unseeingly out of the window.

"Adams, you have convinced me. It is precisely under a
socialist State that the least liberty can exist. Under complete
socialism, in fact, liberty for the individual is simply impossible."[7]

The socialist planner is caught in a dilemma from which he cannot escape: if
people are sufficiently rational and farsighted, they can be trusted to carry out *their
own* plans. (If their plans include using force against someone else, the law is there for
the purpose of stopping them, to protect the liberty of others. And if their plans,
though not violating others' rights, are unwise or scatterbrained or just plain crazy,
they will have to find this out in the course of *their own* experience: the consequences
of their own actions will come down on their own heads, and hopefully cause them
to be a bit saner next time.) But if people are *not* sufficiently rational and farsighted to
be trusted to carry out their own plans, then what superior endowment of wisdom
entitles the politicians to make these plans for them? Are not the politicians human
beings too? If they want to be shepherds and consider the rest of mankind to be
sheep, what evidence can they give of their ability to manage by force the lives of
others? And by what right do they do it even if they do have the ability? If history
teaches us any one thing, is it not the very opposite—that men placed in a position of
power over other people will be not better but worse?

Power does corrupt, and absolute power does corrupt absolutely, and a
man who may be a saint in his relations with his own family may be a power-hungry
manipulator when he is given a chance to govern other human beings. The socialist
state puts such enormous power into the hands of politicians that the thought of
using it is frightening; who among all of mankind can be trusted with that much
power? Will he not abuse it? and even if he exercises it conscientiously, how can he,
or any small group of individuals at the helm of such a government, exercise it wisely

[7]Hazlitt, *Time Will Run Back*, pp. 86–90. Reprinted from *Time Will Also Run Back* by Henry Hazlitt,
published by Arlington House and used with their permission. Copyright © 1951, 1966 by
Henry Hazlitt.

and well, considering the thousands of decisions they would have to make daily affecting the entire population? If you have a hard enough time making decisions for yourself—or yourself and your family—in your own life, consider the difficulties in the case of a government executive who has to make every day countless decisions that affect the lives and welfare of individuals whose unique personalities, situations, and problems he knows nothing about.

> There once was a traveler who arrived in the midst of a tribe of savages when a child had just been born. A crowd of soothsayers and magicians and quacks surrounded the child. One said, "This child will never smell the perfume of a peacepipe unless I stretch his nostrils." Another said, "He will never be able to hear unless I draw his earlobes down to his shoulders." A third said, "He will never see the sunshine unless I slant his eyes." Another said, "He will never stand upright unless I bend his legs." A fifth said, "He will never learn to think unless I flatten his skull." "Stop," cried the traveler; "God has given organs to this frail creature; let them develop and grow strong by exercise, use, experience, and liberty."[8]

The socialists among us are the magicians and quacks in Bastiat's example who would force everyone else into conformity with *their* ideals. But over all social philosophy rules the principle of human rights: the lives (and the livelihood) of others are not theirs (or yours, or mine) to dispose of. The socialist, who wants to build society by forcing others to conform to his plan, is the most flagrant violator of the rights of man.

When one considers the mistakes he has made in regulating his own life, what temerity is involved in the attempt to regulate the lives of others!

> If in these personal affairs, where all the conditions of the case were known to me, I have so often miscalculated, how much oftener shall I miscalculate in political affairs, where the conditions are too numerous, too widespread, too complex, too obscure to be understood. Here, doubtless, is a social evil and there a desideratum; and were I sure of doing no mischief I would forthwith try to cure the one and achieve the other. But when I remember how many of my private schemes have miscarried; how speculations have failed, agents proved dishonest, marriage been a disappointment; how I did but pauperize the relative I sought to help; how my carefully-governed son has turned out worse than most children; how the thing I desperately strove against as a misfortune did me immense good; how while the objects I ardently pursued brought me little happiness when gained, most of my pleasures have come from unexpected sources; when I recall these and hosts of like facts, I am struck with the incompetence of my

[8]Frederic Bastiat, "The Law," in *Selected Essays on Political Economy* (Princeton, N. J.: D. Van Nostrand Co., Inc., 1964), p. 95.

intellect to prescribe for society. And as the evil is one under which society has not only lived but grown, while the desideratum is one it may spontaneously obtain, as it has most others, in some unforeseen way, I question the propriety of meddling.[9]

But the socialist state is simply meddlesomeness exhibited on a large scale, extended to virtually every aspect of human life; its keynote is the regulation of human lives through the coercive force of the political power. On this point no one has spoken more eloquently than Herbert Spencer almost a century ago:

A cardinal trait in all advancing organization is the development of the regulative apparatus. If the parts of a whole are to act together, there must be appliances by which their actions are directed; and in proportion as the whole is large and complex, and has many requirements to be met by many agencies, the directive apparatus must be extensive, elaborate, and powerful. That it is thus with individual organisms needs no saying; and that it must be thus with social organisms is obvious. Beyond the regulative apparatus such as in our own society is required for carrying on national defense and maintaining public order and personal safety, there must, under the regime of socialism, be a regulative apparatus everywhere controlling all kinds of production and distribution, and everywhere apportioning the shares of products of each kind required for each locality, each working establishment, each individual. Under our existing voluntary cooperation, with its free contracts and its competition, production and distribution need no official oversight. Demand and supply, and the desire of each man to gain a living by supplying the needs of his fellows, spontaneously evolve that wonderful system whereby a great city has its food daily brought round to all doors or stored at adjacent shops; has clothing for its citizens everywhere at hand in multitudinous varieties; has its houses and furniture and fuel ready made or stocked in each locality; and has mental pabulum, from halfpenny papers hourly hawked round to weekly shoals of novels and less abundant books of instruction, furnished without stint for small payments: And throughout the kingdom, production as well as distribution is similarly carried on with the smallest amount of superintendence which proves efficient; while the quantities of the numerous commodities required daily in each locality are adjusted without any other agency than the pursuit of profit.
Suppose now that this industrial regime of willinghood, acting spontaneously, is replaced by a regime of industrial obedience, enforced by public officials. Imagine the vast administration required for that distribution of all commodities to all people in every city, town and village, which is now effected by

[9]Herbert Spencer, *Man Versus the State* (Caldwell, Idaho: Caxton Printers, Ltd., 1940), p. 122.

traders! Imagine, again, the still more vast administration required for doing all that farmers, manufacturers, and merchants do; having not only its various orders of local superintendents, but its sub-centres and chief centres needed for apportioning the quantities of each thing everywhere needed, and the adjustment of them to the requisite times. Then add the staffs wanted for working mines, railways, roads, canals; the staffs required for conducting the importing and exporting businesses and the administration of mercantile shipping, the staffs required for supplying towns not only with water and gas but with locomotion by tramways, omnibuses, and other vehicles, and for the distribution of power, electric and other. Join with these the existing postal, telegraphic, and telephonic administrations; and finally those of the police and army, by which the dictates of this immense consolidated regulative system are to be everywhere enforced. Imagine all this, and then ask what will be the position of the actual workers! Already on the Continent, where governmental organizations are more elaborate and coercive than here, there are chronic complaints of the tyranny of bureaucracies, the *hauteur* and brutality of their members. What will these become when not only the more public actions of citizens are controlled, but there is added this far more extensive control of all their respective daily duties? What will happen when the various divisions of this vast army of officials, united by interests common to officialism—the interests of the regulators *versus* those of the regulated—have at their command whatever force is needful to suppress insubordination and act as "saviors of society"? Where will be the actual diggers and miners and smelters and weavers, when those who order and superintend, everywhere arranged class above class, have come, after some generations, to inter-marry with those of kindred grades, under feelings such as are operative in the existing classes; and when there have been so produced a series of castes rising in superiority; and when all those having everything in their own power, have arranged modes of living for their own advantage: eventually forming a new aristocracy far more elaborate and better organized than the old? How will the individual worker fare if he is dissatisfied with his treatment, thinks that he has not an adequate share of the products, or has more to do than can rightly be demanded, or wishes to undertake a function for which he feels himself fitted but which is not thought proper for him by his superiors, or desires to make an independent career for himself? This dissatisfied unit in the immense machine will be told he must submit or go.[10]

Such a worker has become a slave—a slave to the coercive regulations of government. Indeed, as Herbert Spencer pointed out,

[10]*Ibid.*, pp. 69–71.

All socialism is slavery.

What is essential to the idea of a slave? We primarily think of him as one who is owned by another. To be more than nominal, however, the ownership must be shown by control of the slave's actions—a control which is habitually for the benefit of the controller. That which fundamentally distinguishes the slave is that *he labors under coercion to satisfy another's desires.*

The relation admits of sundry gradations. Remembering that originally the slave is a prisoner whose life is at the mercy of his captor, it suffices here to note that there is a harsh form of slavery in which, treated as an animal, he has to expend his entire effort for his owner's advantage. Under a system less harsh, though occupied chiefly in working for his owner, he is allowed a short time in which to work for himself, and some ground on which to grow extra food. A further amelioration gives him power to sell the produce of his plot and keep the proceeds. Then we come to the still more moderated form which commonly arises where, having been a free man working on his own land, conquest turns him into what we distinguish as a serf; and he has to give his owner each year a fixed amount of labor or produce, or both, retaining the rest himself. Finally, in some cases, as in Russia before serfdom was abolished, he is allowed to leave his owner's estate and work or trade for himself elsewhere, under the condition that he shall pay an annual sum. What is it which, in these cases, leads us to qualify our conception of the slavery as more or less severe? Evidently the greater or smaller extent to which *effort is compulsorily expended for the benefit of another instead of for self-benefit.* If all the slave's labor is for his owner the slavery is heavy, and if but little it is light.

Take now a further step. Suppose an owner dies, and his estate with its slaves comes into the hands of trustees; or suppose the estate and everything on it be bought by a company; is the condition of the slave any the better if the amount of his compulsory labor remains the same? Suppose that for a company we substitute the community; does it make any difference to the slave if the time he has to work for others is as great, and the time left for himself is as small, as before? The essential question is: how much is he compelled to labor for other benefit than his own, and how much can he labor for his own benefit? The degree of his slavery varies according to the ratio between that which he is forced to yield up and that which he is allowed to retain; and *it matters not whether his master is a single person or a society.* If, without option, he has to labor for the society, and receives from the general stock such portion as the society awards him, he becomes a slave to the society. Socialistic arrangements necessitate an enslavement of this kind; and towards such an enslavement many recent measures, and still more the measures advocated, are carrying us.[11]

---

[11]*Ibid.,* pp. 41–43. Italics mine.

Such measures were characterized as enslavement by Spencer when he wrote these lines in 1884. Yet they are liberty itself compared with what they are today, and they are likely to be still worse on the arrival of Orwell's prophetic year, 1984.

Equality of Opportunity

"But even if all men shouldn't be forced to be equal in income, because of their differing efforts and achievements, still shouldn't they all have equality of opportunity? Isn't it unfair that some young people, born let us say to poverty-stricken parents, start on life's journey with an enormous handicap as compared with others who are born with a silver spoon in their mouths?"

First let us consider: how would you enforce equality of opportunity if you decided to make it a national policy? Clearly, the son of a man who earns three thousand dollars a year has a great disadvantage compared with the son of a man who earns thirty thousand dollars a year. (At least, he has a financial disadvantage—he may have other compensating advantages, such as parental love which is not forthcoming from the father who is too busy earning money to pay much attention to his growing son. But of course it may go the other way also: the son of the wealthier man may be more favored in parental confidence and affection than the poor man's son.) Now, how could one change this advantage? Obviously one could do it by taking income away from the rich man and putting it into the hands of the poor man; and this, as a regular policy, could be done only by the government. And what would happen as a result? The story is predictable: perhaps for a while the rich man would work that much harder to recoup his losses, while the poor man took an extended vacation on his sudden unearned income. Within a year the first man would have a much higher income than the second—there would be inequality again, which the state would equalize once more. It wouldn't take long before the rich man got the idea: "If I work it will only be taken away from me—so why work?" So he closes down his plant, and lets his employees go. The employer waits to receive his handout from the state, and the employees, now discharged, do the same—and who will now support them both? Compulsory equalization of income will kill incentives and close down the business which made the rich man rich, thus making the poor man poorer.

It is surely plain that the cure is worse than the disease: not only because of the poverty that would result from everyone trying to live off of everybody else, but because it would take a police state with a huge and expensive bureaucracy to sustain it.

A man, even after he has earned enough to keep him going for the rest of his life, may still be motivated to keep producing, hiring new personnel, etc., in the hope that he may pass it on to his son. And when this hope is justified, productive industries will be kept functioning. Besides, if the man earned the money, he has the right to pass it on to his son if he so chooses. Who has the right to dispose of the money he has earned if he himself doesn't?

How great an advantage does the son of a rich man have? Some—for a time. If he is able and industrious, the industry he has inherited will prosper and he can make money more quickly than if he had had to start from scratch. If he is idle and wasteful, the money will pass through his fingers soon enough. And much depends on what it is that he has inherited: more often than not he does not inherit cash as much as a going industry, which will see deficits very quickly unless he is able to make the right decisions. (The Ford Company almost went under after Henry Ford died.) Those who inherited railroad companies were often worse off than those who started the airline companies from nothing. Besides, the great achievers in industry (just as much as in the arts and sciences) owed very little to their immediate ancestors:

> When he began, Ford knew nothing of gasoline engines; Rockefeller knew nothing about oil refining; Carnegie knew nothing about steel making; Vanderbilt did not go into railroading until he was 68 years old, and 90 of the 100 millions he died with were gained in the fifteen remaining years of his life. The almost invariable record [is] that the richest men have started as poor boys, as a rule devoid of any special opportunity. . . .[12]

The important thing is not for everyone to have equal opportunity in the sense of equal income available from his parents; the important thing is *leave the lines open* from poverty to affluence, so that anyone has a *chance* to rise, as high as his ability can carry him. A man may grow up poor, but if he has ability and ingenuity and industry, he may end up a millionaire if that is what he wants to be. *That* is the condition that must be preserved—and it is precisely this condition that is threatened by socialism. With its emphasis on enforced equality, it makes it infinitely more difficult for people of ability to rise, for they are blocked at all turns by an entrenched and inefficient bureaucracy, and a crippling income tax which they have to pay from the inception of their labors, making any rise from a state of poverty enormously more difficult.

The Springs of Socialism

Why do people come to believe in such socialistic schemes?

One reason is the belief that they will get *something for nothing*. It is the allure of the magic word "Free!" in advertisements. They have been treated by government propagandists and liberal commentators (is there a difference?) to vilifications of the rich exploiters, greedy capitalists, and the like, and this provides, in their minds, a moral justification for fleecing them—which they can do via taxation with "soak the rich" policies. They do not, of course, see the end-results of these policies—the loss of incentive, the decline of industry, the rise of unemployment, the decline of consumer goods. But as a way of "getting even" with their supposed enemies, the appeal to "something for nothing" may often succeed. The price paid, however, will

[12]Carl Snyder, *Capitalism the Creator* (New York, Macmillan Co., 1940), p. 241.

be enormous: the people will think they are getting more out of the government than they pay in taxes because the rich are paying more and getting less—and for the moment this may be true. But because of it, in the long run the most productive and successful people will reduce their efforts or throw in the towel entirely—and then the same people who voted these schemes in will experience a lower standard of living, unemployment, an industrial blight settling over the land like a miasma. They will wonder why. They will know that something has gone wrong, but they will not usually see that the cause lies in the very policies they voted for. Their shortsighted greed has boomeranged. This chapter of their endeavors might well be called "the case of the cheated cheaters."

There are, as Albert Jay Nock pointed out in the 1920s, two ways by which human beings can satisfy their needs and desires.

> One is by work—i.e., by applying labor and capital to natural resources for the production of wealth, or to facilitating the exchange of labor-products. This is called the *economic* means. The other is by robbery—i.e., the appropriation of the labor-products of others without compensation. This is called the *political* means. The State, considered functionally, may be described as *the organization of the political means, enabling* a comparatively small class of beneficiaries to satisfy their needs and desires through various delegations of the taxing power, which have no vestige of support in natural right. . . .
>
> It is the primary instinct of human nature to satisfy one's needs and desires with the least possible exertion; everyone tends by instinctive preference to use the political means rather than the economic means, if he can do so. . . . This instinct—and this alone—is what gives the State its almost impregnable strength. The moment one discerns this, one understands the almost universal disposition to glorify and magnify the State, and to insist upon the pretense that it is something which it is not—something, in fact, the direct opposite of what it is. One understands the complacent acceptance of one set of standards for the State's conduct, and another for private organizations; of one set for officials, and another for private persons. One understands at once the attitude of the press, the Church and educational institutions, their careful inculcations of a specious patriotism, their nervous and vindictive proscriptions of opinion, doubt, or even of question. One sees why purely fictitious theories of the State and its activities are strongly, often fiercely and violently, insisted on; why the simple fundamentals of the very simple science of economics are shirked or veiled; and why, finally, those who really know what kind of thing they are promulgating, are loath to say so.[13]

It is the nature of man's situation on this planet that he must work to make

---

[13]Albert Jay Nock, *Anarchist's Progress*. Quoted in William F. Buckley, Jr. (ed.), *Did You Ever See a Dream Walking? American Conservative Thought in the Twentieth Century* (Indianapolis: Bobbs-Merrill Co., Inc., 1970), p. 140.

provision for himself and his future; but if a person thinks he can get the rewards without the effort, he usually submits to the temptation to do so—particularly when he can do it by means of government, so that he himself need not use a gun to hold anyone up, and the people from whom he takes are an anonymous mass who cannot easily be identified individually, and who therefore cannot rise to accuse him of any crime.

Many people, of course, do know the economic facts of life—that man must produce to live, that you can't get something for nothing, that all production is the outcome of man's work, and that interfering with the source of production will cause it to falter—but the number of people who are aware of this is so small in comparison to the total population, that there is little they can do: when they try to point out the economic facts of life, they are condemned by an irate populace as selfish exploiters of the poor. And then, of course, they are outvoted at the polls. And so the morally brainwashed majority carries us all forward on the road to ruin.

Another reason for the voting in of socialistic schemes is a shortsighted and misplaced humanitarianism. Welfare to the poor—"they need it so much"—but the causes for their being poor are seldom investigated, but taken as a given, a simple fact of life. Government ownership of railroads, of steel, of utilities, and countless other things—true, it may be less efficient but "at least other people won't be making profits off of us." Minimum-wage laws—"otherwise the employer will never pay the poor man enough." Subsidies for various industries to lower prices—again, "to lower prices for us and keep the rich bastards from making so much profit." And so on, and so on—we have considered many too many examples in the preceding pages to need to recite them again. Every bit of reasoning, of course, tragically mistaken; but all of it justified in the minds of the unthinking proponents of these government schemes under the general banner of humanitarianism. If this be humanitarianism, then by all means give us selfishness and the profit motive—that way the goods will be produced, profits will be made, prosperity will permeate the economy, and the poor will find, again without knowing why, that their standard of living has risen and they can now look out for themselves.

The professional humanitarian, the philanthropist who would be the benefactor, with large masses of the population grateful for his beneficence, often sees this and tries to avoid it. As Isabel Paterson says in her chapter "The Humanitarian with the Guillotine":

> If the primary objective of the philanthropist, his justification for living, is to help others, his ultimate good *requires that others shall be in want*. His happiness is the obverse of their misery. If he wishes to help "humanity," the whole of humanity must be in need. The humanitarian wishes to be a prime mover in the lives of others. . . .
> But he is confronted by two awkward facts; first, that the competent do not need his assistance; and second, that the majority of people, if unperverted, positively do not want to be

"done good" by the humanitarian. When it is said that everyone should live primarily for others, what is the specific course to be pursued? is each person to do exactly what any other person wants him to do, without limits or reservations? and only what others want him to do? What if various persons make conflicting demands? The scheme is impracticable. Perhaps then he is to do only what is actually "good" for others. But will those others know what is good for them? No, that is ruled out by the same difficulty. Then shall A do what he thinks is good for B, and B do what he thinks is good for A? Or shall A accept only what he thinks is good for B, and vice versa? But that is absurd. Of course what the humanitarian actually proposes is that *he* shall do what he thinks is good for everybody. It is at this point that the humanitarian sets up the guillotine.

What kind of world does the humanitarian contemplate as affording him full scope? It could only be a world filled with breadlines and hospitals, in which nobody retained the natural power of a human being to help himself or to resist having things done to him. And that is precisely the world that the humanitarian arranges when he gets his way. When a humanitarian wishes to see to it that everyone has a quart of milk, it is evident that he hasn't got the milk, and cannot produce it himself, or why should he be merely wishing? Further, if he did have a sufficient quantity of milk to bestow a quart on everyone, as long as his proposed beneficiaries can and do produce milk for themselves, they would say no, thank you. Then how is the humanitarian to contrive that he shall have all the milk to distribute, and that everyone else shall be in want of milk?

There is only one way, and that is by the use of *the political power in its fullest extension.* Hence the humanitarian feels the utmost gratification when he visits or hears of a country in which everyone is restricted to ration cards. Where subsistence is doled out, the desideratum has been achieved, of general want and a superior power to "relieve" it. The humanitarian in theory is the terrorist in action.[14]

The socialist dreamer with "humanitarian" ideals, and the tough, no-nonsense government planner, hungry for power in planning other people's lives—these two strike up a natural alliance. The second's power-lust only implements the "idealistic" dreams of the first, and provides him with a moral alibi. The rationale is left to the humanitarian, who tries not to notice while the power-luster moves others about on his chessboard, causes the poverty, sees the blood flow from his victims—all in implementation of the humanitarian's plan. The productive people, both managers and workers, are the ones who have to pay the costs and take the blame.

[14]Isabel Paterson, *The God of the Machine* (New York: G. P. Putnam's Sons, 1943. Reprinted by Caxton Printers, Ltd.: Caldwell, Idaho, 1964), pp. 253–54.

Power: Nature vs. Man

Many people are strongly opposed to any exercise of power. They consider power itself to be an evil. But there is power and power: they do not draw the distinction between *power over nature* and *power over men.*

Power over nature is the touchstone of human progress; on it civilizations are built. The record of man's climb from savagery is the record of the advance of that power: power to invent, to build, to produce, to use nature for man's benefit. But power over men does not raise mankind's standard of living or improve the quality of his life: for clearly, only *some* men can wield power over other men. And the remainder must be the *victims* of that power.

> Governmental power is the faculty to beat into submission all those who would dare to disobey the orders issued by the authorities. Nobody would call government an entity that lacks this faculty. Every governmental action is backed by constables, prison guards, and executioners. However beneficial a governmental action may appear, it is ultimately made possible only by the government's power to compel its subjects to do what many of them would not do if they were not threatened by the police and the penal courts. A government-supported hospital serves charitable purposes. But the taxes collected that enable the authorities to spend money for the upkeep of the hospital are not paid voluntarily. The citizens pay taxes because not to pay them would bring them into prison and physical resistance to the revenue agents to the gallows. . . . Governmental power means the exclusive faculty to frustrate any disobedience by the recourse to violence. . . .
>
> Economic power . . . is the capacity to influence other people's behavior by offering them something the acquisition of which they consider as more desirable than the avoidance of the sacrifice they have to make for it. In plain words: it means the invitation to enter into a bargain, an act of exchange. I will give you *a* if you give me *b.* There is no question of any compulsion nor of any threats. The buyer does not "rule" the seller and the seller does not "rule" the buyer.[15]

Every human being does to varying extents achieve power over nature, even if he is a simple peasant growing crops and extracting his foodstuffs from the soil. The only way that man can advance himself is to conquer nature—"to transform the face of the earth to satisfy his wants."

> Only such a conquest is productive and life-sustaining. Power of one man over another cannot contribute to the advance of mankind; it can only bring about a society in which plunder has

[15]Von Mises, "The Elite Under Capitalism," *The Freeman* 12, no. 2 (January 1962): 8.

replaced production, hegemony has supplanted contract. Violence and conflict have taken the place of the peaceful order and harmony of the market. Power of one man over another is *parasitic* rather than creative, for it means that *the nature-conquerors are subjected to the dictation of those who conquer their fellow men instead.*[16]

Productive men have always tried to advance man's conquest of nature. And always other men have tried to widen the scope of political power in order to seize for themselves the fruits of that conquest. Political power is the power of man over man—that is why we should minimize it and reduce it to nothing if possible; economic power is the power of man over nature. History is a race between the two kinds of power. The power of capitalism and the free market lies in an ever-increasing standard of living resulting from the conquest of nature. The reascendance of power over man, the political power, is what reduces us again to the level of savages.[17]

The three billion people that the earth now holds—and the larger number presumably still in store—can, as we have seen, be kept alive in comparative safety, and with some reserve for emergencies, only on a free-market economy. The further they move toward a non-market (coercive) economy, the smaller the incentive to production, the greater the shortages, the greater the chance of something going wrong in a critical place at a critical time, and the more frequently mass starvation and famine will occur. The British scientist-novelist C. P. Snow has predicted that before the end of this century "many millions of people in poor countries are going to starve to death before our eyes. We shall see them doing so upon our television sets."[18] The countries most affected, of course, will be those which either have a primitive barter economy and already live on the edge of starvation (as in the jungle or the Arctic), and those with a centrally controlled economy—that is, the socialist countries of the world, whose economic systems cannot solve the huge problems of production, supply, and distribution to an ever-increasing population.

If this happens, many among us will tell us that *we* are guilty, that we should try to equalize incomes all over the world, that the others are starving because we are too stingy. And if we act on their advice, we will finally starve ourselves in a vain attempt to keep them from starving. The whole thing would be fruitless unless we can come to grips with the *cause* of starvation—the coercive statist economies under which these populations live, the forced collectivism by which a man who would gladly work hard to support his wife and family becomes discouraged at having to share the benefits with 200 million others, in which matters of life and death are left to bureaucrats as incapable of handling them as a child would be in calculating the trajectories of spaceships as now done by computer. The fate of these people could

[16]Murray Rothbard, *Power and Market* (Menlo Park, Calif.: Institute for Humane Studies, 1970), p. 172.

[17]See Rothbard, *Power and Market*. pp. 172-73.

[18]*Life* magazine, September 14, 1970, p. 64.

be avoided if they could have free-market economies; but most of the victims of the suffering and death will not even know that their fates are avoidable. Only a capitalistic economy could solve their problems, and many of them have never been permitted to learn about capitalism.

Just as a capitalist economy is "an incredible bread machine,"[19] providing amply for the needs of millions, so the socialist economy, in the face of a burgeoning population, is a guaranteed starvation machine which needs only time to perfect its deadly work. Why do you suppose that Soviet Russia permits the 3 percent of its land area to remain privately owned? Because the garden and agricultural plots of this 3 percent produce 48 percent of Russia's foodstuffs, and its leaders well know that without it Russia would starve.

But the danger does not end there: the danger is that by the end of the century we ourselves may have fallen victim to the same kind of starvation machine that is already afflicting them. Once our citizens no longer question the policies of centralized control, deficit spending, inflation, and social insecurity which they now appear to favor, even the strong economic reserve generated by a century and a half of economic freedom will at last break down. And if this happens, it is we who will turn on our television sets and watch the starvation of our own people. Our own formulas for disaster will have come back to haunt us, but by that time it will be too late. By the time catastrophe strikes, a military dictator will probably take over the country, with "sweeping emergency powers," and for those of us who remain alive, our heritage of liberty will have vanished.

In the face of all this, student groups in the United States are almost all fiercely opposed to capitalism. Of the dozens of confusions and fallacies about the nature and functioning of a free market, they fall victim to one after another; no slogan is too false for them to repeat as if it were an obvious truth. What account will they give of their present views if mass starvation stalks the world?

Perhaps, one suspects, it was what some of them wanted all along: the poverty of millions means little to those with an insatiable appetite for power. The vast majority of them, of course, desire no such terrifying outcome; they are simply misguided idealists who know nothing about how production can be generated to fulfill human needs. Totally ignorant of the role of liberty in economic matters, they chant any slogans they hear as long as they have a humanitarian ring. But in the end they will be simply cannon-fodder, to be used by their leaders as long as they are useful, and then thrown on the trash-heap when the time for power comes.

[19]See Richard Grant's excellent book, *The Incredible Bread Machine*. (Privately printed, 1966.)

Suggestions for Further Reading

The Concept of Justice

Plato. *The Republic.* Translated by Francis Cornford. New York: Oxford University Press, 1945.

Pieper, Josef. *Justice.* London: Faber and Faber, 1957.

Perelman, Chaim. *Justice.* New York: Random House, 1967.

Vlastos, Gregory. "Justice and Equality." In *Social Justice,* edited by Richard Brandt, pp. 31–72. Englewood Cliffs, N. J.: Prentice-Hall, 1962.

Feinberg, Joel. "Noncomparative Justice. *The Philosophical Review* (1974): 297–338.

Liberal Justice

The Contractual Tradition

Rousseau, Jean-Jacques. *The Social Contract and Discourse on the Origin of Equality.* Edited by Lester Crocker. New York: Washington Square Press, 1967.

Richards, David. *A Theory of Reasons for Action.* Oxford: Clarendon Press, 1971.

Buchanan, James. *The Limits of Liberty.* Chicago: The University of Chicago Press, 1975.

Daniels, Norman, ed. *Reading Rawls.* New York: Basic Books, 1975.

Nielson, Kai, and **Shiner,** Roger, eds. *New Essays on Contract Theory. Canadian Journal of Philosophy* (1977).

The Utilitarian Tradition
    Sidgwick, Henry. *The Methods of Ethics.* New York: Dover Publications, 1966.
    Narveson, Jan. *Morality and Utility.* Baltimore: The Johns Hopkins Press, 1967.
    Quinton, Anthony. *Utilitarian Ethics.* New York: St. Martin's Press, 1973.
    Gorovitz, Samuel, ed. *Mill: Utilitarianism.* Indianapolis: The Bobbs-Merrill Co., 1971.
    Smart, J.J.C., and **Williams,** Bernard. *Utilitarianism For and Against.* Cambridge: Cambridge University Press, 1973.

Libertarian Justice

    Rand, Ayn. *Capitalism: The Unknown Ideal.* New York: The New American Library, 1946.
    Friedman, David. *The Machinery of Freedom.* New York: Harper & Row, 1973.
    Mack, Eric. "Liberty and Justice." In *Justice and Economic Distribution,* edited by John Arthur and William Shaw, pp. 83–93. Englewood Cliff, N. J.: Prentice-Hall, 1978.
    Singer, Peter. "The Right to Be Rich or Poor," *The New York Review of Books,* 6 March 1975, pp. 19–24.
    Lyons, David. "Rights Against Humanity," *The Philosophical Review* (1976): 208–215.

Socialist Justice

    Engels, Friedrich. "Socialism: Utopian and Scientific." Reprinted in *Essential Works of Marxism,* edited by Arthur Mendel, pp. 45–82. New York: Bantam Books, 1961.
    Sweezy, Paul. *Modern Capitalism and Other Essays.* New York: Monthly Review Press, 1972.
    Macpherson, C. B. *The Life and Times of Liberal Democracy.* New York: Oxford University Press, 1977.
    Heilbroner, Robert. *Between Capitalism and Socialism.* New York: Random House, 1970.
    Miller, David. *Social Justice.* Oxford: Clarendon Press, 1976.